COMMERCE AND GOVERNMENT

*Considered in Their*

*MUTUAL RELATIONSHIP*

*Étienne Bonnot, Abbé de Condillac*

# COMMERCE AND GOVERNMENT

## Considered in Their
## *MUTUAL RELATIONSHIP*

~~~~~~

*Étienne Bonnot,*
*Abbé de Condillac*

### TRANSLATED BY SHELAGH ELTIS

With an Introduction to His Life
and Contribution to Economics
*by Shelagh Eltis and Walter Eltis*

LIBERTY FUND
*Indianapolis*

This book is published by Liberty Fund, Inc.,
a foundation established to encourage study of the
ideal of a society of free and responsible individuals.

𒂼𒄄

The cuneiform inscription that serves as our logo and as the
design motif for our endpapers is the earliest-known written
appearance of the word "freedom" (*amagi*), or "liberty."
It is taken from a clay document written about 2300 B.C.
in the Sumerian city-state of Lagash.

© 2008 by Liberty Fund, Inc. *Commerce and Government*, originally published by
Edward Elgar Publishing in 1997, copyright 1997 by Shelagh Eltis and Walter Eltis.
Reprinted by permission of Edward Elgar Publishing

Cover art: "Mr. L'abbé Condillac," from the Prints & Photographs Division,
Library of Congress, LC-USZ62-130299

Frontispiece from the Musée Dauphinois de Grenoble,
reprinted by permission of Edward Elgar Publishing

Printed in the United States of America
All rights reserved
1 3 5 7 9 C 10 8 6 4 2
1 3 5 7 9 P 10 8 6 4 2

Library of Congress Cataloging-in-Publication Data

Condillac, Étienne Bonnot de, 1714–1780.
[Commerce et le gouvernement considérés rélativement l'un à l'autre. English]
Commerce and government: considered in their mutual relationship
Étienne Bonnot, Abbé de Condillac; translated by Shelagh Eltis;
with an introduction to his life and contribution to economics
by Shelagh Eltis and Walter Eltis.
p.      cm.
Originally published in 1997 by Edward Elgar Pub.
Includes bibliographical references and index.
ISBN 978-0-86597-702-0 (alk. paper)
ISBN 978-0-86597-703-7 (pbk.: alk. paper)
1. Economics.   2. Commercial policy   3. Condillac, Étienne Bonnot de, 1714–1780.
I. Eltis, Shelagh, 1937–   II. Eltis, Walter, 1933–   III. Title.
HB 153.C7413   2008
381.01—dc22                              2006052873

Liberty Fund, Inc.
8335 Allison Pointe Trail, Suite 300
Indianapolis, Indiana 46250-1684

# CONTENTS

# PREFACE

WE BOTH read *Commerce and Government* for the first time in 1990, and we were astonished that such a brilliantly written and powerfully argued book had made so little impact, and that it had never been translated into English. We resolved then, six years ago, that we would produce the first English language edition.

*Commerce and Government* was published in the same year as Adam Smith's *Wealth of Nations,* and their analysis and implications for policy have much in common. It was presented with the comparative brevity and precision of a distinguished philosopher of the French Enlightenment, who was one of the first to base value on utility, an achievement which was recognised after the marginal revolution of the 1870s.

Eighteenth-century France was not fertile ground for the demolition of dirigisme, and the advocacy of the universal benefits of competition was resisted everywhere by vested interests. The physiocrats who controlled an economic journal in which the book was reviewed took exception to Condillac's powerful demonstration that industry and commerce and not merely agriculture contributed to the wealth of France. The reviews were dismissive, the great preferred Colbert, so *Commerce and Government* made little headway in France, and British political economists of the eighteenth century were unaware of it, so there was no demand for an immediate translation. The abbé Morellet sent a copy to the Earl of Shelburne, the future British Prime Minister, with the accolade that "in every part of it you will find freedom of commerce sustained." There may have been an occasional nineteenth- or twentieth-century British Prime Minister who could plausibly be expected to wish to read 90,000 words of French political economy in French, but the eighteenth century was another world.

After 1990 we pursued detailed research, on Condillac's life: Chapter 1 (by Shelagh Eltis) is the result; and on the impact of his economics, which is outlined in Chapter 2 (by Walter Eltis). This was preceded by conference papers on his economics in the École Normale Supérieure in St-Cloud, Paris, and in the University of Birmingham, with the subsequent publication of articles on Condillac's economics in French and English language journals.

Condillac's life is a revelation. He combined the respect and friendship of Voltaire and Rousseau (he is prominent in the *Confessions*) with the high regard of the King and the Church. He was appointed Director of Studies to Louis XV's grandson, the Bourbon heir to the throne of Parma, and after the success of that assignment, he was invited to go on to supervise the education of the three royal children who subsequently reigned in France: Louis XVI, Louis XVIII and Charles X. He declined that invitation which could have changed the world if he had had any impact.

In 1796, after the Revolution, the Minister of the Interior, no less, believed that education in France would be advanced by a complete edition of Condillac's works which made use of all his posthumous papers. Orders were given for the preparation of an edition which appeared in 1798 in twenty-three volumes and included *Commerce and Government*. The story is outlined in Chapter 3. It takes a certain kind of genius to earn the admiration of liberal philosophers, a monarchy and a post-revolutionary government.

It will give us great pleasure if this first English language translation increases the attention which Condillac's economics deservedly receives. We have had valuable help from the Taylorian Library in Oxford, the Direction des Archives Municipales in Grenoble, Professor Ramon Tortajada of the University of Grenoble, Professor Gloria Vivenza of the University of Verona, Dr Adam Brown, and the participants at the conferences in St-Cloud and Birmingham.

SHELAGH ELTIS
WALTER ELTIS
*Oxford*

# THE LIFE AND CONTRIBUTION
## TO ECONOMICS OF THE
### ABBÉ DE CONDILLAC

# 1 Étienne Bonnot, Abbé de Condillac, 1714–1780

## BIRTH AND FAMILY

Étienne Bonnot, known to posterity as the abbé de Condillac, was born in Grenoble on 30 September 1714.[1] He was the youngest child of a large family. His parents both came from families of lawyers and officials which entered the *noblesse de robe* in the early eighteenth century. The *noblesse de robe* was an aristocracy built on the purchase of offices under the monarchy. Such offices could be very expensive to purchase. In 1705, Gabriel Bonnot, Étienne's father, paid 10,000 livres for that of Secretary of the King in the Court of the Parlement of the Dauphiné, which brought him noble rank with the title vicomte de Mably. Local importance, tax exemptions, freedom from having soldiers billeted on one's household, and the income from fees payable to such officeholders all made such investments worthwhile. For the monarchy it brought desperately needed short-term income and an opportunity to recruit fresh talent.

Gabriel Bonnot amassed a fortune through this and other posts such as receiver of tailles—the main land and personal tax—and as registrar of births, etc., for the Oisan; he was also a royal castellan, though jealousy probably forced him to resign the latter two offices in 1714. He invested heavily in royal stock and in land: it has been calculated that he invested more than 85,000 livres in government stock, and, significantly, he seems to have reached the peak of his fortune in 1720. In 1719 he bought the domain of Mably for 300,000 livres and the following year that of Condillac, near Romans.

Gabriel Bonnot died in September 1726 leaving his wife and dependent children comfortably off, despite losses in his investment income following the collapse of Law's system. Each son was bequeathed the sum of 25,000

---

1. Condillac's birth date is established beyond question by his baptismal certificate, which says on 1 October 1714 that he was born on the previous day (see Jean B. Sgard, ed., *Corpus Condillac* [Geneva and Paris: Slatkine, 1981], 31). Yet many accounts of his life, such as that in Auguste Lebeau, *Condillac: Économiste* (Paris, 1903), erroneously give the year of his birth as 1715.

livres on attaining the age of twenty-five. Their mother also held a life interest in annuities in their names. The income from both these sources, reckoned at 1,300 livres a year, would have given Condillac a modest competence. It also meant that he was not to be forced into the Church as a younger
son whose family lacked means.

At his father's death Étienne was nearly twelve years old and, according to the 1836 *Encyclopédie des gens du monde,* unable to read because his
very weak eyesight had forbidden study. The same source states that he
then began his studies under a good curé and learnt fast. On 29 August 1728
Étienne acted as proxy godfather to his sister Anne's firstborn. The baptismal certificate is interesting as the first record of his using the title de Condillac, marking him out as a noble.[2] Condillac's eldest brother Jean was known
as M. de Mably from 1727 at least, and his brother Gabriel became famous as
the abbé de Mably.

### THE YOUNG PHILOSOPHER

Condillac's life is largely obscure until he emerges as a very successful
philosopher in the 1740s. The *Encyclopédie des gens du monde* says that aged
sixteen he joined Jean de Mably at Lyons where the latter held the office of
Provost General of the Maréchaussée, or constabulary, for the Lyonnais,
Forez and the Beaujolais, purchased in 1729 with his mother's assistance.
Lyons was the second city in France, and Condillac's brother a man of standing in it. However, by 1733 Condillac had joined his brother Gabriel, six
years his senior, in Paris, a new world for the young provincials, and un-
charted territory for the family.

Condillac registered in the Faculty of Arts at Paris. At his graduation as
an MA two years later, he is described as a *clericus* of Grenoble, so he will
have received the tonsure in that diocese. This should not lead to the assumption that a career in the Church was already inevitable as many of the
literary confraternity began as tonsured clerks, including Marmontel who

---

2. The above account of Condillac's family and early years is drawn from Sgard,
*Corpus Condillac,* which also has a family tree and much more detailed information about
his wider family.

married late in life, and many eighteenth-century abbés led secular lives after entering orders. Indeed, it was with this background in mind that in 1910 his family biographer, Count Baguenault de Puchesse, was eager to stress Condillac's proper wearing of clerical garb, regular attendance at mass and general orthodoxy in a century when to some the name *philosophe* seemed synonymous with free-thinker.[3]

The stages of his studies in Philosophy, Physics, Mathematics and Theology and his studies for the priesthood have been traced across documents by the authors of *Corpus Condillac,* a group of scholars who have assembled all the documentary evidence they could find for his life.[4] It seems probable that Condillac was at the Collège Mazarin, also known as the Four Nations, for his first two years, pursued theological studies at the Faculty of the Sorbonne and was in a Paris seminary, perhaps St Sulpice, for his preparation for the priesthood. He became a priest in 1741, though he never held cure of souls and is thought never to have said a mass.

Diderot and d'Alembert, distinguished *philosophes* with whom Condillac was to have close ties, had a similar education but finished their theological studies after three years and did not proceed, as did Condillac, Turgot and Morellet, to the "licence" in Theology, which required another two years' study and the day-long defence of a thesis.

This account of his studies shows that Condillac was the very opposite of a self-taught man as his own comment that one had to begin one's studies afresh on leaving the schools led some to suppose falsely. His remark indicated rather that he saw education as a life-long process, a view underlined when he wrote to his former pupil, the prince of Parma:

> It is for you Monseigneur, to instruct yourself alone from now on. I have already prepared you for that and even made you used to doing so . . . for the best education is not that which we owe to our teachers; it is that which we have given ourselves. (Condillac, *Oeuvres de Condillac,* 20:540–41)

3. Count G. Baguenault de Puchesse, *Condillac, sa vie, son oeuvre, son influence* (Paris: Plon-Nourrit, 1910), 9, 20.

4. This is under the editorship of Jean Sgard and is referred to as Sgard, *Corpus Condillac.*

In April 1740 Jean-Jacques Rousseau entered the household of Condillac's eldest brother, Jean Bonnot de Mably, at Lyons, as tutor to his small sons, and it is from his *Confessions* written in the late 1760s that some human detail about the abbé de Condillac and his brothers, Jean and Gabriel, emerges.

Many of Rousseau's friends and acquaintances commented on his prickliness and persecution complex. His time in the Mably household saw him caught pilfering wine from the cellar, in addition to which he says he was a failure as a tutor and fell in love with Mme de Mably. Yet he left voluntarily a year later and revisited the family in 1742. He says of M. de Mably that he behaved honourably and sensibly in the matter of the wine, that "he was a very courteous man; beneath a severity of manner in keeping with his employment he concealed a really gentle disposition and a rare kind-heartedness. He was just and equitable and—strange though this may seem in a police officer—he was also most humane" (Rousseau, *Confessions*, 255). Rousseau struck up a friendly acquaintance with the two abbés in Lyons, and their contacts continued over many years, in Condillac's case until about a year before Rousseau's death.

Through their recommendation of Paris lodgings to him we learn that at some point Condillac and his brother had lodged in the rue des Cordiers near the Sorbonne in what Rousseau called "a wretched room, in a wretched house, in a wretched street" (ibid., 266), student life no less! More interesting is his comment in *Émile* that "at a fairly advanced age" Condillac passed within his family and among his friends as of limited intelligence (*esprit borné*). Considering the great success of the abbé Mably, who gained European fame for his writings on history and government, and the worldly success of Jean and François Bonnot, intellectual and conversational standards must have been high in their company. It will not be surprising that Étienne, the much younger brother whose education had been delayed, preferred to keep his own counsel. Rousseau added, "Suddenly he showed himself as a philosopher and I do not doubt that posterity will mark out an honourable and distinguished place for him among the best reasoners and the most profound metaphysicians of his century" (Rousseau, *Émile*, 102).

Referring to the year 1745, Rousseau said in his *Confessions:*

I had also become intimate with the abbé de Condillac, who, like myself, cut no figure in the literary world, but who was born to be what he has become to-day. I was the first, perhaps, to see his stature, and to estimate him at his true worth. He seemed also to have taken a liking to me; and whilst I was confined to my room in the Rue Jean-Saint-Denis near the Opera, writing my Hesiod act, he sometimes came to take a solitary Dutch treat of a dinner with me. He was then engaged on his *Essai sur l'origine des connaissances humaines* which was his first work. When it was finished, the problem was to find a bookseller who would undertake it. Paris booksellers are hard and overbearing with authors who are just beginning; and metaphysics, not then in fashion, did not offer a very attractive subject. I spoke to Diderot about Condillac and his work; and introduced them to one another. They were born to agree, and they did so. Diderot induced Durand the bookseller to take the Abbé's manuscript, and that great metaphysician received from his first book—and that almost as a favour—a hundred crowns [300 livres], which perhaps he would not have earned but for me. As we all lived in widely different quarters the three of us met once a week at the Hôtel du Panier-Fleuri. These little weekly dinners must greatly have pleased Diderot; for though he almost always failed to keep his appointments, even with women, he never missed one of them. (324)

Their friendship must have become less close for a while, since a decade later Rousseau says, "Lacking a single friend who would be entirely mine, I required friends whose energies would overcome my inertia. It was for this reason that I cultivated and strengthened my relationship with Diderot and the Abbé de Condillac" (ibid., 387).

In the 1740s Condillac saw much of his brother Gabriel, the abbé de Mably, himself the author of a very successful work, *Parallèle des romains et des français par rapport au gouvernement*, published in 1740. The abbé de Mably worked as secretary for the minister, Cardinal de Tencin, from 1742 to around 1747. The Cardinal's sister, Mme de Tencin, a former nun and mistress of the Regent Orléans, held a renowned salon where the two brothers met such distinguished men of letters as the baron de Montesquieu, the abbés Prévost and de St Pierre, the playwright Marivaux and the historian Duclos, who was still close to Condillac twenty years later.[5] D'Alembert, the

5. Puchesse, *Condillac*, 15.

mathematician and *philosophe*, a Member of the Académie from 1754, was her unacknowledged, illegitimate son.

Until the publication of Condillac's first book in 1746, his brother will doubtless have seemed his mentor. However, the abbé de Mably separated himself increasingly from the *philosophes* and moved out to Marly, while Condillac with his further philosophical publications was in close contact with Diderot and d'Alembert.

In 1748 Condillac had published anonymously the dissertation *Les monades*, with which he won a prize awarded by the Academy of Berlin. Maupertuis, the French President of the Academy of Berlin, may have been influential in securing Condillac's election to the Academy in 1749. Condillac wrote to him on Christmas Day 1749 to express his pleasure and gratitude at being elected to that body. Their correspondence corrects the mistaken later date of Condillac's election given by Puchesse.[6]

In the letter Condillac said that it was a friend, M. d'Alembert, who had given him the news. In two more letters in 1750 to Maupertuis, Condillac refers to d'Alembert, saying in a postscript to that of 12 August from Segrez, "We shall just make one parcel of our letters, M. d'Alembert and I: we are at the home of Monsieur the Marquis d'Argenson where one meets the best society" (Condillac, *Oeuvres de Condillac*, 2:535). D'Alembert was known to all as the wittiest of guests, so those later writers who have wished to show Condillac as dry, retiring and boring have to explain away their pleasure in each other's company. Marmontel, speaking of Mme Geoffrin's salon wrote, "Of that gathering, the gayest, most animated man, the most amusing in his gaiety, was d'Alembert . . . he made one forget in him the philosopher and scholar, to see only the lovable individual" (Marmontel, *Mémoires*, 1:300). When a false rumour of Condillac's death circulated in 1764 d'Alembert wrote to Voltaire that had it been true, "for my part I should have been distraught" (Voltaire, *Correspondance*, 57:4).

An important correspondent of Condillac's in the late 1740s was the Genevan mathematician and philosopher Gabriel Cramer. Cramer was ten years

---

6. L'abbé Étienne Bonnot de Condillac, *Oeuvres philosophiques de Condillac*, ed. Georges Le Roy, vol. 33 of *Corpus générale des philosophes françaises* (Paris: Presses Universitaires de France, 1947–51), 2:533.

older than Condillac and had an international reputation: he was a member of the Royal Society of London and of the Academy of Berlin. Condillac welcomed his comments on his philosophical ideas and hoped to visit him in Geneva in the autumn of 1749, but events precluded this.

Their correspondence mentions an especially close friend of Condillac's, Mlle Ferrand, a mathematician who commanded respect.[7] It has been suggested that she may have been the model for Mlle de la Chaux, Diderot's *"femme savante,"* shown by Laurence Bongie to be a fictitious character, though her salon is one that Puchesse had Condillac and Mably attending.[8] Condillac gave Mlle Ferrand the credit for exposing logical problems in his early work, and said that, though she had no pretensions to authorship, hers was the major contribution to his *Traité des sensations*, published in 1754, after her death.[9] This work has been the most highly regarded of Condillac's philosophical writings. It received favourable scholarly attention in the Jesuit *Journal de Trévoux*, while the readership of the *Gazette littéraire* was informed of it by the Chevalier Grimm whose generally hostile and patronising tone may reflect cooling relations between his close friend Diderot and Condillac. Reviewing this work Grimm attacked Condillac's celebrated device of gradually giving life to a statue, saying, "This idea, in itself poetic, has not been embellished in this Treatise by the decoration of poetry, nor by the wealth of a brilliant imagination. Our author has treated it with all the wisdom of a philosopher, and all the subtlety of a metaphysician" (Raynal et al. *Correspondance Littéraire*, 2:438). Buffon too had a statue in his *Histoire naturelle* which Grimm preferred, "The first movement of M. de Buffon's statue is to stretch out its hand to seize the sunshine. What a notion! what poetry!" (ibid., 442).[10]

7. L'abbé Étienne Bonnot de Condillac, *Lettres inédites à Gabriel Cramer*, ed. Georges Le Roy (Paris, 1953), 35, 52, 59, 77.

8. Laurence L. Bongie, "Diderot's femme savante," in *Studies on Voltaire and the Eighteenth Century* (Oxford: The Voltaire Foundation at the Taylor Institution, 1977), 166:149–63, and Puchesse, *Condillac*, 13.

9. L'abbé Étienne Bonnot de Condillac, *Traité des sensations*, in *Oeuvres de Condillac* (Paris, 1798), 3:52.

10. Eighteenth-century taste valued poetry very highly, and Turgot wrote a lot of it, while it launched Marmontel on his career when he won a prize which brought him

None the less Grimm was clearly moved by Condillac's dedication of the work. He wrote, "If we believe M. l'abbé de Condillac, Mlle Ferrand had a very large hand in the *Traité des sensations,* and I do not know if this admission does more honour to her or to the person who makes it. What is certain is that the introduction is not the least interesting part of the *Traité.* Our Philosopher, in speaking of Mlle Ferrand, delivers the eulogy from his own heart, and one likes to read an author who has the fortune to know the price of friendship" (ibid., 438).

The dedication of the 1754 book was to the comtesse de Vassé who lived in the same house as Mlle Ferrand, her close friend, and held a salon alone after Mlle Ferrand's death. The two women sheltered the Young Pretender, who was supposed to have been expelled from France as a term of the 1748 peace treaty between Britain and France. We are told that he listened in concealment to the conversations at their salon.[11] Mlle Ferrand left Condillac 6,000 livres in her will in 1752 to buy books. Mme de Vassé was to die in 1768 in Condillac's Paris home.

The salon of the wealthy bourgeoise Mme Geoffrin was for the 1750s what Mme de Tencin's had been a decade earlier. Puchesse relied on Lemonnier's painting entitled *Une soirée chez Mme Geoffrin en 1755* to assert that Condillac attended her salon in the distinguished company shown. Unfortunately, this picture is worthless as an historical record and was only composed for the Empress Josephine half a century later. It may simply be taken as indicating those who were regarded as the most distinguished Frenchmen of the mid-century.[12]

## Philosopher with an International Reputation

By the mid-1750s Condillac was a philosopher with an international reputation. He was an admirer of Locke, whose works he had only read in trans-

---

to Voltaire's attention (Jean François Marmontel, *Oeuvres complètes,* vol. 1, *Mémoires* [Paris: Amable Costes, 1819], 87, 118).

11. L'abbé Raynal, baron Friedrich Melchior Grimm, and Denis Diderot, *Correspondance littéraire,* ed. Maurice Tourneux (Paris: Garnier Frères, 1877), 12:343.

12. John Lough, "Lemonnier's painting, *Une soirée chez Mme Geoffrin en 1755,*" *French Studies* 45, no. 3 (1991): 268–78.

lation, as he himself stated.[13] He demanded a scientific approach based on observation.

In 1749 his *Traité des systèmes* appeared. This, we learn from Condillac, in a letter to Cramer, particularly impressed Diderot.[14] In 1755 his *Traité des animaux* was published, seen primarily as an attack on Buffon. His dissertation on freedom of December 1754 is often not separately mentioned, as it was described as an extract from his *Traité des sensations*. Jacques Proust deals at length with the controversy on human free will as against determinism which involved many men of letters at the time and ended with the publication of Voltaire's *Candide* in 1759. He concludes, "Condillac like Locke and Diderot absolutely rejects the traditional theory of freedom . . . But while Diderot, in reaction, radically affirms determinism, Condillac keeps the notion and the name of freedom, without however making the useful distinction Locke made between freedom and free-will." Proust regards Condillac's position as "lame, philosophically contradictory, and in addition lacking in clarity" (Proust, *Diderot et l'Encyclopédie*, 321).

This was all dangerous territory. Diderot was imprisoned for some time in Vincennes by order of a *lettre de cachet* after the publication of his *Lettre sur les aveugles* in 1749. So one may wonder whether Condillac was thinking in part of the censorship. Yet here one might quote what Condillac wrote of himself in 1747 to Cramer, "I follow experience, when it leaves me, I no longer have a guide and I stop. That is all I can do as a philosopher. As a theologian, faith comes to my aid when experience ceases to enlighten me" (Condillac, *Lettres inédites*, 82).

The best known publication of these years in France was the *Encyclopédie* which was principally Diderot's undertaking, though d'Alembert and a host of other scholars were involved. The first volume appeared in 1751. It has been reckoned on grounds of style and content that many entries could be by Condillac, but all that is certain is that in the entry *Divination* Diderot gives a free résumé of Condillac's *Traité des systèmes*, and refers to him by name.[15]

---

13. L'abbé Étienne Bonnot de Condillac, *Oeuvres de Condillac*, vol. 1, *l'Essai sur l'origine des connoissances humaines* (Paris, 1798), 230.

14. See Condillac, *Lettres inédites*, 54.

15. Denis Diderot, *Oeuvres complètes*, vol. 15 (Paris: Le Club Française, 1973), 224.

Bongie comments that Condillac's and Diderot's friendship lapsed soon after the mid-century. However, they were closely studying each other's work during the 1750s, and Diderot commended Condillac's later *Cours d'études* to the Empress Catherine of Russia in 1775, calling it an excellent work of an excellent instructor (Diderot, *Oeuvres complètes*, 15:814–15).

Bongie comments that Diderot himself said of his *Lettre sur les sourds et muets*, addressed to the abbé Batteux, that it could just as well have been addressed to the abbé de Condillac or to M. du Marsais. He regards Diderot as having let Condillac down by not defending him against the charges of plagiarism levelled at him by Grimm, Buffon and Fréron. He points out that Condillac's letter of 12 August 1750 to Maupertuis shows that he was already working on his statue. Condillac's own words to Maupertuis in the same letter indicate how his way of going about his writing could have delayed publication. He wrote:

> I have several works that I set about in turn: the one I am concerned with at present deals with the origin and generation of feeling. It is a statue which I bring to life step by step. I have found some problems in it, but I think I have overcome them. I am going to leave it to one side for a few months in my usual way. (Condillac, *Oeuvres philosophiques*, 2:535)

## Condillac and the Censorship

The intellectual excitement of that decade alarmed the orthodox and conservative. The case of the abbé Prades alerted the censorship, not all hostile to the encyclopedists and *philosophes*. The thesis of the abbé Prades had been accepted by the Sorbonne in December 1751, but in early 1752 the Parlement of Paris, or supreme law court, hastened to attack it as undermining the miracles of the Gospels. The thesis was condemned to be burned, and the abbé had to leave France. Since the abbé's earlier theses had won golden opinions and he had been seen as a promising theologian, the Parlement's reaction might seem strange. The abbé's known collaboration in the *Encyclopédie* is plausibly thought to have brought the censorship troubles upon him.[16] Mo-

---

16. John S. Spink, "Un abbé philosophe: l'affaire de J.-M. de Prades," *Dix-huitième siècle* 3 (1971): 157–59.

rellet commented that after the Prades incident he continued to see Diderot, but in secret.

Voltaire wrote to Helvétius in 1766, when falsely denying that he was the author of a book attributed to a long-dead abbé, "It is doubtless better to be ignored and in peace than to be known and persecuted" (Helvétius, *Correspondance générale*, 3:264–65). Rousseau was about to be arrested when he fled France in 1762 after the publication of *Émile*, and Voltaire spent many years abroad, fearful to return to France, though his reputation and readership grew in his absence.

Condillac himself had some trouble with the censorship: the abbé de Mably wrote to a friend in May 1744 that the censor was holding up Condillac's first book, *Essai sur l'origine des connoissances humaines*, for a long time. But it was not only the government censorship that had the power to have books banned, confiscated or burned and their authors pursued. In 1759, following the uproar over Helvétius's book *De l'esprit*, seen as atheistic, the Parlement of Paris undertook a general revision of all the "dangerous" books that had appeared in the previous ten years. The Procurator General, Joly de Fleury, intended to denounce the *Encyclopédie*, *De l'esprit*, Diderot's philosophical works *Lettre sur les sourds et muets* and *Lettre sur les aveugles*, some works by Voltaire, Rousseau's *Discours sur l'origine et la fondation de l'inégalité*, and Condillac's *Traité des sensations*. On further reflection he omitted Diderot's and Condillac's works, and the Parlement's decree was declared inoperative for encroaching on the Chancellor's authority. The Chancellor was none other than the father of Malesherbes, who was in charge of the printing houses and whom he had appointed.

The legislation in force in eighteenth-century France regarding the production and distribution of books was draconian. As an example, the declaration of April 1757 punished with death all authors, editors, printers or bookcarriers of works tending to attack religion, to excite opposition and undermine the king's authority. It condemned to the galleys for life or for a period of time anyone who had not obeyed all the formalities. All authors were supposed to submit their completed manuscripts to a royal censor and to obtain letters of privilege for them, or, in the case of cheap works or short leaflets, from the lieutenant of police. The privileges were registered, and printing was not permitted until all the written formalities had been completed. There were more than a hundred censors, all in Paris, who were supposed to have specialist knowledge. Diderot and Condillac themselves worked as censors.[17] After the censor had given his approbation he could be in trouble as much as the author if the work caused a stir.

Practice modified the law. Already towards the end of Louis XIV's reign, tacit permissions were introduced. They were given by the censor who signed the approval and signed the manuscript or a printed copy. The list was held at the Syndical Chamber of the Parisian booksellers. But as they were not sealed with the Great Seal, and as they were not printed at the end of the work, the public did not know who had given the approval. This was the only way for foreign printers to bring themselves within the law. As Belin said, in general the censors were not very hard on these foreign editions which it was difficult to modify and often cruel to prohibit. Often the author's nationality and his religion were taken into account, and a book was authorised which would not have been approved if its author had been French, because it was the work of a non-Catholic republican. And then certain over-bold passages were ignored in consideration of the difficulty of asking for corrections.

The practice of French authors to pretend that their works had been printed abroad or were even by pretended foreign authors can be understood in the light of this. Malesherbes explained the "simple tolerances":

> Often the need to allow a book was felt and yet one did not want to admit that one was permitting it; so one did not wish to give any express permission: for example that was what happened when a foreign edition had been made of some books which displeased the clergy and hence some cardinal minister, and this edition had spread in France despite obstacles placed in its way.
>
> In that case and in many others one took the course of saying to a bookseller that he could undertake his edition, but secretly; that the police would pretend to be unaware of it and would not have it seized; and since one could not foresee just how far the anger of the clergy and the law would go, one warned him always to be on the ready to make his edition disappear as soon as he was warned, and he was promised advanced warning before his premises were searched. (Malesherbes, *Mémoire*, 254)

17. See Sgard, *Corpus Condillac*, 63–64.

It is not known how Condillac navigated these treacherous waters, but he obtained warm reviews from the Jesuit *Journal de Trévoux* for all his philosophical works. About his 1749 *Traité des systèmes* the reviewer wrote, "This essay bears all the characteristics of works which deserve to pass to posterity, great clarity in style, much force and exactness in reasoning, and an exact and rigorous analysis" ( *Journal de Trévoux*, 44:469). Though the reviewer did not share Condillac's aversion to systems, he praised him for his examples, which he said did more than prove: "they enlighten, instruct and develop very tricky questions which needed to pass through the crucible of the metaphysical and geometrical spirit of M. l'abbé de Condillac." Described as "An avowed partisan of Locke, he has attacked the thought of Descartes and Malebranche with more method, clarity and success than the English philosopher; but like the English philosopher he is happier destroying than building." By 1755 the *Journal* notes that Condillac's *Traité des sensations* is seen by some critics as exuding materialism, "a hateful suspicion" which the reviewer does not share and which should not be advanced without the strongest proof (ibid., 60:165). In Condillac's defence he says, "Besides the author holds forth so learnedly on the Creation and on revelation that in all these respects his orthodoxy seems beyond attack." However, in the same year at the end of a very long review of Condillac's *Traité des animaux* the reviewer concludes, "One hopes that he will set out in full what one finds here in the two chapters, the one on 'The existence and attributes of God' and the other on 'Principles of Morality'; and that he will also work on a truth which is only stated at the end of the seventh chapter of the second part, namely that *true Philosophy cannot be contrary to Faith*" (ibid., 726).

## Director of Studies to the Prince of Parma

Don Philippe, the Duke of Parma, was the husband of Louis XV's eldest daughter, Louise Élisabeth. He was also son of the Bourbon King of Spain by his second wife, Elisabeth Farnese. The appointment of a tutor to their son was therefore of interest to both courts. Enlightenment had secured a hold in the French court where, in Mme de Pompadour's time as official royal mistress, Quesnay and Marmontel were among those who benefited from her patronage. Official Spanish and Italian circles were less receptive. Madame Élisabeth was well aware that the Jesuits would be put out at Condillac's appointment as he would displace one of their number. She wrote to her husband that she had consulted many people on Condillac's fitness for the post with regard to his orthodoxy and noted that there was murmuring about his rather metaphysical book (she is almost certainly referring to the *Traité des sensations*), but she adds firmly, "Our son must be a good catholic and not a doctor of the Church: it would be pointless for him to study all the controversies" (Bédarida, *Parme et la France*, 412). Since the Queen and the powerful minister the duc de Choiseul are also said to have wanted Condillac, he took up this prestigious position.

Condillac was at the same time seen by the doyen of the *philosophes,* Voltaire, as one of them. In a letter of 1756, Voltaire wrote to him saying that at last he had had time to read Condillac with the attention he merited. Voltaire knew the *Essai sur l'origine des connaissances humaines,* the *Traité des sensations* and the *Traité des animaux.* He suggested that Condillac might consider writing another work bringing together the ideas in these books. He goes on to say that the country is better than Paris for bringing thoughts together and diffidently suggests that Condillac might like to come to his home. Voltaire was ready to be Condillac's "elderly disciple" and offered his niece, Mme Denis, as a younger one, adding that Condillac would find plenty of people ready to take his dictation. The letter is important evidence that Condillac's problems with his eyesight were chronic. As Voltaire wrote, "I know that physically speaking you have eyesight as weak as the eyes of your mind are penetrating" (*Correspondance,* 30:142). In 1758, when the news that Condillac was to be tutor to the Prince of Parma had reached him, Voltaire wrote to Mme de Dompierre asking her if she knew whether the Prince was to be taught in Paris or whether Condillac was to go to Parma. In the latter case he hoped she would have the courage to persuade him to travel via Geneva and Turin, in which case Voltaire planned aloud to meet him at Lausanne, take him to his home, "Les Délices," and then meander to the Duchy (ibid., 33:78–79).

In a letter to d'Alembert of 1760 Voltaire is in no doubt of the acceptability of the education that the Prince will receive, "It seems to me that the Parmesan Prince is well encircled. He will have a Condillac and a Leire [Deleyre, later a regicide]. If with that he becomes a bigot, grace must be strong" (ibid., 44:159). Nothing had caused Voltaire to change his mind by December

1764 when false rumours of Condillac's death were current. Then, writing to Count d'Argental, representative of the court of Parma at Versailles, and his wife, Voltaire said, "We lose in him a good philosopher, a good enemy of superstition" (ibid., 66:198).

The Duchy, in which Condillac arrived in April 1758 to instruct his seven-year-old pupil, already had a considerable French presence. Its chief minister Dutillot, marquis de Felino, had begun his career attached to the Spanish court, but he was a major figure of the French Enlightenment and brought the latest books to the Duchy. Bédarida states that Dutillot knew Quesnay's *Tableau économique* from 1758 and his *Maximes générales* from 1760.[18] The ducal library had works by Voltaire, subscribed to the *Encyclopédie* and the *Gazette littéraire de l'Europe* and bought an *Essai sur le luxe,* which Bonnet, the Duke's Parisian banker and man of affairs, said was essential reading. Seventeenth-century classics were well represented in the library, which also acquired new works such as Rousseau's, his *Julie, ou la nouvelle Héloïse,* his *Lettres de la montagne,* and we are told by Mme de Chenonceaux that Condillac had his young pupil studying the *Contrat social.*[19] Father Paciaudi, himself a noted bibliophile, was busy adding to the library classical texts, French history and legal collections besides building up a renowned collection of English works. These are said in part to have come to Parma because of Condillac's reputation in England.

Dutillot was anxious to improve Parma's economy, its agriculture and industries by introducing more up-to-date French practice. He was also ready to learn from England, and received Duhamel's treatise on Jethro Tull's method of cultivation in 1751. In 1756 he wanted a subscription to Du Pont de Nemours's *Journal de l'agriculture, du commerce et des finances.* He head-hunted the famous printer Giambattista Bodoni to set up a press that would be the envy of other states. Though Bodoni and Condillac were not at Parma at the same time, it was his press that was to print the *Cours d'études,* the works based on Condillac's lessons to the Prince. The books of that press are now collectors' items.

---

18. H. Bédarida, *Parme et la France de 1748 à 1789* (Paris: Champion, 1928), 89.

19. Jean-Jacques Rousseau, *Rousseau, ses amis et ses ennemis, correspondance,* ed. M. G. Streckeisen-Moultou (Paris, 1865), 237.

Condillac was to receive every consideration at Parma. He had an annual income of 12,000 French livres. He seems to have had carte blanche with regard to books for his pupil, and he rapidly set about getting the very expensive (2,400 livres), and exceedingly rare, *Ad usum Delphini,* the course of studies written for the Grand Dauphin. From 1761 he had Deleyre, the young friend of Rousseau, to help him by making résumés of books too long for his pupil. Deleyre should have helped with the latter's historical instruction but does not appear to have been up to the task, so Condillac enlisted the help of his own brother, the abbé de Mably. In 1761 he received an early version of Mably's *Observations sur l'histoire de France,* and the volume *Étude d'histoire* in the *Cours d'études* was by Mably's hand though it is thought Condillac toned down some republican enthusiasms. Mably was handsomely thanked and rewarded by the Prince in December 1765.[20]

Claude Bonnet had instructions from Dutillot that Condillac was to be among a favoured few whose parcels could go by the official courier, saving expense and four days' delay. In 1765 Condillac was specially mentioned with Keralio and the bailli de Rohan as a person to whom the newly appointed French ambassador, baron de La Houze, should pay attention.[21]

While at Parma Condillac seems to have found plenty of congenial company. In later years he was still in touch with his colleague the under-governor, baron Keralio, jokingly known as "the Ogre." Condillac had his own nickname, "the Great Grumbler," which he happily applied to himself. The picture some have given of an austere and unsympathetic teacher is belied by Condillac's letter to Dutillot of 31 January 1761. Self-mockingly he begins, "Monsieur, I should really like to grumble." His plaint is of postal delays between the Minister's residence at Colorno and the capital, Parma. He goes on to say that the dismantleable "plan of defence" that Louis XV's engineers had made so that the little Prince could study the art of war had arrived. He continues:

20. Bédarida, *Parme et la France,* 257.

21. Bédarida, *Parme et la France,* gives an exhaustive account of the French presence in Parma based on archival material.

All is executed with great clarity and great precision. Nothing is more in-
structive; and that makes me want to learn warfare. We are agreed that the
Prince will give me lessons when he has profited from those of M. de Keralio. If he makes a good pupil out of me he will not be ignorant. (Bédarida,
"Lettres inédites," 243–44)[22]

He got on well with the Jesuit mathematicians Fathers Jacquier and Le Sueur
and with the librarian Father Paciaudi. Letters between Deleyre, Rousseau
and their and Condillac's mutual friend Mme de Chenonceaux show him
walking in the park at Colorno with Deleyre and his wife. The visiting phy-
sician, Tronchin, took him to task after he had eaten twelve small birds, or-
tolans, at one sitting, and noticed that the lesson had some effect as he only
ate six at the next meal![23] He became a member of an Arcadian assembly
with the name Auronte, and the poet Frugoni noted his fondness for wine
in a poem he wrote to celebrate the philosopher's recovery from smallpox.[24]
Condillac's letter to his good friend and patron Louis Jules Mancini Mazarin,
duc de Nivernais, when the latter had been looking for accommodation for
Condillac on his return to Paris, said, "I prefer a few more bottles of wine in
my cellar and less splendour in my furnishing and lodgings."[25] This letter is a
reminder that, though Condillac had not yet learnt that he was to have a life
pension in addition to the income from his abbey, he was never to know the
wealth of an abbé Véri with his countless servants and six-horse coach. Condillac said he would just take on two lackeys on his return to France.

It would be wrong to think that Condillac was deprived of intellectual
stimulation in Parma. The ducal family was intelligent. Before her marriage
to the Habsburg Archduke Joseph, they were searching for a German trans-

22. In *Émile* (234), Rousseau advocated that the tutor learn a new craft alongside his
pupil, as the only sure way of seeing that the pupil learnt well. Condillac probably expected his correspondent to be aware of this.

23. Sgard, *Corpus Condillac*, 72.

24. Bédarida, *Parme et la France*, 446, summarises the poem in French. The original
Italian poem is in Carlo I. Frugoni, *Opere poetiche*, collected and published by P. Manara
and C. C. Rezzonico (Parma, 1779), 7:339–46.

25. Condillac, *Oeuvres philosophiques*, 2:545.

lation of Racine's "Télémaque" so that Don Ferdinand's sister, the Infanta Isabelle-Marie, could learn the language. Don Ferdinand was such an apt pupil that already in 1763 the end of Condillac's task was seen as approaching. Don Philippe and his son were keen on the theatre, and they and many courtiers read a great deal. The duc de Nivernais teasingly pitied Condillac for only being able to hear concerts three or four times a week.[26]

Throughout his time in Parma Condillac and Nivernais kept up a regular correspondence. The Duke was ambassador to the court of Frederick of Prussia in 1756 and a plenipotentiary for France in the negotiations with England which led to the Peace of Paris of 1763. He was also highly regarded as a man of letters, and he was a Member of the French Academy from 1743. Their correspondence reads as letters between friends for all the careful respect for rank. Condillac nevertheless had in the Duke a powerful acquaintance who could use his influence both for Condillac and, at his request, for his family.

Family ties and obligations were important to Condillac throughout his life. In 1761 a very awkward problem had to be resolved when the duc de Choiseul gave the succession to the post of Provost of the Maréchaussée, held by the recently deceased M. de Mably, to his son-in-law and not to one of his sons. The recipient was later to be officially separated from his wife and may have misrepresented the family's wishes. Apparently the abbé de Mably should have handled the matter. Condillac was left to sort it all out from a distance. Nivernais gave sensible advice and all was put right, so an important source of income was not lost to Condillac's nephews. It can be seen from Condillac's letter that he had already had other correspondence about this.[27] Again the help of well-placed persons was invoked to gain entry for his niece, Mlle de Marsan, to the exclusive school of Saint-Cyr. Dutillot, d'Argental and Nivernais all worked to this end, and the young girl was admitted in April 1762 accompanied by the Parmesan Minister Plenipotentiary.[28]

26. Sgard, *Corpus Condillac*, 151.
27. Ibid., 148, 150.
28. H. Bédarida, "Lettres inédites de Condillac," *Annales de l'université de Grenoble* (1924): 233.

When a promised French benefice was unforthcoming after Condillac had held his post for four years, many important individuals busily pressed his claims on Louis XV and on the bishop of Orléans whose dossier it was. The bishop had to deal with so many claimants that his polite fending off of the representations on Condillac's behalf does not necessarily indicate hostility to the philosopher. Despite the urgings of the Dukes of Nivernais and Choiseul-Praslin, of Dutillot, d'Argental and even Don Philippe, it probably took Condillac's near-miraculous recovery from smallpox to obtain for him in 1765 the titular abbacy of Mureau in the diocese of Toul.[29]

Smallpox was a scourge of even affluent society in the eighteenth century. There was great interest in the risks of inoculation as against its benefits, and several of Condillac's letters show his readiness to obtain information about it for his correspondents who included La Condamine and the Italian nobleman and famous jurist Beccaria.[30] In November 1764 Condillac expected soon to be free from his post, when instead he was fighting for his life. The Court was preparing for the isolation of Don Ferdinand who was to be inoculated. There is no question of Condillac's having caught smallpox from his pupil's inoculation, since such was the fear of the disease that strict isolation of the Prince with the minimum of attendants plus his doctor had been arranged.[31]

Condillac was likewise closely confined in his illness, and, when his life was despaired of, instructions were given for the rapid sealing of his wardrobes and trunks in the event of his death. So close was that supposed to be that the church had already been draped for his burial. The bells of the convent precincts within which his house lay had been kept silent when he was critically ill, a considerate action for which the Duke thanked the abbess. It seems that he would have left many grieving friends and a pious reputation among the common people, since they believed, according to Deleyre, that

29. Ibid., 236–37.

30. See Sgard, *Corpus Condillac,* 152, for the Beccaria letter, and François Moureau, "Condillac et Mably: dix lettres inédites ou retrouvées," *Dix-huitième siècle* 23 (1991): 199, for that to La Condamine.

31. U. Benassi, "Il precettore famoso d'un nostro Duca," *Bollettino Storico Piacentino* 18, no. 1 (1923): 9.

he had gone to Heaven and returned. Certainly concern for his recovery was not confined to Parma. Deleyre gives the touching story of Condillac spending what he thought were his last hours dictating a letter to the Prince, his pupil, and after it was done asking to be left alone. Deleyre added that his recovery was complete. But Deleyre was writing in the following February, and his main point was that Condillac's very weak eyesight had received no further damage.[32] Dutillot, writing to d'Argental at the end of December, spoke of his being in a very weak state.[33]

According to Puchesse, after his recovery Condillac stayed on at Parma in order to attend the marriage of another sister of his pupil, Princess Marie-Louise, to the heir to the Spanish King.[34] This marriage, that of Isabelle-Marie to the future Emperor, and the later one of Don Ferdinand to another daughter of the Empress Maria Theresa show the important role of the Parmesan family in French diplomacy. The Family Compact of 1743 had already strengthened ties between the two major Bourbon houses.

However, Puchesse was mistaken. The wedding was to take place in Spain, and Condillac was not even part of Don Philippe's train accompanying the princess. Condillac still held the position of a gentleman of the Chamber given him by Don Philippe, but he was at leisure to visit Venice with Father Paciaudi in the spring of 1765.[35] They were received by the best company. Condillac was clearly delighted by the *casini*, small apartments that the nobility had near the cathedral of San Marco. In the eighteenth century, women too wanted them as salons for receiving guests, for concerts and for gaming. It seems that their reputation was not always above suspicion.

Writing on his return to Parma to Sagramoso, a Veronese diplomat who had been their guide, Condillac warmly thanks him, hopes that they are beginning a long friendship and asks him to convey his thanks to the Erizzo family.[36] In June, in another letter to Sagramoso, Condillac hopes he may have a

---

32. Sgard, *Corpus Condillac*, 74.

33. Benassi, "Il precettore famoso," 10.

34. Puchesse, *Condillac*, 126.

35. F. Piva, "Condillac a Venezia. Con alcune lettere inedite," in *Studi Francesi*, no. 64, Anno 22 (1) (1978): 77.

36. Ibid., 81–82.

further visit to Venice and writes delightfully, "While waiting, I should like to know just how long Madame Cordemila will be at her country house. It is not that I dare flatter myself that I shall be able to go there, but I may at least occupy myself with the thought, and who knows if it will not come true? A metaphysician can do a lot with ideas" (ibid., 82). Condillac was on the point of leaving for the baths of Lucca and reports from there in mid-July.

However, the death of the Duke, Don Philippe, from smallpox in July 1765 forced Condillac's return to Parma before he had seen anything of Tuscany. In a letter of 18 August to Sagramoso Condillac gives an interesting account of how his pupil reacted to becoming sovereign of the duchy:

> On my arrival I found the young prince like a lion. His situation goads him: he remembers things he has learnt, he explains them to himself, he watches over himself, he wants to do well, he wishes to inform himself; in a word, he is affected by emulation, the only thing he had lacked, since he has intelligence and facility. (Piva, "Condillac a Venezia," 83)

Condillac also informs Sagramoso that his time as tutor has ended. In the autumn he was at Genoa and then Milan, where he met the Marchese Beccaria whose *Dei Delitti e delle pene* gained much attention in France. Beccaria was himself honoured to meet Condillac as he wrote to Morellet.[37] A letter of Father Jacquier shows Condillac in his company at Rome in March. In June Condillac was at Naples, in July at Florence, then at Lucca again and back at Parma in September. He returned to Paris in early March 1767.

## THE ACADEMICIAN

The *Mémoires secrets* chose to see Condillac as returning a disappointed man, no decoration, no bishopric, etc., to obscurity.[38] That was far from the truth. In October his impending election to the Académie française was being talked about, though his brother was thought to be a rival for the place. On 22 October d'Alembert wrote to inform Voltaire that Condillac was to take the chair made vacant by the death of the abbé Olivet. Voltaire applauded the

---

37. Sgard, *Corpus Condillac*, 76.
38. *Mémoires secrets* (London: Adamson, 1777–89), 3:194.

choice.[39] The inaugural ceremony on 22 December was attended by a crowd of fashionable ladies, though one observer considered that only the witty fables of the duc de Nivernais would have saved them from boredom.[40] Voltaire read Condillac's speech and approved it in a letter to Charles Bordes.[41] It is interesting that Voltaire describes the Académie as a company dedicated uniquely to eloquence and poetry, so he has to defend the intrusion of philosophy.

Condillac was paid an unusual favour by being summoned to an audience with the King to present his Académie speech. He was afterwards presented to the Dauphin and the royal children. Lafaye in the nineteenth-century *Encyclopédie des gens du monde* said that the *reine-mère*, though he must have meant Queen Marie Leszcynska, told him she wished he would undertake the education of the sons of the Dauphin, who later ruled as Louis XVI, Louis XVIII and Charles X. "He declined such a dangerous honour, fearing failure . . . and because he did not want to stir up powerful enmities against him" (Sgard, *Corpus Condillac*, 91). Later in his life Condillac crossed out the whole passage dealing with his personal relations with Louis XV from his Académie speech.[42]

As Condillac had tasted freedom in his Italian travels and as he had good company in friends such as Nivernais and Duclos, a quieter life was doubtless inviting. It never seemed likely that the man whose letters show a delight in company would flee it on his return to France. Fortunately the team of scholars who produced *Corpus Condillac* have seen the Registers of the Académie française which contradict Puchesse's assertion that he did not often attend its sessions.[43] In fact he was present at 316 sessions, and his attendance only drops markedly in 1774, by which time he was living in Flux. Even so it is only in the last two years of his life that he attended just once a year.[44]

39. Voltaire (François-Marie Arouet), *Correspondance*, ed. Theodore Besterman (Geneva: Institut et Musée Voltaire, and University of Toronto Press, 1968), 70:127, letter 14319.

40. *Mémoires secrets*, 4:177–80.

41. Voltaire, *Correspondance*, 71:21.

42. Puchesse, *Condillac*, 140–41.

43. Ibid., 18.

44. Sgard, *Corpus Condillac*, 92.

*Philosophes* were strongly represented in the Académie when Condillac joined it, though the King expected to have a veto over appointments to its ranks, and this became an issue when Suard was first elected. The *philosophes* were accepted in society, whereas the Jesuits were being expelled from country after country. At the reception given for the Danish monarch on 20 November 1768 Condillac was in the company of d'Alembert, l'abbé Barthélemy, Bernard, Diderot, Grimm, Helvétius, d'Holbach, Marmontel and Morellet among others.[45] Voltaire could be confident that d'Alembert would pass on to Condillac suggested material for his acceptance speech to the Académie.

Condillac seems to have had an uninterrupted friendship with d'Alembert, whereas the absence of any mention of him in the correspondence between Mme d'Epinay and the abbé Galiani covering the years after Condillac's return from Italy until he moved from Paris to the Loire valley in 1773 indicates that he was distanced from the society of Diderot and Grimm.

A passage from the count d'Angivilliers' memoirs, *Épisodes de ma vie,* quoted in a footnote to Helvétius's correspondence, says that Mme de Vassé, whose character he could not praise too much, had bound him in close friendship with the brothers Mably and Condillac, her close friends who had fallen out with each other. There is no detail of the quarrel nor of its seriousness. Happily, d'Angivilliers says that he and she reunited the brothers. Mme de Vassé died from cancer in Condillac's Paris home on 2 June 1768 in the presence of d'Angivilliers and Condillac.[46] D'Angivilliers adds that she was equally a friend of the "fanatic and madman, Helvétius." He was writing after the Revolution when the *philosophes,* especially those whose books had offended, were held responsible for it. It seems quite likely that Condillac saw something of Helvétius too. What is certain is that in 1776 Condillac was staying with the widowed Mme Helvétius at Auteuil when he wrote to the Marquis Rangoni.[47]

45. Claude-Adrien Helvétius, *Correspondance générale* (Oxford: Voltaire Foundation and University of Toronto Press, 1991), 3:264–65.

46. Ibid., 304. Her death may have been the sad circumstance referred to in Condillac's letter of 9 October 1768 to the Prince of Parma (Condillac, *Oeuvres philosophiques,* 2:549).

47. Sgard, *Corpus Condillac,* 154–55.

The general view held in philosophical circles was that, though Condillac had done an excellent job in educating his Prince, the latter was a dull and ungrateful pupil. In this context it is particularly interesting to look at letters that Condillac wrote to Don Ferdinand from Paris in 1767 and 1768. In one of May 1767 Condillac tells how he was received at Court and questioned about his pupil. He says that he related the positive things about his pupil but kept quiet about the negative ones. He challenges his former pupil to apply himself so that this picture of him may become true. He continues:

> it would be a mortal disappointment for me if the public did not estimate you to the extent that I love you. Try, Monseigneur, to write some letters to me in which there will be something to show how you are thinking, that you are reflecting and that you are occupying yourself usefully. Your style must show that you find pleasure in your diversions, that you find pleasure in your occupations, that you apply yourself to everything, and that you do nothing with indifference. (Condillac, *Oeuvres philosophiques*, 2:547)

An August letter shows that the now sovereign Duke had written to Condillac, who, after giving him much instruction on his Latin, goes on to tell him that he has shown the letter to the duc de Nivernais, the comtesse de Rochefort, the historian Duclos and assembled company where he was dining. It met with approval in that distinguished company, but Condillac still thought exhortations to continue improving were necessary. He gave advice on letter-writing. Here the contemporary practice of handing round letters and even writing them for publication should be held in mind: "letters and conversations should only be an exchange [commerce] of enlightenment, of friendship, of entertainment, there should be no constraint, for the absence of freedom is the ruin of trade [commerce]" (ibid., 548). The metaphor seems revealing for the later author of *Le Commerce et le Gouvernement*.

When Condillac writes in October of the same year, he thanks the Duke for the dinner service he has been given and says he has sent more history notebooks and will continue to do so in order that Don Ferdinand may have enough to read in the winter. He again praises him for his letter which he has shown to the same named individuals. The next letter is a year later, and his praise is this time for the Duke's feeling when Dutillot's life was in danger. He also praises his bearing during a visit to Mantua. He writes:

you conducted yourself like an angel, and I have been delighted at it. However I have kept on delaying complimenting you on it because I found myself in very sad circumstances, but, Monseigneur, you must always scold your tutor when he does not write to you; because if you do not make me reproaches I shall be in the right to reproach you, I shall say that you do not care about having my news, since you do not ask me for it, so you see that my silence puts you in the wrong. You must realize that sovereigns are often obliged to make the first moves, and that no one goes up to them unless they cover half the way, or even more . . .

What, Monseigneur, are your pursuits and your entertainments? For I am interested in both. As for me, I am waiting with impatience for the news of your marriage, then I shall have the pleasure of paying court to you, and it will be a real holiday for me. I hope it will be for next Spring, I shall see the start of the happiness you promise yourself; you will be happy, Monseigneur, I hope and I wish for it with all my heart. (Ibid., 2:549)

The relationship between them sounds affectionate at this point, and the Duke is still ready to make an effort for his former tutor. However, later events such as Don Ferdinand's sanction of the interference with the printing of the *Cours d'études* show that the Duke turned against Condillac. The usual explanation is that under the influence of his Habsburg wife, Don Ferdinand became a bigoted Catholic: it is not documented by further correspondence between them.

During the 1770s Condillac's presence has been noted at several salons, those of Mlle de Lespinasse and Mme du Bocage and also "*chez* Collé" twice a week. Nivernais had arranged for him to have the use of two small boxes at the Comédie française. None of this fits the picture of a man who avoided society and was awkward in it that some nineteenth-century accounts, and some twentieth-century accounts relying on them, would have one see.[48]

---

48. The first chapter of Sgard, *Corpus Condillac*, "Réalites et légendes," summarises many different and sometimes contradictory accounts of his personality given in mostly nineteenth-century works. Modern scholars have had as varied views as Roger Lefèvre, who entitled his book *Condillac, ou la joie de vivre* (Paris: Seghers, 1966), and Isabel Knight (*The Geometric Spirit: The Abbé de Condillac and the French Enlightenment* [New Haven, Conn., 1968], 6), who saw his life as austere.

Julie de Lespinasse was a remarkable woman. Like d'Alembert, she was the illegitimate child of an aristocrat. Her mother had her educated, but she was left with little money on her mother's death, and Mme du Deffand's patronage rescued her from work as a governess.[49] She helped with her salon from 1754 to 1764, until a quarrel with her patroness led to her setting up her own. Marmontel in his memoirs sang her praises in encouraging conversation, adding, "And take good note that the heads which she stirred at her will were neither feeble nor frivolous; Condillac and Turgot were among them; d'Alembert was like a simple docile child in her company" (Marmontel, *Mémoires*, 1:415). Others who attended her salon were Condorcet, Suard, Morellet, Galiani, Mably, Shelburne, d'Argenson, Diderot, Thomas.[50] This does not mean that all were attending at the same time; Galiani, for instance, had had to leave France in June 1769 on the orders of the duc de Choiseul.

Condillac, the Academician, writer and man in society, was also commendatory abbot of Mureau in the diocese of Toul. Business connected with the abbey, the reward for his service as tutor to Louis XV's grandson, took some of his time in these years. It is thought improbable that he ever visited Mureau. However, he had to employ lawyers to represent his and the community's property interests in tithes.[51] His income from the abbey was 8,000 livres a year, the same as his pension from Parma, and together with other investment income will have enabled him to keep up his accommodation at Paris and pursue his writing without financial worries.

## RETIREMENT TO FLUX AND FINAL PUBLICATIONS

A major development in Condillac's later life was the purchase in April 1773 of the property of Flux near Beaugency which bordered the river Loire. It was Condillac's money in large part which enabled this house with chapel and land to be acquired by Mme de Sainte-Foy, his niece. The property is thought to have been bought with serious cultivation in mind. It was his chief home until his death, though for a number of years he also kept a Paris

---

49. Mme du Deffand was the correspondent of Horace Walpole over many years.

50. Julie de Lespinasse, *Lettres inédites*, introduction by M. Charles Henry (1887), 8.

51. See Sgard, *Corpus Condillac*, 82–85, for some details of the management of the abbey.

apartment, and he continued to visit Paris even when he no longer had any place there. Family tradition, as given by his great-great-nephew, Count Baguenault de Puchesse, the grandson of Mme de Sainte-Foy, has it that life in the country stimulated his interest in economic debate.

Condillac had trouble in publishing his *Cours d'études* which was to establish him as an enlightened educator and make his pupil famous. Initially all went well. Bodoni began work on it shortly after his arrival in Parma in 1768, which indicates Dutillot's personal interest in the task. Condillac busied himself with correcting manuscripts and began receiving volumes from the Bodoni press with a view to an additional French edition.

Dutillot was brusquely dismissed in mid-1771; but his Spanish successor, Llano, let the printing continue, and the great enterprise was finished by the end of 1772. However, the Church could operate its separate censorship. Count Lalatta, bishop of Parma, opposed publication. The work was given to Father Andrea Mazza to examine. He found in it the mark of a free-thinker, bold comments on the Church's deeds and great scorn towards the Spanish and their rulers. No printed volumes could leave Bodoni's workshops.[52]

If de Loynes d'Autroche was correct, Condillac was faced with a huge task as some of his manuscripts of volumes in the *Cours d'études* had been lost in transit from Parma to France, and he had to begin them afresh since his request for printed versions was refused. By that time he is believed to have had just four of the printed volumes.[53] Condillac's industriousness was remarkable as he managed none the less to have a French edition prepared, which came out in 1775. The coincidence in time with Turgot's ministry is surely significant. The decision to allow publication infuriated the authorities in Parma, and a proclamation in the Duke's name denied the false and calumnious pretence that the works had issued from the Duchy's press and ordered any copies found to be surrendered. However, in 1782, after Condillac's death, the Parma edition eventually appeared, though with the false date of the French Deux Ponts edition.[54]

*Le Commerce et le Gouvernement* also had problems with the censorship.

52. Bédarida, *Parme et la France*, 417.
53. Ibid., 417 footnote.
54. Ibid., 418.

Since the edict of 1764 that allowed the export of grain from France, a debate had raged on that policy and on the wisdom or otherwise of keeping
police regulation of grain sales and movements. This is discussed in detail in
the next chapter (pp. 45–50). Another matter which involved people of importance was the revocation of the *Compagnie des Indes'* monopoly of trade
with India and the Indies. Condillac has much to say about both these controversial matters, though he does not enter into personalities. While Turgot's views will have carried influence, he was not all-powerful in matters
of censorship,[55] and even the *philosophes* had been split over free trade in
grain. Diderot defended his friend the abbé Galiani's *Dialogues sur le commerce des bleds,* which Turgot and the abbé Morellet, whom he encouraged to
write against it, saw as pernicious. So it is hardly surprising that there were
those in official circles who would not welcome the intervention of such a
distinguished scholar in this debate. Grimm's review in the *Correspondance
littéraire* noted that the book gained attention for having been held up at the
Syndical Chamber.[56] This is a useful reminder that then as now knowledge
that a book was considered controversial could considerably aid its sales.
Turgot may have helped to have it released to the censor. Senneville gave
it a tacit permission which is on record, as customary. His conclusion was,
"This work can only be useful. The author has never crossed the borders of
the discussion and truth can only gain from such works." He gave some indi-
cation why Condillac's book may have met with opposition when he speculated that theologians and the *dévots* were likely to protest at the chapter on
usury. But he cheered himself with: "I know that people with an axe to grind
do not find me zealous enough, but I am what I am" (Belin, *Le commerce des
livres,* 32).[57]

   Other evidence confirms that its publication was delayed for at least seven

55. Turgot, as a friend and colleague of Malesherbes, preferred public opinion to
judge works, provided they were not seditious or blasphemous; and as a man eager to
extend toleration into religious matters, he was hesitant to use his influence to have work
censored even when it was opposed to his policies. Thus he allowed Necker's *De la législation et du commerce des grains* to pass the censors in 1775.

56. Raynal, Grimm and Diderot, *Correspondance littéraire,* March 1775, 11:53ff.

57. Belin gives the mss. no. of the Archives de la Chambre syndicate des libraires et
imprimeurs de Paris 22016, 273.

months. Before the end of July 1775, Diderot wrote in his *Plan d'une université* for Catherine the Great of Russia that "M. l'abbé de Condillac has just published the elements of commerce considered in relation to government. It is a simple, clear and exact work" (Diderot, *Oeuvres complètes,* 11:815). Later, in December 1775, Diderot wrote to Catherine that she had not received *Le Commerce et le Gouvernement* because it had not yet appeared (ibid., 1124). It was actually published in February 1776, but Diderot had known of its general content, the subject of the next chapter, at least seven months previously.

Despite difficulties with the censorship and advancing years, Condillac was not ready to rest on his considerable laurels as a scholar. He was only too happy to provide a new text on logic for the Poles. His brother, the abbé de Mably, had written a constitution for the Polish state, and French influence was significant in Poland. Count Potocki approached Condillac in September 1777, after an international competition in 1775 to provide books for the Palatinate schools had failed to produce a work of sufficient quality. On completion of the manuscript in June 1778—true to his promise it was ready before the deadline of December 1779—Condillac wrote to Potocki saying that he had sent it to Keralio in Paris from whom it could be collected or who would forward it if requested. He said that, while not wanting to make them wait for the work, he had not rushed it. He was eager to show that he had given it great thought and tailored it to their needs. The Education Commission seems to have been delighted as he was given two gold medals as well as the 100 gold florins promised in the competition.[58]

Condillac's friendship with mathematicians has been noted, and his last, posthumously published work was the *Langue des calculs.* The *Mémoires secrets* also mention in September 1780 that when he died he was writing a dictionary which they called a vast task which had daunted all the other *philosophes.*[59] This is the *Dictionnaire des synonymes* which his niece found among his papers at Flux. Puchesse saw it as ready for publication, but it probably missed being

---

58. It forms volume 22 of the 1798 edition of Condillac's *Oeuvres.* Count Potocki's invitation and Condillac's reply are printed on pp. 199–202. Sgard, *Corpus Condillac,* 101–2, gives an excerpt from the third letter. Condillac's brother Mably thought highly of the work (see letters to Wielhorski, quoted in Sgard, *Corpus Condillac,* 121).

59. *Mémoires secrets,* 16:10.

included in the twenty-three-volume 1798 *Oeuvres* as it was not among the corrected manuscripts intended for a full edition of all his works that passed to the abbé de Mably on Condillac's death. Condillac had obtained a privilege in his own name for the publication of his complete works in 1778.[60]

During Condillac's time in Parma, news and advice was passing from him to Rousseau through their mutual friends such as Mme de Chenonceaux and Deleyre. Only a fraction of Condillac's correspondence survives,[61] so it is impossible to know how far they subsequently kept in touch. However, in 1776 Rousseau was desperate to bring his *Dialogues*, which he considered his masterpiece, to the attention of the world. He saw himself beset by schemers and initially had the notion that he would circumvent them by leaving the manuscript on the high altar of Notre Dame and that this would bring it to the King's attention. Thwarted by finding access to the altar barred, he soon persuaded himself that his idea had been absurd and suddenly thought of his old friend Condillac whom he had not seen for some time and who was opportunely visiting Paris. He left the manuscript with the abbé, expecting on his return to be greeted with the excitement that recognition of a masterpiece warranted. He regarded himself as betrayed when Condillac merely received him courteously and offered to undertake the production of an edition of Rousseau's collected works. Rousseau saw this helpful offer as a sign that Condillac had been influenced by his enemies and rejected it. Even so he recounted that he saw his old friend a few more times, and it was to Condillac that he entrusted the manuscript for safe-keeping with instructions that it was not to be opened until the next century.[62] This undertaking may indicate some courage on Condillac's part, to judge from the extreme reluctance of the abbé de Reyrac to accept custody of it from Condillac on his deathbed.[63]

---

60. Sgard, *Corpus Condillac*, 101.

61. The Sgard catalogue of his letters mentions fifty-eight, but it is clear both from their content and from what some of his correspondents wrote to him that he was a busy and quite chatty letter-writer.

62. Rousseau wrote his own account of these events, the *Histoire du précédent écrit* (1782). It is printed with his *Dialogues* in *Rousseau, Juge de Jean Jacques*, texte présénté par Michel Foucault (Paris: Armand Colin, 1962), 321–22.

63. This is referred to in *Mémoires secrets* (vol. 22, for 10 Jan. 1783). The abbé Reyrac is said to have taken the manuscript, while trembling, only on the assurance that it contained nothing against the state, morals or religion. He later handed it over to the family.

Puchesse describes Condillac in his last years as "Always serious, thought-ful, preoccupied" (Puchesse, *Condillac,* 166–67),[64] but this sits uneasily with the statements which he quotes from Condillac's friend Claude de Loynes d'Autroche who delivered the customary eulogy to the Royal Agricultural Society of Orléans in 1781. D'Autroche had been made a member of the So-ciety on the same day as Condillac, 5 February 1776. He wrote of his friend:

> To escape the distressing sight of ever-growing corruption in the Capi-tal, near the end of his days the abbé de Condillac chose a country retreat in our district: it is here that in the midst of the nature that he loved, he whiled away days that were as peaceful and as pure as his heart; it is in this refuge, beautified by his taste, that he loved to entertain and that he received real friends with such true warmth, and with such affecting satis-faction . . . (Puchesse, *Condillac,* 166)

D'Autroche was thirty years younger than Condillac and a great traveller; he was interested in the classics and later translated Horace's *Odes.* He owned extensive lands and a fine château dominating the Loire valley. Other friends were local clergy and magistrates who included Le Trosne, the economist.[65]

Later disputes between Mme de Sainte-Foy and her family over the Flux estate have brought speculation that Condillac's last years may have been unhappy, and his shortness of temper in these years is commented upon.[66] What seems certain from their own words is that he retained the affection of his two surviving elder brothers, Mably, who was to be his literary executor, and Saint-Marcellin.[67]

---

This source contains the inaccuracy that the abbé de Condillac was Rousseau's pupil. It was his nephew, M. de Mably's son, also known as Condillac, whom Rousseau found an unsatisfactory pupil.

64. Though Baguenault de Puchesse can speak of family tradition about his distin-guished ancestor, it must be noted that he was writing over a century after Mme de Sainte-Foy's death in 1807. On the abbé's character the testimony of d'Autroche, speak-ing to an assemblage of intelligent men who will have had some acquaintance with Con-dillac, carries more weight.

65. Puchesse, *Condillac,* 166.

66. Sgard, *Corpus Condillac,* 102, 106.

67. Ibid., 107. Mably's letter of 6 January 1780 to a cousin, printed in Puchesse, *Con-dillac,* 273–74, shows that the brothers kept in touch, though by that time Condillac's visits to Paris where Mably lived were very brief. In a letter to a Polish count after Con-

Condillac's death on 3 August 1780 was sudden and occurred shortly after his return from a visit to Paris. Accounts of it are incompatible. The family tradition given by Puchesse is that Condillac ascribed his last illness to a bad chocolate drink he had at Condorcet's house. As he says that Condillac disliked Condorcet this may just have been a grumbling reaction when the abbé felt unwell on his journey home.[68] A medical account has it that he fell victim to a fever that was going through the neighbourhood of Flux.[69]

Accounts of his funeral tally well. It was movingly described by Lablée, a local lawyer who said he was present: "It was at harvest-time. His corpse escorted by a man of affairs had been carried across the fields to the small parish of the burgh of Lailly. Bare-legged peasants wearing chasubles sang the mass. The corpse was buried without the slightest mark, in a small cemetery open on all sides, and I doubt one will be able to find any trace of it" (Rousseau, *Correspondance générale*, 20:368–69). Several local clergy witnessed the burial certificate. Mme de Sainte-Foy's absence is not noteworthy, as it was not customary at the time for women to attend funerals.

Condillac's posthumous reputation has rested chiefly on his philosophical works. Puchesse, who traced his posthumous reputation, says that his *Traité des systémes* was on university syllabuses in the early years of this century.[70] Since the Second World War, there appears to have been a revived interest in his philosophy in Italy as well as in France. On a recent visit to Grenoble we learnt that his works are on the syllabus of the university of his native town. The *New Cambridge Modern History* devotes equal space to his contributions to education and to philosophy. The significance of *Commerce and Government* has received less attention. Its reception by the physiocrats when it appeared, and its growing reputation in the nineteenth and twentieth centuries, are discussed in the next chapter.

---

dillac's death, he spoke of his sharp sorrow on the loss of his brother whom he loved tenderly (Sgard, *Corpus Condillac*, 121), and for Bonnot de Saint-Marcellin, see ibid., 22.

68. Puchesse, *Condillac*, 23–24.

69. Sgard, *Corpus Condillac*, 102–3.

70. Puchesse, *Condillac*, v.

### CONDILLAC'S DECISION TO WRITE
### "COMMERCE AND GOVERNMENT"

In March 1776, when Condillac published *Commerce and Government,* he was sixty-one years old, the same age as François Quesnay when he first published on economics. When he returned from Parma in 1767 he devoted the next eight years to the seventeen-volume *Cours d'études,* his summary of everything a prince needed to know to govern well. This took him for the first time towards economics because there are reflections on how economies should be governed. The following statement is of especial interest because it differs so startlingly from the Colbertian dirigisme which had dominated French economic policy during most of the previous century:

> Governing an economy requires a comprehensive genius who knows everything, who weighs everything, and who directs all the resources of government in perfect harmony. It would be difficult, or rather impossible to find such a genius. The best intentioned and most skilful statesmen have made mistakes through ignorance or through over hasty action, for it is difficult to see all and bring all together without sometimes falling into error . . . statesmen never do more harm than when they wish to interfere in everything. It is wisest to confine oneself to preventing abuses and otherwise to pursue a policy of laissez-faire. (Condillac, *Cours d'études,* 20:488)

A year later, in 1776, Adam Smith, who knew Condillac's philosophy, produced a strikingly similar statement in *The Wealth of Nations:*

> The statesman, who should attempt to direct private people in what manner they ought to employ their capitals, would not only load himself with a most unnecessary attention, but assume an authority which could safely be trusted, not only to no single person, but to no council or senate whatever, and which would nowhere be so dangerous as in the hands of a man who had folly and presumption enough to fancy himself fit to exercise it. (456)

Condillac's advice to a future sovereign therefore led him towards the non-interventionist *laissez-faire* approach to economic policy which Adam Smith went on to establish so commandingly.

After the publication of the *Cours d'études,* Condillac followed his contributions to philosophy and a royal education with an account of economics and of economic policy, which he presented, like much of his philosophy, in a single elegant volume.

The first part of *Commerce and Government* is entitled "Elementary Propositions on Commerce, determined according to the assumptions or principles of Economic Science," and it provides a step-by-step statement of economic principles to establish the political economy which will most advance the wealth of nations. One of Condillac's notable philosophical works, his *Traité des sensations,* had opened with the celebrated initial assumption, referred to in the previous chapter, that human beings are statues. Condillac then relaxed this assumption in successive chapters to arrive at a clear account of complex human sensations. His economics follows a similar methodology. He opens Chapter 1 with a corn model (with corn the only commodity that is produced and consumed), and he gradually relaxes the assumptions to provide a general account of a real economy.

He believed that political economy could be presented simply and comprehensibly by creating a clear language for the representation of economic analysis (which up to then had been lacking) and by using this to move forward, chapter by chapter, to provide a comprehensive account of complex economies. *Commerce and Government* opens with a striking claim in Condillac's first paragraph:

> Each science requires a special language, because each science has ideas which are unique to it. It seems that we should begin by forming this language; but we begin by speaking and writing and the language remains to be created. That is the position of Economic Science, the subject of this very work. It is, among other matters, the need which I propose to meet. (*CG* 93)[71]

71. *Commerce and Government* is abbreviated to *CG* hereafter; page references are to the edition presented in this volume.

In the edition published posthumously in 1798 in the twenty-three-volume collection of his *Oeuvres,* Condillac adds the footnote:

> Since the first edition of this work I have shown in my *Logic* that the art of dealing well with a science comes down to the art of creating its language well. Also, when I said that the language of Economic Science needed to be created, the public, for whom this science was still often no more than an indecipherable code, had no difficulty in believing this: because it thought, justly, that a language that is not understood is a badly con-structed language. (*CG* 93)

These are statements with which philosophers will have more sympathy than will economists, who still produce "indecipherable codes."

Condillac's approach is very much that of a philosopher of the first rank who is seeking to establish a sound basis for economic analysis, and he completes his First Part account of economic principles in 55,000 words. The considerably shorter 35,000-word Second Part, entitled "Commerce and government considered in relation to each other following some assumptions," has the same title as he gives to his book, with the addition of the words "following some assumptions." Condillac uses the analysis he develops in the First Part to elucidate the practical questions he is addressing. The expositional method he uses is generally a comparison between abstract countries in which some pursue disastrous policies while others adopt correct policies and perform far more successfully. But the pretence that it is hypothetical countries he is comparing is discarded in Chapter 15, subtitled "Obstacles to the circulation of grain when the government wishes to restore to trade, the freedom it took from it," which is concerned with the actual impact of the attempted reform of food markets by the great economist-administrator Anne Robert Jacques Turgot who became Controller-General of Finances in 1774 and still held that position when the book was published. In a Third Part, which Condillac foreshadowed in 1776 but never completed, he proposed to consider what he had established in the First and Second Parts "according to the facts in order to rest as much on experience as on reasoning" (*CG* 93). Richard Cantillon is said to have followed his largely theoretical *Essai sur la nature du commerce en générale* (1755) with an empirical second volume which has not survived,[72] and it has been suggested that Karl Marx's plan for the third volume of *Capital* (which he did not live to complete) included an empirical account of the trade cycle in nineteenth-century Britain.[73] Condillac might have found it equally challenging to provide an account of "the facts" to conclude *Commerce and Government,* but this is actually complete as it stands. The theoretical First Part and its development in the Second Part to illuminate practical questions and especially Turgot's proposed reforms produce a wholly coherent book.

On 9 October 1776, seven months after its publication, Condillac wrote to the marquis de Rangoni about the circumstances which had led him to write and publish *Commerce and Government:*

> I only began to occupy myself with political economy when I wished to produce my work on commerce and government. I worked to inform myself, I had absolutely no preconceptions and I saw nothing but disorder and confusion in the writings being produced in France. You see by this, Monsieur, that I am not sufficiently well versed in this genre to flatter myself that I can be as useful to you as I would wish. I have shown abuses, I have shown the order that must be substituted, and that part was easy: the difficulty is to show the way to set about this problem. I have not known how to involve myself in this question, perhaps I shall deal with it in the third part [of the book] on which I shall not begin to work for the time being. Perhaps also, it may only be possible to indicate the means in a very imprecise fashion, as they must vary with circumstances.
>
> I have long been convinced that a science that is well treated comes down to a well constructed language and I have applied myself to the creation of the language of economic science. Unfortunately I was obliged to work in haste to take advantage of a favourable opportunity, for I foresaw that if there were changes in the ministry, I would not be able to get to press. That is why I have not always put all the precision I should have liked into this work. I have just made some essential corrections to it . . . In

72. A. Murphy, *Richard Cantillon: Entrepreneur and Economist* (Oxford: Oxford University Press, 1986), 251.

73. Z. Kenessey, "Why Das Kapital Remained Unfinished," in *Perspectives on the History of Economic Thought,* ed. William J. Barber, vol. 5, *Themes in Pre-Classical, Classical and Marxian Economics* (Aldershot, Hants.: Edward Elgar, 1991).

any case these changes bear on points of detail which change no essentials and which are only needed to prevent awkward difficulties. (Sgard, *Corpus Condillac*, 154–55)

The previous chapter describes how the publication of the *Cours d'études* was much delayed by censors in both Parma and Paris, and Condillac evidently expected that Turgot's reforming ministry would have sufficient influence to minimise interruptions to the publication of *Commerce and Government*. It was shown in the previous chapter that its publication was none the less delayed, but perhaps by no more than seven months. As Condillac had envisaged, the lively national interest in political economy during Turgot's ministry offered him the best chance of publishing *Commerce and Government* uncensored.

Since 1761 Turgot had been a reforming Intendant in Limoges, in effect head of local government there. In 1769 he had published one of the great classical economic texts, *Réflexions sur la formation et la distribution des richesses*, and his numerous publications commanded high respect. He corresponded regularly with Condorcet and Du Pont de Nemours, the father of the founders of the United States chemical empire. He had always been close to the *philosophes* and the *encylopédistes* as well as to the leading physiocrat *économistes*, and he was elected President of the Académie des Belles Lettres in 1778. He was well known to Benjamin Franklin, Edward Gibbon and Adam Smith. His personal *cabinet* included Du Pont, and room was also found for Quesnay de Saint-Germain, a grandson of the founder of physiocracy.[74]

The appointment of this distinguished philosopher-economist to administer the finances of France with a personal *cabinet* which included leading *économistes* aroused great contemporary interest in economic analysis and policy. It was widely understood that a further attempt would be made to apply the economic analysis of the dominant physiocratic school to the problems of the French economy. The physiocrats believed that the economy's taxable surplus originated in agriculture, so this was where taxes must come from, and that increasing the prosperity of France depended above all on raising agricultural profitability through free trade in food. It was evi-

74. Gustave Schelle, *Turgot* (Paris, 1909), 154.

dent that a further attempt would be made to liberalise food markets: reforms had been introduced in 1763–64, but these had been reversed in 1770 when they led to large price increases. The renewed attempt to implement policies based on these doctrines aroused much debate, and those like Condillac who were outside the administration naturally wished to participate in the accompanying excitement and interest in political economy.

Peter Groenewegen has suggested in *The New Palgrave: A dictionary of economics* that Condillac wrote *Commerce and Government* "to assist his friend Turgot in the difficulties he faced in 1775 as finance minister over the grain riots induced by his restoration of free trade in food" (Groenewegen, "Condillac," 1:565). The above letter to Rangoni includes the more general intention to add a book which clarified the foundations of political economy to his extensive published contributions. The level of interest in economics in 1775–76 created the opportunity to combine this with a highly relevant contribution to contemporary debate. No personal correspondence between Turgot and Condillac has been found, but they moved in similarly distinguished circles; it was shown in the previous chapter that they both belonged to Julie de Lespinasse's salon (and doubtless to others), and there may well have been personal friendship in addition. The economic principles which were to emerge from Condillac's study of political economy were actually close to Turgot's. It will emerge that Condillac derived his understanding of the nature of the efficient food markets on which the success of Turgot's reforms depended from his new theory of value and utility, the core of the theoretical First Part of *Commerce and Government*.

## CONDILLAC'S INNOVATIVE ANALYSIS OF VALUE AND UTILITY

The most original contribution of *Commerce and Government* is Condillac's theory of value and utility. Here Condillac the philosopher produced a new theoretical approach which only began to be appreciated nearly a century after his death.

Terence Hutchison concluded in his magisterial *Before Adam Smith* that "Condillac's work represented the crowning achievement in the long and distinguished line of Italian and French theorists of utility and subjective value," and that "it is Condillac, with his emphasis on ignorance, uncertainty and erroneous expectations, who has stronger claims than anyone else to be regarded as the founding father of subjectivist analysis in economic theory" (331). It will emerge below (p. 71) that in the 1870s, Stanley Jevons, Carl Menger and Léon Walras, the originators of the marginal revolution, each recognised the importance of Condillac's contribution. Condillac's account of the relationship between the utility derivable from commodities, the demand for them, and the impact this had on the motivation to produce was nearly one hundred years ahead of its time.

Condillac the subjective philosopher sought to explain the motivation of producers and consumers, and he did this by suggesting that producers work to obtain utility. Farmers and manufacturers produce to generate "value" for themselves which depends on the personal utilities they derive. In his first chapter Condillac explains that "The value of things is . . . founded on their utility" (*CG* 99), and he goes on to say: "it is natural that a more strongly felt need gives things a greater value, and that a less pressing need gives them less value. The value of things therefore grows with scarcity and decreases with abundance." The marginal utility of a single commodity can indeed fall to zero: "Value can even diminish in abundance to vanishing point. For instance, a surplus good will be without value every time that one can do nothing with it, since then it would be completely useless" (*CG* 100).

Farmers will only increase their output of grain if they can exchange their surplus over their own needs, which offers them no value because it has no marginal utility, for something else that they desire, and the same is true of the producers of all other commodities. Wherever production is surplus to a farmer's own needs, an absence of adequate opportunities to market an excess will remove any incentive to produce beyond the level which satisfies the farmer's personal desires. The absence of adequate markets will therefore have highly adverse effects on their incentive to produce and hence on the supply side of the economy. Cultivators' food that is surplus to their own requirements will only have value for them if they can exchange it for something else which will actually provide utility:

> The surplus [of farmers] . . . is wealth, so long as they can find an outlet for it; because they procure for themselves something that has value for them, and they hand over something which has value for others.

If they were unable to make exchanges, their surplus would stay with them, and it would have no value for them. (*CG* 121)

Farmers' incentives to produce beyond their own needs will depend on what they can consume with the money they receive from the sale of their surplus produce and the utility they derive from the goods they are entitled to buy, which will include manufactures. Cultivators of the land will obtain utility from manufactures as well as food, so their motivation to produce food will be influenced by the availability and cost of manufactures. There is indeed a mutual interchange between farmers who produce products that manufacturers require and manufacturers who produce products which farmers will find useful. Merchants are needed to arrange the exchange of surplus food for the products of artisans:

> Now merchants are the channels of communication through which the surplus runs. From places where it has no value it passes into places where it gains value, and wherever it settles it becomes wealth. . . .
>
> A spring which disappears into rocks and sand is not wealth for me; but it becomes such, if I build an aqueduct to draw it to my meadows. This spring represents the surplus products for which we are indebted to the settlers [colons], and the aqueduct represents the merchants. (*CG* 121)

As a result of this process whereby merchants arrange the marketing of the agricultural surplus, cultivators are induced to raise their level of production:

> If one compares the state of deprivation our tribe is in, when, without artisans, without merchants, it is confined to goods of prime need, with the state of plenty in which it finds itself, when, through the hard work of artisans and merchants, it enjoys goods of secondary need, that is, of a host of things that habit turns into needs for it; one will understand that the work of artisans and merchants is as much a source of wealth for it, as the very work of the farmers. . . .
>
> It is therefore proved that in the final analysis industry is also a source of wealth . . . It has been much obscured by some writers. (*CG* 125)

This statement was provocative to the *économistes* who held that agriculture was the sole source of wealth. Condillac argues in contrast in a much quoted passage that farmers, manufacturers and merchants combine to create wealth:

> All the groups, each busy with its own tasks, come together in competition to increase the mass of wealth, or the abundance of goods which have value. . . .
>
> It is the farmer who provides all the primary material. But such primary material, as would be useless and without value in his hands, becomes useful and obtains value when the artisan has found the way to make it serve the needs of society.
>
> With each skill that begins, with each advance it makes, the farmer thus acquires new wealth, because he finds value in a product which previously had none.
>
> This product, given value by the artisan, gives a fresh spur to commerce for which it is a new stock in trade; and it becomes a new source of wealth for the farmer because, as each product acquires value, he makes new consumption for himself.
>
> Thus it is that all, farmers, merchants, artisans, come together to increase the mass of wealth. (*CG* 124–25)

Condillac is arguing that the free exchange of commodities within an economy, each exchange benefiting both seller and buyer, leads to continual advances in the range of products available to the population and to increases in wealth. His account of a competitive economy generalises into a detailed multi-sectoral presentation:

> The farmer, busy in the fields, would not have the time free to make himself a coat, to build a house, to forge weapons, and he would not have the aptitude because these jobs require knowledge and a skill he does not possess.
>
> Several groups will therefore form. Besides that of the farmers, there will be tailors, architects, armourers. . . .
>
> When I distinguish four classes it is because we must choose a number. The tribe may and even must have many more. They will multiply in proportion as the arts come into being, and make progress. (*CG* 124)

all the citizens are given a wage with regard to each other. If the artisan and the merchant are paid by the farmer to whom they sell, the farmer is in his turn paid by the artisan and the merchant to whom he sells, and each of them gets paid for his work. (*CG* 127)

This mutual financial interdependence of farmers, merchants and artisans reads admirably in the late twentieth century. Condillac's analysis shows how each class, generating utility for itself, interacts with others to create a highly effective economy.

In addition to arguing that the free domestic exchange of goods will always raise economic welfare, he extends his argument internationally and suggests that countries will always gain from unrestricted trade. He indicated that in 1776 no country had free trade in food and that France would gain by being the first to free both exports and imports:

> France, we assume, is alone in giving export full, complete, permanent freedom without restriction, limitation or interruption. All her ports are always open and no one ever demands any duty on entry or exit there.
>
> I say that, on this assumption, the trade in grain must be more profitable for France than for any other nation. (*CG* 230)

> Whether she sells or whether she buys grain, France will, on our assumption, thus have a great advantage over the nations which forbid export and import . . . Because by forbidding export, they reduce the number of purchasers, and consequently they sell at a lower price; and by forbidding import they buy at a higher price, because they reduce the number of those selling to them. (*CG* 231)

He argued that the same would be true for each European nation:

> We may conclude that if the states of Europe persist in denying complete freedom to trade, they will never be as rich or as populous as they might be; that if one of them gave complete and permanent liberty, while the others only allowed a temporary and restrained freedom, it would be, other things being equal, the richest of all; and that finally, if all ceased to place obstacles in the way of commerce, they would all be as rich as they could be; and then their respective wealth would depend . . . on the fertility of the soil and the hard work of its inhabitants. (*CG* 231)

Thus the removal of all barriers to trade would maximise the wealth of each country. Condillac's economic reasoning led him to comprehensive support for domestic and international competition and the belief that this would make countries "as rich as they could be." That was the most that economic policy could contribute; the rest would depend on "the fertility of the soil and the hard work of its inhabitants."

Working from the analysis of human motivation which was subsequently adopted by most twentieth-century economists, Condillac provided the intellectual foundations for the establishment of the conditions for the maximisation of wealth, both nationally and internationally. With free markets, the free exchange of commodities would contribute to the utility and add to the wealth of all. It was this that led the French Nobel Prizewinner in Economics, Maurice Allais, to comment that Condillac had developed "a general theory of the generation of surpluses, of general economic equilibrium, and of maximal efficiency" (Allais, "General theory," 174).

## "COMMERCE AND GOVERNMENT" AND TURGOT'S REFORM PROGRAMME

The policy analysis of the Second Part of *Commerce and Government* follows the theoretical presentation of the First Part with an account of how the existence of adequate markets plays a central role in providing sufficient incentives for the supply side of the economy. Condillac's 1776 account of the practical difficulties of Turgot's reform programme is dominated by the absence of sufficient well-informed merchants to allow markets to work effectively.

In France from the 1750s onwards an influential circle of economic writers had been arguing the case for freeing agricultural markets. Local famines were frequent, and much of the population lived on the borderline of subsistence. Above all, Paris, the centre of political power, where discontent could most easily undermine governments, needed to be fed.[75] Governments accepted an obligation to feed Paris, which often involved expensive purchases of grain by vast state-funded organisations and its sale at controlled prices which the people could afford.

---

75. Steven Kaplan (*Bread, Politics and Political Economy in the Reign of Louis XV* [The Hague: Martinus Nijhoff, 1976]) provides a detailed and authoritative account of French policy with regard to grain from the 1750s to the 1770s and the particular impact of the need to feed Paris. This has much influenced the account which follows.

The consequent network of government purchasing and price controls was buttressed by a system of supervision of grain markets: Condillac describes its condition at the time Turgot became Controller-General in August 1774, when it was:

> forbidden to all persons to undertake trade in grain without having obtained permission for it from officials appointed for that purpose.
>
> forbidden to all others, farmers or landowners to interfere directly or indirectly in carrying out this trade.
>
> Any association between grain merchants was forbidden unless it had been authorized.
>
> forbidden to pay a deposit on corn or to buy corn unripe, standing, before the harvest.
>
> forbidden to sell corn other than in the markets.
>
> forbidden to make hoards of grain.
>
> forbidden to let it move from one province into another without having obtained permission. (*CG* 292–93)

The disadvantages were compounded by corruption, for:

> You could not carry on the corn trade at all without having obtained . . . permission. But it was not enough to ask for it in order to get it; you also needed to have protection; and protection was hardly ever granted except to those who would pay for it, or who would give up a share in their profit. (*CG* 295)

From the 1750s onwards many economic writers had begun to compare the dirigisme of French grain markets with the comparative freedom of England's, where competition reinforced by tariff protection to establish a minimum price for farmers allowed people to be fed without famine and without any need for an apparatus of government control. When Quesnay first published "Fermiers" and "Grains" in the *Encyclopédie* in 1756, Vincent Gournay and Claude-Jacques Herbert, in his *Essai sur la police générale des grains* (1753), had already argued for the benefits from deregulated food markets. Quesnay went on to invent the *Tableau économique* (according to Marx "an extremely brilliant conception, incontestably the most brilliant for which political economy had up to then been responsible": Marx, *Theories of Surplus Value*, 1:344) which formed the core of a complex economic model that demonstrated how the finances of France could be enhanced through agricultural reforms in which the freeing of food markets was of central importance.[76] These combined influences led to a first attempt at liberalisation in 1763. The special attraction of the liberalisation of grain to those who governed France was the claim that freeing agricultural markets would sharply raise rents and therefore government revenues, which would place the finances of the Kingdom on a sound basis.

Clément-Charles-François de Laverdy, the Controller-General who attempted to liberalise food markets in 1763–64, called upon Turgot and Du Pont, who were to be central to the 1774 reforms about which Condillac writes in *Commerce and Government,* to draft the relevant decree.[77] They both believed that Laverdy's reforms did not go far enough. Laverdy retained the obligation to feed Paris, and he retained the bureaucratic apparatus to intervene to protect consumers whenever he judged this necessary. That meant that farmers and merchants who had correctly foreseen shortages could find that the exceptional profits which might have resulted from their superior foresight would be wiped out because the state could come in and undercut them by provisioning markets at a loss. Turgot and Du Pont insisted that markets must become entirely free if they were to work as they should. Laverdy also only offered limited and localised freedom to export. The liberalisers believed that France would only become entirely free from famine if a regular export surplus provided a cushion for home consumption in years of poor harvests. The higher prices exports offered would also raise agricultural profits and rents and therefore royal revenues.

Laverdy's reforms produced disappointing results; food prices rose sharply immediately afterwards, and there were years of famine. The reforms had

76. Perhaps the most succinct account of the physiocrat reform programme is to be found in *Philosophic rurale,* where, with Mirabeau, Quesnay shows in twenty-two pages how freeing food markets and substituting the taxation of rents for all other taxes could double the capital of France in nine years (Marquis de Mirabeau [Victor Riqueti] and François Quesnay, *Philosophic rurale* [Amsterdam, 1763; reprinted in 1972 by Scientia Verlag Aalen], 2:354–75). Their argument is explained in Walter Eltis, "The *Grand Tableau* of François Quesnay's economies," *European Journal of the History of Economic Thought* 3, no. 1 (1996): 21–43.

77. Kaplan, *Bread, Politics,* 141–42.

been welcomed in the agricultural regions which had benefited from higher food prices, but consumer-dominated Paris, which was politically far more important, had been hostile throughout. Laverdy was dismissed in 1768, and from 1770 to 1774 his reforms were reversed: while the liberalisers blamed their failure on their incompleteness.

In 1770 Ferdinando Galiani published a scathing assault on the reformers in *Dialogues sur le commerce des bleds* which had a great impact, especially because of its wit. Voltaire told Diderot that he had found it a mixture of Plato and Molière: "no one has ever reasoned better nor more amusingly" (Kaplan, *Bread, Politics,* 593). Galiani especially emphasised the arrogance of the liberalisers who believed that they had practical solutions to all problems, and he drew particular attention to the starvation of those whom free markets temporarily overlooked.[78] One of his most quoted remarks denounces the liberalisers' argument that free markets would rapidly move food from where it was abundant to where it was scarce: "beware that it takes time to send word from a deficit town to a surplus town that grain is lacking and still more time for this grain to arrive. 'The theory goes well but the problem goes badly,' for after a week of waiting 'this insect called man' will die of hunger" (Galiani, *Dialogues sur le commerce,* 221–23).

Faced by the practical failure of Laverdy's reforms and powerful published assaults on the liberal analysis, the new Controller-General, Joseph-Marie Terray, entirely restored the previous system of regulation and even sought to widen its scope: he asked for detailed statistics of grain production and consumption from every region of France to provide the foundations for a national food policy.[79] But the vast expense of his provisioning policies and their relative ineffectiveness led to another change of policy in 1774. The liberalisers succeeded in persuading the new King, Louis XVI, that Laverdy's reforms had failed because of their incompleteness and that Turgot, one of the principal advisers in 1764, should be given the opportunity to carry the reform programme forward to an extent where it could become effective.

---

78. See G. Faccarello, "'Nil Repente!': Galiani and Necker on economic reforms," *European Journal of the History of Economic Thought* 1, no. 3 (1994): 519–50, for an account of Galiani's analysis.

79. Kaplan, *Bread, Politics,* 550–52.

Soon after he became Controller-General, Turgot appointed Du Pont, another of Laverdy's principal advisers, Inspector-General of Commerce.

Turgot's appointment as Controller-General appeared a new dawn to those who favoured reform. D'Alembert wrote, "If good does not come about, one must conclude that good cannot be done" (Turgot, *Oeuvres de Turgot*, 4:20). But Galiani foresaw a very different outcome. He wrote to Mme d'Epinay from Naples on 17 September 1774 immediately he heard of the appointment: "At last M. Turgot is Controller-General. He will stay in place too short a time to carry out his systems . . . He will wish to do good, will meet thorny problems . . . His credit will fall, he will be hated, people will say that he is not up to the task, enthusiasm for him will cool, he will resign or be dismissed, and once and for all one will realise the error of having given a position such as his to a very virtuous and philosophical man in a monarchy such as yours. Free export of corn will be what will break his neck. Remember that" (Galiani, *Correspondance*, 4:183–84).

Turgot was appointed on 24 August 1774, and just three weeks later on 13 September he persuaded the King to issue an edict which allowed anyone to trade in food throughout France however and whenever he wished, and to forbid interference with commercial activity under all circumstances by all officials. Turgot even ordered that Terray's statistics, which were to form the foundation for a national food policy, should no longer be collected.[80] Since newly liberalised markets would provide the food the French people needed without even occasional interventions, the government had no need for information about harvests and the quantity of food in granaries.

Turgot accompanied the 13 September decree with a 3,000-word preamble which provided a comprehensive account of the economic reasoning behind his liberal approach to food markets. This was indeed the same as that of the physiocrats and Condillac.

According to this introduction, each province from time to time grew less or more food than it needed because of the vagaries of harvests, and suffered from alternations of distress and glut (non-valeur) when it could not sell its harvest for an adequate price. There were two ways of dealing with the difficulty: "by means of commerce left to itself, or through the intervention

80. Ibid., 552.

of government." The preamble continued, "Reflection and experience prove alike that in order to furnish the needs of the people, the approach of free commerce is the most certain, the fastest acting, the least costly and the least subject to inconvenience" (Turgot, *Oeuvres de Turgot,* 4:203).

Turgot's preamble went on to claim scope for the merchants of France to respond to market forces which much exceeded what Condillac judged to be their actual condition in 1776, when he wrote that the people:

> regarded the grain merchants as grasping men who took advantage of their needs. Once that opinion was rooted, a person could not engage in this trade if he cared for his reputation: it had to be left to those vile creatures who counted money for everything and honour for nothing. (*CG* 300)

In contrast Turgot asserts that:

> Merchants, through the huge amount of the capital that they have at their command, and the extent of their connections with other merchants, by the promptitude and exactness of the advice they receive, by the economy that they understand how to place in their operations, by their practical experience in all matters of commerce, have the means and resources lacking to the most far-sighted, clear thinking and most energetic administrators. (Turgot, *Oeuvres de Turgot,* 4:203)

Turgot's merchants are not recognisably drawn from the same citizens as Condillac's, and Turgot's assumption that this wealthy, sophisticated, well-informed and competitive merchant class already existed was to prove a fatal error in Condillac's account of the failure of his policies. But Condillac entirely agreed on the importance of a well-informed merchant class if grain markets were to function effectively:

> Driven by . . . self-interest, merchants, great and small, multiplied by reason of our needs, will cause the corn to circulate, will put it everywhere at a level, everywhere at the true price [*vrai-prix*]. (*CG* 196–97)

> In dealing with the circulation of cereals we have seen that it can only be carried out by a host of merchants spread everywhere. These merchants are so many canals through which the grain circulates. Now these canals had been broken and it was time to to mend them.

Indeed, to succeed in any type of trade it is not enough to have the freedom to carry it on; one must . . . have obtained contacts, and these contacts can only be the fruits of experience, which is often slow. One must also have capital, stores, carters, agents, correspondents; in a word one must have taken many precautions and many measures. (*CG* 298)

Condillac therefore entirely shared Turgot's analysis that a large, well-informed merchant class was necessary, but he doubted its effectiveness until time and experience had created the infrastructure that successful markets require.

In the preamble to the September 1774 decree, Turgot went on to explain how freely functioning markets could not be relied upon to remedy food shortages if the state's humanitarian response as under previous Controllers-General was to supply food to the needy at a price below the one that markets would establish:

when the government takes upon itself the task of providing for the people's subsistence by carrying on the grain trade, it will be participating alone in this trade, because, since it is able to sell at a loss, no merchant can without foolhardiness expose himself to its competition. (Turgot, *Oeuvres de Turgot*, 4:204)

Turgot believed that governments could only hold grain prices down briefly and intermittently:

Whatever means the Government employs, whatever sums it lavishes, experience has shown on all occasions that it can never prevent corn from being expensive when harvests are bad.

If, by forceful means it succeeds in delaying this necessary effect, this can only be in a particular place, for a very short period; and in believing it can come to the relief of the people, it will only ensure their wretchedness and aggravate their condition. (Ibid., 206)

The artificially low prices are "alms to the rich" at least as much as to the poor, because the well-off consume large amounts of grain themselves and through their households, while the greedy will buy as much as they can at the low prices and store it. Then the authorities will seek to punish such behaviour through terrifying searches of the houses of citizens.

An organisation which seeks to use the resources of government to provision cannot succeed, because:

> Its attention is divided between too many objects, and it cannot be as active as merchants who are occupied with their trade alone.
> Its operations, nearly always precipitous, will be conducted in a wasteful manner.
> The agents it employs, having no interest in economy, buy more dearly, transport at much greater expense, store the grain with less care; much grain is lost and goes mouldy.
> These agents may through lack of skill or even fraud, excessively inflate the cost of their operations.
> Even when they are totally innocent they cannot avoid being suspected and the suspicion always rebounds on the Administration which employs them. (Ibid., 204)

So for Turgot, as for Condillac, there is no alternative to an attempt at a market solution, but both acknowledge that the price of grain has to be high enough to create the necessary incentive to supply. Turgot insists that competition will prevent the emergence of any monopoly and hold merchants' profits down, "from which it arises that in years of dearth the price of grain incorporates little more than the inevitable increase which comes from the costs and risks of transporting or guarding the grain in times of need and hunger" (ibid., 204).

Condillac fully acknowledges that the *vrai-prix* which would follow the establishment of free markets might well be higher than the one which had prevailed previously: "it must be seen that that high price is not dearness; it is the true price fixed by competition, a true price which has its high, its low and its middle limit" (*CG* 230), while in his introduction to the September 1774 decree Turgot only accepts that prices will be high after bad harvests.

Partly because Turgot wrongly assumed the influence of a competitive merchant class which did not as yet exist, he underestimated the possibility that the freeing of markets would lead to substantial price increases. The price of corn began to rise immediately after the September 1774 decree took effect, and it became 50 per cent higher in 1775 than in 1774.[81]

81. Turgot, *Oeuvres de Turgot*, 4:45.

By being able to sell corn in provinces other than their own, farmers were able to receive higher prices, and those who bought bread had to pay more. In May 1775 a series of provincial bread riots reached Paris: as a mob was smashing bakers' shops, the comte de Maurepas, Turgot's principal colleague in government, went to the opera and left the mob to rampage. The Paris Parlement met and passed a resolution which asked the King to "take the measures which his good sense and love for his subjects will inspire, to lower the prices of wheat and bread to a level appropriate to the needs of the people." Turgot, regarding it vital to prevent the publication of this subversive decree which asked the King to revoke the laws of market economics, dashed to Versailles in the middle of the night, had the King woken, had a musketeer sent to summon each member of the Royal Council and obtained the King's agreement to prevent the circulation of the Parlement's decree. Several ministers were replaced and order was restored. Two members of the mob were hanged, many were imprisoned and a *curé* who had preached against the food riots received a pension and promotion (to a *bénéfice*).[82]

The attitude of the physiocrats to bread riots is illustrated by the marquis de Mirabeau's statement in a memoir he wrote in 1772, prior to Turgot's reforms, that "Paris will be fed when Paris will pay" (Weulersse, *La Physiocratie*, 158); but as Galiani wrote to Madame d'Epinay on 27 May 1775, "I hope that this event will have taught M. Turgot . . . to know men, and the world, which is not that of the works of the économistes. He will have seen that revolts occasioned by dearness are not impossible as he believed" (Galiani, *Correspondance*, 4:250).

After the crisis, Turgot imposed price controls on bakers, despite the universal belief in the efficacy of markets which he had expressed in his 1774 decree. Joseph Albert, the Lieutenant-General of Police, threatened to hang the first baker who stopped making bread out of dissatisfaction with the inadequate maximum price he was allowed to charge.[83] Turgot's need to feed Paris left him with the fundamental dilemma that the measures necessary

---

82. See Schelle, *Turgot*, ch. 13; Turgot, *Oeuvres de Turgot*, 4:44–55; and E. Faure, *La Disgrâce de Turgot, 12 mai 1776* (Paris: Gallimard, 1961), Part 2, chs. 3–4, for detailed accounts of the bread riots (*"La guerre des farines"*) of 1775.

83. Kaplan, *Bread, Politics*, 509.

to do so undermined his agricultural reforms. He had remarked eight years before he became Controller-General that "the cobblestones of the cities do not produce any grain" (Kaplan, *Bread, Politics,* 681). The fundamental difficulty that the policy of establishing a free market for food would initially raise food prices remained unsolved. Bachaumont speaks of a mob being ready to smash a bust of Quesnay "on hearing that he was the cause of the current dearness of grain through the false theories and the baneful opinions he had inspired in the government" (Hecht, "La vie de François Quesnay," 276).

Turgot retained royal support throughout the crisis of 1775, but in February–March 1776 he proposed six reforming edicts which aroused still greater opposition. These included the replacement of the *corvée,* which obliged peasants to spend a number of days a year on local public works, with the financing of these by local taxation to be paid by landowners. Other decrees proposed to free internal French food markets and to abolish local monopoly privileges. A large number of government posts associated with the administration of the markets Turgot was proposing to free would be abolished, and indirect taxes such as those on salt would be replaced with a territorial tax which landowners and even the Church would have to pay, with a consequent loss of privileges for tax collectors.[84] Turgot knew that great opposition would be aroused by the speed of his reform programme, but he remarked when he became a minister at the age of forty-seven: "In my family we die at fifty" (Schelle, *Turgot,* 211): he was actually fifty-four when he died in 1781.

Maurepas declined to support the six decrees, the Paris Parlement again voiced its opposition, and referred to "The cry for an ill considered freedom" and "a novel system introduced by books and articles, as inexact in their facts as their principles." But Turgot still enjoyed the support of the King, and his six decrees were endorsed by the Council. Paris was illuminated that night; but Turgot's triumph was brief.

He was isolated in the Council. He attempted to appease his opponents by closing down the physiocratic journals, but he failed to persuade the King

---

84. See Schelle, *Turgot,* ch. 14; Turgot, *Oeuvres de Turgot,* 5:1–12; and Faure, *La Disgrâce de Turgot,* Part 3, chs. 4–5, for accounts of the February–March decrees.

to replace Maurepas or in fact to make any ministerial changes which would strengthen his position. There was indeed powerful and widespread opposition to his reforms which did not even enjoy the support of the unprivileged because the price of bread had risen. Many of those in receipt of government incomes saw that the reforms would destroy their jobs and their wealth. The farmers who were beginning to benefit were mostly some distance from Paris. The King opened conversations with another Provincial Intendant, Clugny, who was appointed to succeed Turgot as Controller-General of Finances in May 1776.[85] Clugny proved a tinkerer who rearranged public debt without seeking to pursue policies which would produce sufficient revenues to place government finances on a sound footing. He was succeeded by others, including most notably Necker, who equally failed to achieve the fundamental reforms which were needed.

Turgot actually wrote to Louis XVI immediately before the King replaced him, "Never forget that it was weakness that placed the head of Charles I on the block" (Schelle, *Turgot*, 238). The King had written to Turgot previously: "It is only you and I who love the people" (ibid., 247). But he failed to sustain Turgot in office, and permitted Clugny to reverse the six decrees. His Queen, Marie Antoinette (who followed Louis XVI to the guillotine during the Revolution), wrote to her mother, Maria-Theresa, the Empress of Austria, that she was not sorry Turgot's ministry had fallen. The Empress responded that they had tried to do too much too quickly.[86] That is always the problem radical reformers face. Gustave Schelle, one of Turgot's principal biographers, has commented that if Turgot had moved more slowly, opposition to his reforms would have had more time to build up, and his position would have been undermined before much could be achieved.[87] The optimum pace of reform when radical change is necessary is never clear. After his reforms encountered difficulties Turgot fell victim to the short-term policy option of all monarchs (and Prime Ministers) that the ousting of a Controller-General (or a Chancellor of the Exchequer) is "one of the few acts by which the King

---

85. See Schelle, *Turgot*, ch. 16; Turgot, *Oeuvres de Turgot*, 5:12–20; and Faure, *La Disgrâce de Turgot*, Part 3, chs. 6–7, for accounts of Turgot's fall.

86. Schelle, *Turgot*, 251–52.

87. Ibid., 252.

could please the vast majority of his subjects without taking into consideration any of their specific grievances" (Kaplan, *Bread, Politics,* 249).

Condillac published *Commerce and Government* two months before Turgot's fall, but the fate of the reform programme was already clear. Many of the later chapters of *Commerce and Government* are a thinly veiled indictment of the vast range of anti-competitive institutions and policies which proliferated in France and which undermined the effectiveness of the economy and the King's finances. He was especially concerned by the dirigisme in the market for grain which was so prominent in Turgot's programme. Writing contemporaneously with the reforms which he utterly supported, and perceiving the initial opposition they aroused, Condillac provides insights into the failure of Turgot's policies. His description of the French grain market and his account of the conditions in which Turgot's policies were pursued underlines the initial difficulties he faced.

Condillac comments on the adverse reaction to the price increases that followed the freeing of food markets. People remarked: "'Look at what freedom produces.' That is how the common people reasoned, and they were almost the entire nation. They thought that the dearness was a result of freedom." They did not appreciate that prices would only fall when there were "enough merchants" to establish cereals "at their true price". But they said, "we need bread every day" (*CG* 298–99). They believed that:

> the one task of government was to procure them cheap bread . . . So every time that it became dearer the people asked the government to have the price lowered.
>
> There were only two ways to satisfy them. The government had to buy grain itself to sell again at a loss, or it had to force merchants to deliver their corn at the price it had fixed.
>
> Of these two ways the first tended to ruin the state; the second was unjust and odious; and both accustomed the people to think that it was for the government to obtain cheap bread for them. (*CG* 299)

In Condillac's judgment the people saw the problem of obtaining cheap bread as a conflict of "The rights of humanity opposed to the rights of property" (to which Condillac replied, "What gibberish!"); and everyone said "the most absurd things to oppose the operations of the new minister . . . It seemed that everyone was condemned to reason badly on this matter." Turgot's opponents, many of whom had favoured the policy of freeing food markets until the uncomfortable consequences of higher prices emerged, now included, according to Condillac, "poets, geometricians, philosophers, metaphysicians, in a word almost all literary men, and especially those whose trenchant tone hardly allows one to take their doubts for doubts, and who do not permit one to think differently from them" (*CG* 300).

The *philosophes* had welcomed the physiocrat policy of freeing food markets when this appeared to be a contribution to greater freedom in general, but much of their support was withdrawn as soon as it became clear that greater market freedom meant higher prices. When the freeing of food markets as a consequence of physiocrat advocacy had produced localised famine in 1770, Voltaire wrote that: "I have a desire to carry my protests to the *Éphémérides des Citoyens*" (Kaplan, *Bread, Politics*, 504), while Diderot's response to the argument that higher food prices would eventually raise the supply of food was: "I eat badly when I only have potential bread" (Diderot, *Apologie*, 115).

Opposition to Turgot also came from the vast bureaucracies which government had created to administer regulated markets and to exploit monopolistic privileges in international trade. Condillac writes:

> In the capital they need administrators, directors, clerks, employees: they need other administrators, other directors, other clerks, other employees wherever they form establishments. They also need, in addition to the counters and the warehouses, buildings as a monument to the vanity of the directors they employ. Forced to such outlays, how much will they not lose in embezzlement, in negligence, in incompetence? They pay for all the errors of those they employ to serve them; and all the more arise, as the administrators who succeed each other at the whim of faction, and who each see differently, never allow a sensible, sustained plan to be made. They form badly contrived enterprises: they carry them out as though randomly; and in an administration that seems to tie itself up in knots, they employ self-interested men to complicate it further. The direction of these companies is thus necessarily vicious. (*CG* 314)

Those with vested interests in the perpetuation of these bureaucracies added their voices to the opposition to Turgot's reforms. According to Condillac, "the new minister showed courage," but "Such are the chief obstacles in the way of the re-establishment of freedom. Time will remove them if the government perseveres" (*CG* 300–301). It became evident two months after the publication of *Commerce and Government* that Turgot would not be allowed to persevere. After just twenty months, the opposition Condillac describes led to his fall and the reversal of his reforms. As Condillac remarked, "when disorder has reached a certain point, a revolution, however good it may be, is never accomplished without causing violent shocks" (*CG* 298).

The physiocrats fell with Turgot. Du Pont was ordered to leave Paris, and the editors of the physiocratic journals which Turgot had closed in a vain attempt to appease his opponents were exiled. But what had occurred became central to economic debate. The *économistes* had had an opportunity to give practical effect to their theories and they had failed. The reasons for Turgot's fall, which Condillac illuminates in *Commerce and Government*, have aroused continuing interest, including a major work by Edgar Faure, a President of the National Assembly and member of several twentieth-century French governments.

There is much in Condillac's account of the difficulties that Turgot's reforms encountered as a consequence of their immediate adverse impact on vested interests and food prices which foreshadows the obstacles that similar reforms have encountered in post-communist Eastern Europe.[88] In the eighteenth century and in the twentieth, prices rose sharply when markets were first freed, and the extent of the price increases was accentuated because the large numbers of merchants and traders required to exploit freer markets were absent. Some of the movement and trading of food and consumer goods fell into the hands of the semi-criminal because the numerous middle-

---

88. See Faccarello, "'Nil Repente!'," for an account of the contemporary explanations of Galiani and Necker for the practical failure of Turgot's reforms, and the general implications for price reform programmes—in eighteenth-century France and in twentieth-century Eastern Europe. See also Walter Eltis, "France's free market reforms in 1774–5 and Russia's in 1991–3: the immediate relevance of L Abbé de Condillac's analysis," *European Journal of the History of Economic Thought* 1, no. 1 (1993): 5–19.

men and the small traders which efficient distribution requires had not yet emerged. In the eighteenth century and in the twentieth, new policies were obstructed by inefficient bureaucracies with vested interests in the prevention of reform which undermined their privileges.

Like the leading physiocrats, Condillac entirely supported Turgot's reform programme, and his account of the contemporary reasons for its failure should have made sense to them. His theory of value with which his book opened has earned high praise in the twentieth century. But how did his contemporaries, and above all the physiocrats, react to the book on its first publication in 1776?

## THE CONTEMPORARY REACTION TO "COMMERCE AND GOVERNMENT"

The publication of a book on economics by this well-connected and distinguished philosopher and man of letters was bound to arouse great interest. He had known François Quesnay well,[89] and common ground has been found in their approaches to the philosophy of science, on which both published in the 1750s,[90] but Quesnay had died in 1774, two years before the publication of *Commerce and Government*. The professional reaction would come from the physiocrat followers of Quesnay. Economic thought advances and a new contribution by a distinguished writer would inevitably refine and develop what had already been published. Condillac was in complete agreement with the two principal physiocrat policy proposals: the freeing of food

89. According to J. Hecht, "La vie de François Quesnay," in *François Quesnay et la physiocratie* (Paris: Institut National d'Études Démographiques, 1958), 252, Condillac was a frequent visitor (*habitué*) to Quesnay's entresol in the Palace of Versailles.

90. Philippe Steiner ("L'économie politique du royaume agricole François Quesnay," in *Nouvelle histoire de la pensée économique*, edited by Alain Béraud and Gilbert Faccarello [Paris: Éditions la Découverte, 1992], 227–28) refers to similarities between the article "Évidence" which Quesnay contributed to the *Encyclopédie* in 1756 and the *Traité des sensations* and the *Traité des animaux* which Condillac published in 1754 and 1755, and suggests that Quesnay's article is borrowed largely from Condillac. According to Louis Salleron (editorial notes in *François Quesnay et la physiocratie*, 397), Quesnay's article is developed from fundamental ideas which he first presented in his *Essai phisique sur l'oeconomie animale* (1736; 2nd ed., Paris, 1747), so the priority for some of the argument is Quesnay's.

markets and the use of the agricultural surplus as the only sustainable source of tax revenues. He opens his analysis of the sources of taxation by stating that only landowners have the resources to pay taxes:

> There are in general only two classes of citizen: that of the landowners to whom all the land and all the products belong; and that of the paid workers [*salariés*] who, having neither land nor produce of their own, subsist on the wages that are due for their work.
>
> The first class can easily contribute; since, with all the products belonging to it, if it does not have all the money, it has more than the equivalent and besides it passes entirely through its hands. (*CG* 220)

When he says that everyone is either a landowner or a paid worker, Condillac is saying that everyone either owns land so that he is financially independent, or else depends for his livelihood on the production of a good or service. In this sense the paid workers sell their labour (which may be extremely skilled) or the products of their labour in the market place for their livelihood. Because the incomes of paid workers ultimately have to be paid by landowners, any shortfall in such incomes must eventually fall on the landowners who will bear the burden of any tax:

> So there you have, in a state such as France, several millions of citizens who are forced to cut back on their consumption. Now I ask whether the land will return the same income, when people sell a smaller amount of their produce to several million citizens. So whether the wage-earners are totally reimbursed, or whether they are only partially reimbursed, it is clear that, in the one case as in the other, the tax that one places on them falls equally on the owners.
>
> Indeed, the landowners must certainly pay for the wage-earning class, since it is the landowners who pay the wages. In a word, no matter how one approaches it, they must pay everything. (*CG* 221–22)

While Condillac totally supported the principal policy proposals of the physiocrats, his new theory of value and utility on which his analysis was ultimately based had led to the conclusion that "farmers, merchants, artisans come together to increase the mass of wealth," and even more provocatively that this had been "much obscured by some writers."

Because his analysis endorsed Quesnay's principal policy proposals, the physiocrats could have regarded this contribution by a distinguished philosopher and member of l'Académie française as a constructive contribution to the analysis of their school. They had accepted the economics of Turgot, who had been heterodox enough to suggest that industry as well as agriculture generates an economic surplus: in the form of profits, which only appear tangentially in Quesnay's writings.[91] Turgot was welcomed as at least a "fellow traveller," and physiocrats were delighted to have the opportunity to serve with him in government. They none the less censored his writings via extensive editorial amendments by Du Pont before these could be allowed to appear in *Les Éphémérides du citoyen.*[92] A school of knowledge which is still alive can accommodate debate. This will generally enrich its analysis through the Hegelian process of thesis-antithesis-synthesis. Would Condillac's book be similarly welcomed as a basis for debate on the development of

91. G. Vaggi (*The Economics of François Quesnay* [London: Macmillan, 1987]) shows from a careful interpretation of detailed physiocratic sources (including especially Quesnay's articles "Grains" and "Hommes") that farmers gain profits wherever the current price of corn exceeds the fundamental price (*prix fondamental*) and that there is a general tendency for profits to arise from this source. Walter Eltis ("François Quesnay: a reinterpretation, 1: The *Tableau économique,*" *Oxford Economic Papers* 27 [1975]: 176–77) shows that the equilibrium incomes of large farmers necessarily include the equivalent of a normal profit on the large capital sums they have to invest in *la grande culture*. It none the less requires considerable textual exegesis to find profits in Quesnay. In most of his writings incomes consist only of the revenues of landowners and the earnings of those who work in the productive and sterile sectors.

92. Turgot's *Réflexions* . . . appeared in three successive issues of *Éphémérides* (1769, vols. 11 and 12, and 1770, vol. 1), and Du Pont made such extensive changes to his text that Turgot wrote on 2 February 1770, "I insist absolutely that you conform to my manuscript from now on . . . the passage on *avances foncières* has caused me particular heartache; you know how I argued on this subject with l'abbé Baudeau in your presence; I may be wrong, but we each wish to be ourselves and not someone else" (Turgot, *Oeuvres de Turgot,* 3:374). It was none the less Du Font's version of the *Réflexions* . . . and not one based on Turgot's manuscript which he republished in 1808–11 in his nine-volume *Oeuvres de M. Turgot*. Peter D. Groenewegen (*The Economics of A. R. J. Turgot* [The Hague: Martinus Nijhoff, 1977], xx), following Schelle's account in Turgot (*Oeuvres de Turgot,* 3:373–84), suggests that "all these changes and additions were designed to give the *Réflections* a greater Physiocratic flavour and to remove conflicts between Turgot's economics and Physiocratic thought." See also Robert L. Meek, *Turgot on Progress, Sociology and Economics* (Cambridge: Cambridge University Press, 1973), 37–38.

physiocracy? The physiocrats would have found it technically challenging to absorb his analysis of human motivation into their system's already rich analysis, but a successful synthesis of the economics of Quesnay and Condillac would have produced a stronger theory.

Contemporaries of the physiocrats have remarked on their dogmatism. For instance, in 1769 David Hume wrote to Morellet, who would soon be commissioned by the Administration to write a book to rebut Galiani, "crush them, and pound them, and reduce them to dust and ashes," for they are "the most chimerical and arrogant [set of men] that now exists" (Hume, *Letters*, 2:205). Would the leading physiocrats succumb to such arrogance and dogmatism in their reaction to Condillac?

When *Commerce and Government* first appeared it was received with interest. According to the abbé Nicholas Baudeau, Du Pont's successor as editor of *Les Ephémérides*, the book was published with "the highest praise" (Baudeau, "Observations," 432), while according to Guillaume-François Le Trosne, another prominent physiocrat, it had impressed "many people" (Le Trosne, *De l'intérêt social*, 886). In April 1776 Morellet sent a copy across the Channel to the future British Prime Minister, the Earl of Shelburne, and remarked in his accompanying letter, "I am however sending you an admirable book by one of our men of letters, the abbé de Condillac. You no doubt have his treatise on education, but this is an elementary economic work where the ideas are in general true and the principles wise. In every part of it you will find freedom of commerce sustained" (Morellet, *Lettres*, 1:339).

Some of the most distinguished physiocrats were members of the Société royale d'agriculture d'Orléans, and Condillac was invited to read chapters from his book to this society in February and March 1776. In the minutes of the 306th meeting on 14 March 1776 it was noted that the society had seen with satisfaction that "the practical conclusions aimed to guide every administration that intends the public good being found in perfect conformity with those of economic science, fewer problems than advantages are to be expected from the publication of this work" (Lebeau, *Condillac*, 41). On 21 March the society continued to read and discuss Condillac's book, but on 25 April 1776 the first part of a critical review article by Baudeau appeared in *Les Nouvelles Éphémérides*, and this was discussed in place of further chapters of Condillac's book. Then on 27 February 1777 Le Trosne came to the

331st session of the society to read chapters of his new book, *De l'intérêt social,* which included an extensive critique of *Commerce and Government.* The flavour of Baudeau's and Le Trosne's responses to *Commerce and Government* can be judged from Baudeau's statement that:

> True économistes can easily be distinguished by one simple characteristic in a manner that the whole world can understand. They recognise one master, Dr Quesnay, one doctrine (that of *Philosophie rurale* and *l'Analyse économique*), classic texts (*la Physiocratie*), and a single formula (*le Tableau économique*), and they use technical terms in the same way as the ancient scholars of China. (Baudeau, "Observations," 433)

Le Trosne complained that Condillac had departed from doctrines which had been "published, proved and demonstrated in several works in the last fifteen years" (Le Trosne, *De l'intérêt social,* 886). After further readings from Le Trosne's critique, the society concluded that he had succeeded in "dissipating the clouds in which the subtle metaphysician, M. l'abbé de Condillac, appeared to wish to obscure this science that is so important to the well-being and stability of political societies. The Society has thanked M. Le Trosne" (Lebeau, *Condillac,* 43).

In addition to their dogmatic hostility, Baudeau and Le Trosne had criticisms of substance, which were sufficient to persuade the Royal Agricultural Society of Orléans to condemn the book.

Both Baudeau and Le Trosne drew attention to Condillac's statement that there were, in general, "only two classes of citizens: that of the landowners . . . and that of the paid workers" (*CG* 220). They could not accept Condillac's radical concept of a multi-sectoral and mutually interdependent economy.

Their detailed criticisms concerned Condillac's sketchy (to the physiocrats' confused) account of the creation of the agricultural surplus which was central to physiocracy. The landowners provided the sole source of taxable revenues. But could the entrepreneur-farmers who invested their own capital in farms which they leased and whose success or failure determined whether France would grow or decline be regarded as belonging to the same class, paid workers (*les salariés*), as farm labourers? Condillac generally describes those who farm as "*colons*" or "*fermiers.*" In the early chapters where he describes a very primitive society (*peuplade*) these plausibly own their own land, but as soon as the argument is developed and landowners congregate in cities where they receive rent, can those who actually organise agriculture be sensibly described as belonging to the same class as farm labourers? It would be entirely natural to speak of both farm labourers and farm managers as employees if farming was conducted on a *métayer* basis where all farm capital is owned by landowners, while those who actually farm on their behalf are allowed to keep a fraction of the harvest, corresponding via competition to the subsistence wage.

But Quesnay insisted in his first publications that to achieve the level of agricultural surplus which France required and England was actually achieving, it was necessary that agriculture should evolve to a condition where the management of farms was in the hands of capitalist tenant farmers. These would take farms on long leases, own all movable capital such as horses, ploughs and farm animals, finance all the costs which precede harvests and own the harvests net of their obligation to pay an agreed rent to landowners. Quesnay called this manner of farming "*la grande culture*" as opposed to the *métayer* system which he labelled "*la petite culture.*"[93] Condillac's two-class society comfortably accommodates *la petite culture* in which *les salariés* are easily recognisable, but he nowhere brings the considerable technical advantages of *la grande culture* fully into his argument. Condillac's father was a prominent provincial lawyer, while Condillac himself lived as a philosopher who advised princes. Quesnay grew up the son of a farmer, who understood the significance of capital-intensive farming with horses rather than labour-intensive farming with ox-drawn ploughs: Condillac never discusses the details of efficient farming which were so central to the principal physiocratic texts. Baudeau and Le Trosne complained that by calling both entrepreneur-farmers and day-labourers *salariés*, Condillac had obscured the economic significance of the entrepreneur-farmers on whom the well-being of France predominantly depended in mainstream physiocracy.

Condillac actually distinguishes the entrepreneur-farmers from labour-

---

93. Quesnay's detailed accounts of *la petite culture* and *la grande culture* are set out in the articles "Fermiers" and "Grains" which he published in the *Encyclopédie* in 1756 and 1757. Their significance and the interconnections between methods of farming and the extent of the agricultural surplus are set out in Eltis, "François Quesnay."

ers in his chapters "The origin of towns" and "Of the right of ownership" (*CG* 135–40), where he sets out several ways in which agriculture can be organised. Landowners may receive their rents through farm managers who will also sometimes themselves farm; or directly from large farmers who themselves lease the land from the landowners, provide initial and annual advances and hire day-labourers, which is Quesnay's *la grande culture;* or farming may be organised through *métayer* systems of output sharing. He does not bring these distinctions into the remainder of the book, and he makes no reference to Quesnay's insight that only some systems of land tenure are compatible with *la grande culture* where horse-drawn ploughs produce a rate of surplus three times as great as the ox-drawn ploughs of *la petite culture*. Condillac's passages on alternative systems of land tenure are slightly extended in the passages he added to the 1798 edition in response to the criticisms of Baudeau and Le Trosne, but again there is no impact on the remainder of the book.[94] Condillac therefore still neglected to bring the physiocrat supply-side arguments about agricultural efficiency and what actually determines the extent of the agricultural surplus directly into his argument.

But his detailed analysis of agriculture is entirely in line with his general approach to economic efficiency. The incomes of farm managers, farmers and day-labourers are all determined by competitive market forces, and the land is capable of delivering a growing supply of agricultural produce as new demands for this are created through the development of new industrial products. Quesnay's world, where horse-drawn ploughs yield a surplus on annual advances of 100 per cent and ox-drawn ploughs a surplus of 36 per cent, is essentially one of fixed coefficients. Condillac has no fixed coefficients. Instead, provided that the markets for farm managers, farmers, day-labourers and food are competitive, agriculture will be conducted in the best possible manner to maximise productive efficiency. The supply side will organise itself through market forces which must be allowed to operate entirely freely, and it will then operate as effectively as possible. With this general approach, he does not need to follow Quesnay, Baudeau and Le Trosne in having more categories of employees in agriculture than in other sectors. It is enough to say that throughout an efficient economy there are

94. Lebeau (*Condillac,* 138–47) discusses the significance of the new passages.

landowners and the *salariés,* who are all those who are market-dependent, be they managers, farmers or labourers.

Le Trosne was highly critical of Condillac's multi-sectoral view of the economy, but he accepted that his argument had led him to policy conclusions which were as sound (they were indeed the same) as those of the physiocrats:

> I admit only one source of wealth, and M. l'abbé de Condillac admits as many as there are kinds of work . . .
>
> However when he moves on to the practical, the fairness of his intellect redeems his argument. He establishes perfectly the single tax, freedom of industry, freedom of commerce both internal and external, the effects of monopoly and the dangers from prohibitions. The theoretical lines of thought he has developed do not influence his results. (Le Trosne, *De l'intérêt social,* 933)

Le Trosne writes equally warmly that "I shall bring to this discussion, which has the sole object of instructing the public, the high respect the author merits, and I dare flatter myself that there will be no weakening in the friendship he has been ready to show me" (ibid., 886).

Baudeau complains that Condillac made no use of Quesnay's *Tableau économique:*

> you would destroy to nothing the *Tableau économique,* this masterpiece of the Master, this valuable summary of economic doctrine. You certainly had no intention to do this wrong to knowledge, nor to the memory of Dr Quesnay of whom you were a disciple and friend before me. ("Observations," 443)

The unwillingness of Baudeau and Le Trosne to accept Condillac's book as a contribution to economic debate which deserved to be added to the literature meriting discussion by the dominant physiocratic school sufficed to limit its contemporary impact.[95] The physiocrats could have absorbed into their system the most fundamental element of Condillac's contribution: utility and its impact on human motivation. Condillac was not the first to see a powerful

---

95. See Daniel Klein, "Deductive economic methodology in the French Enlightenment," *History of Political Economy* 17, no. 1 (1958): 52–53, for a similar account of the

connection between value and utility. Galiani had found one in *Della Moneta* in 1751, and Condillac's attention was drawn to this work while he was tutor to the Prince of Parma.[96] Turgot also set out an analysis of the influence of utility on value in 1769 in an unfinished paper, "Valeurs et monnaies," which was published posthumously by Du Pont, but the extent of its manuscript circulation during his lifetime is unknown.

Condillac's readily available published account of the connection between value and utility is more coherent and comprehensive than Galiani's and Turgot's,[97] and it was therefore from him that the physiocrats had an outstanding opportunity to absorb the influence of utility upon value and human motivation into their analysis, almost a century before this became the universal approach of economists throughout the world.

## "Commerce and Government" in the Nineteenth and Twentieth Centuries

Adam Smith published *The Wealth of Nations* three months after *Commerce and Government,* and it established an overwhelming case for competitive market economics and the removal of trade barriers. The policy conclusions of *Commerce and Government* are similar, and Maurice Allais and

---

rejection of the economics of *Commerce and Government* by Baudeau and Le Trosne. He does not refer to the extent of Condillac's common ground with the physiocrats so that, as with Turgot, they could have welcomed his support and acquiesced in the differences.

96. Terence Hutchison, *Before Adam Smith: The Emergence of Political Economy, 1662–1776* (Oxford: Basil Blackwell, 1988), 324.

97. In 1769 Turgot elegantly derived the relationship between the relative marginal utilities of commodities and their relative values in exchange in his uncompleted "Valeurs et monnaies." His rigorous analysis took the form of two persons trading two commodities. The influence of the opportunity cost of producing the commodities and the generalisation of the argument beyond two persons and two commodities are sketchily indicated. It is not known if Condillac saw Turgot's manuscript; if he did, he certainly extended the argument, which is why he is widely credited with the principal French originality in the development of the relationship between utility and value, and its implications for an efficient economy. Turgot's analysis of utility, value and demand is set out and discussed in detail in G. Faccarello, "Turgot et l'économie politique sensualiste," in *Nouvelle histoire de la pensée économique,* vol. 1 (Paris: Éditions la Découverte, 1992), 254–88.

Friedrich von Hayek, French and German Nobel Prizewinners in economics, have bracketed it with *The Wealth of Nations*. Hayek has remarked that "the great strides" in economics "always came from outside—and for the most part in opposition to—the schools" which, like the physiocrats, are "more likely to hinder than to advance progress." He refers in contrast to the lasting gain to science in 1776, "the year in which the works of Adam Smith and Condillac were published" (Hayek, "Richard Cantillon," 267). Allais has described *Commerce and Government* as "definitely superior to Smith in theoretical analysis and logical systemization of ideas" (Allais, "General theory," 37).

But in 1776 and subsequently, the impact of *The Wealth of Nations* was immeasurably greater. A key to the contemporary success of Smith's book and Condillac's failure to arouse widespread attention may be found in Spencer Pack's interpretation of the relevance of Smith's *Lectures on Rhetoric and Belles Lettres* to the success of *The Wealth of Nations*. Smith advises that when an author is writing for those already receptive to what he has to say, a deductive method of presentation with a logical derivation of conclusions from axioms which readers are already prepared to acccept is appropriate. It is by far the easiest to follow and it is the most elegant. But when an author is writing for the unconverted, he should argue inductively, moving step by step from known facts to the conclusions he wishes to establish. Tariffs, restrictions on trade and detailed government interventions proliferated in both Britain and France in 1776, so both Condillac and Smith were addressing the unconverted, but Smith adopted the method of presentation he had prescribed for such a situation:

> keep as far from the main point to be proved as possible, bringing on the audience by slow and imperceptible degrees to the thing to be proved, and by gaining their consent to some things whose tendency they cant discover, we force them at last either to deny what they had before agreed to, or to grant the Validity of the Conclusion . . . if they are prejudiced against the Opinion to be advanced; we are not to shock them by rudely affirming what we are satisfied is disagreeable, but are to conceal our design and beginning at a distance, bring them slowly on to the main point and having gained the more remote ones we get the nearer ones of consequence. (Smith, *Wealth of Nations*, 146–47)

Pack reminds us with this passage in mind that Smith only reached his critique of mercantilist policies after more than 500 pages replete with convincing empirical detail.

Condillac in contrast used the deductive methodology of a distinguished philosopher and moved faultlessly and elegantly from proposition to proposition,[98] but he failed to carry the vast majority of his French readers. His initial chapters lacked Smith's empiricism, and his French readers were unprepared to accept that a deductive argument, which moved from premises they did not recognise as relevant, could arrive at conclusions which sensibly related to their country. Because of the consequent lack of recognition by his own countrymen, unlike much important French economics of the eighteenth and nineteenth centuries, *Commerce and Government* was not immediately translated into English. This limited the scope for international recognition in the warmer environments for deductive argument and free market conclusions that was offered by the economics profession in Britain and later the United States.

There were occasional citations of Condillac in the nineteenth-century French literature. In 1803 Jean-Baptiste Say found Condillac insufficiently empirical in his "Discours préliminaire" to his *Traité d'économie politique:*

> almost all the French writers of some reputation who have concerned themselves with matter relating to Political Economy from 1760 to around 1780 without positively marching under the banner of the physiocrats have nonetheless allowed themselves to be dominated by their opinions . . . One can even count Condillac among their number although he sought to devise his own system. There are some good ideas to be discovered among the ingenious chatter of his book; but he passed by the most fruitful truths without noticing them. Just like the physiocrats, he almost always bases a principle on a gratuitous assumption: now an assumption may serve as an example but not as a fundamental truth. Political Economy only rose to the level of the sciences when, like the other sciences, it made a study solely of what is. (xviii–xix)

98. The deductive nature of Condillac's methodology is emphasised in Klein, "Deductive economic methodology."

A. F. Théry repeated Say's judgement that *Commerce and Government* is insufficiently empirical to make a significant contribution to economics in his introductory article on the life and works of Condillac for the second edition of the complete *Oeuvres de Condillac* published in Paris in 1821–22. It was Théry's judgement and doubtless that of his contemporaries that Condillac was an important philosopher but an insignificant economist.

The 1844 edition of Say's *Cours complet d'économie politique* was published with a "Bibliographie raisonnée de l'économie politique" by A. Blanqui, who claimed that he had omitted no book essential to the study of economics, but he failed to include *Commerce and Government* among the 600 titles he listed.

A passage from *Commerce and Government* none the less attracted condemnation from two economists, Say and Marx, who do not ordinarily cohabit. Both strongly criticised Condillac's statement that:

> it is false that in exchanges one gives equal value for equal value. On the contrary, each of the contracting parties always gives a lesser value for a greater value . . . Indeed, if one always exchanged equal value for equal value, there would be no gain to be made for either of the contracting parties. Now, both of them make a gain, or ought to make one. Why? The fact is that with things only having value in relation to our needs, what is greater for one person is less for another, and vice versa. (*CG* 120)

In the *Cours complet d'économie politique* Say declared that "This doctrine . . . does not explain in any way the variety of phenomena which commercial production presents . . . I confront the same errors in social discourse, and even in books" (part 2, ch. 13).

Marx's reaction is to be found in the first volume of *Capital:* "We see in this passage, how Condillac . . . confuses use-value with exchange-value . . . Still, Condillac's argument is frequently used by modern economists, more especially when the point is to show, that in the exchange of commodities in its developed form, commerce, is productive of surplus-value (part 2, ch. 5).

Condillac's argument which both Marx and Say condemned was that the value of commodities depends on their utilities, and that when a good is sold, the total utility the seller sacrifices is less than the total utility the buyer gains, and vice versa. He drafted a further five paragraphs to explain this analysis further after the publication of the 1776 edition, and these are included in the posthumous 1798 edition (and on pp. 121–22 of the present text). Marx cites Condillac from Daire's 1847 edition, which includes none of the posthumous material (see p. 79 below), while it is not clear whether Say used the 1798 edition, which included the additional material. Marx and Say may have condemned Condillac without reading all he had to say on this question.

The concepts of consumers' and producers' surplus were developed well after his death, but the statement which both Marx and Say objected to is compatible with that later development of economic theory, and Condillac comes close to it in the posthumous paragraphs. In the twentieth century it came to be understood that the buyer of a commodity for final consumption gains a consumer's surplus, while the producer gains a producer's surplus. Theorems have been formulated to establish that the sum of these will be maximised when the relevant commodities and factors of production are sold entirely freely in competitive markets. Condillac's economics is in line with these twentieth-century developments.

How close he came to understanding that there were actually rigorous proofs for his propositions is naturally unclear, but in chapter after chapter he reiterates the benefits an economy derives from the free exchange of goods in competitive markets.

Condillac began to receive serious attention after the marginal revolution of the 1870s when Stanley Jevons and Carl Menger discovered that there was much where Condillac had been before them. In 1871 in his *Theory of Political Economy*, Jevons credited him with "the earliest distinct statement of the true connection between value and utility" (xxviii). Also in 1871 in his *Grundsätze der Volkswirthschaftslehre*, Menger referred to his fundamental view that utility is the measure of a good's use value which has "frequently reappeared since that time in the writings of English and French economists" (Menger, 297). He has eight references to Condillac, more than to any other French economist apart from Say, and more than to any British economist other than Adam Smith.[99] Walras was less warm. In his pathbreaking *Eléments d'économie pure* of 1874 he writes:

99. Erich W. Streissler, "The influence of German economics on the work of Menger and Marshall," in *Carl Menger and His Legacy in Economics,* edited by Bruce J. Caldwell, Annual Supplement to vol. 22 of the *History of Political Economy* (1990), 35.

The science of economics offers three major solutions to the problem of the origin of value. The first, that of Adam Smith, Ricardo and Mc-Culloch, is the English solution, which traces the origin of value to *labour*. This solution is too narrow, because it fails to attribute value to things which, in fact, do have value. The second solution, that of Condillac and J. B. Say, is the French solution, which traces the origin of value to *utility*. This solution is too broad, because it attributes value to things which, in fact, have no value. Finally, the third solution, that of Burlamaqui and my father, A. A. Walras, traces the origin of value to *scarcity* [*rarité*]. This is the correct solution. (201)

Walras at least places Condillac among the originators of one of the leading approaches to the theory of value.

After the 1870s, with the significance of Condillac's contribution to the theory of value and utility firmly established, several French economists recognised the importance of *Commerce and Government*. In particular, Condillac's condemnation by the physiocrats was reassessed, and several preferred his analysis to theirs. That was the early twentieth-century judgement of Charles Gide and Charles Rist, the authors of *Histoire des doctrines économiques depuis les Physiocrates jusqu'à nos jours,* which appeared in seven French and two English editions between 1909 and 1948. They wrote, 140 years after Condillac's death, "it is above all in Condillac's book that we must seek the closing of the gaps and the correction of the errors of the Physiocrats" (3rd ed., 55).

Writing in 1912, Émile Morand examined the psychological theories of value of Galiani, Turgot and Condillac, and described Condillac as "the most eminent man of his century on this question" (*La Théorie psychologique,* 6). He especially praises Condillac's account of the role of commerce in the creation of value:

the aqueduct which, for Condillac, symbolises commerce, becomes as the creator of wealth, the creator of value. (Ibid., 308)

Condillac developing his general theory logically arrives at results which are far more admissible and far more in conformity to economic reality since he recognises that commerce has an immense role in the creation of value. (Ibid., 311)

He sided with Condillac against the physiocrats who insisted that exchanges of goods cannot increase the "value" of production and extolled precisely the passage which Say and Marx condemned. He argued indeed that this controversial passage is at the heart of the originality of Condillac's contribution, and he has extensive passages which show that those who receive goods in an exchange derive more utility from them than those who part with them, and that these potential gains in utility go on to spur real economic activities which raise the value of production.

When he argues that the utility gained from exchanges leads to a consequential increase in productive activity, he quotes the passage where Condillac argues that with each advance made by artisans, farmers acquire "value in a product which previously had none," which gives "a fresh spur to commerce" so that "farmers, merchants, artisans, come together to increase the mass of wealth" (*CG* 125). Morand writes:

> Therefore it is difficult to provide in less space a better and more complete perception of the role commerce plays in production; here again by the exactitude and depth of his insights Condillac far surpasses those of whom he has often been regarded as a disciple. Value being founded on our needs, the appearance of a new need, to which corresponds a good appropriate to satisfy it, creates a new value. (*La Théorie psychologique*, 312)

He identifies "To give less for more" as a phrase which "returns in Condillac's work as a refrain . . . it alone would be enough to distinguish him from the physiocrats" (ibid., 302).

Perhaps the greatest French compliment to the advance of Condillac over the physiocrats is to be found in Georges Weulersse's *La Physiocratie sous les ministères de Turgot et de Necker (1774–81)*, posthumously published in 1950, forty years after his great history of physiocracy.

His account of "Physiocracy under the ministry of Turgot" concludes with the chapter "Attack and defence of the system," which culminates in an account of how Condillac surpassed his predecessors. He opens by remarking that "it was left to a qualified philosopher, a more subtle analyst, to advance the elucidation of the problem," of the role agriculture plays in relation to industry and commerce (*La Physiocratie sous les Ministères*, 229). He welcomes Condillac's statements that industry and commerce add to the mass of wealth. Like Morand, he endorses the statement that each party to an exchange always gives up a lesser for a greater value (neither refers to its condemnation by Say and Marx):

> this is the precious distinction between the psychological value in use to the individual and the social market value in exchange which the physiocrats were inclined to consider too exclusively. (Ibid., 230)

Weulersse emphasises that a very different natural social order emerges as soon as it is accepted that industrial and commercial as well as agricultural activity add to the value of output.

He remarks that, "according to our philosopher, a society consists of a kind of universal salariat, a conception altogether strange to the [physiocratic] school." He quotes Condillac's statement that "all the citizens are given a wage with regard to each other. If the artisan and the merchant are paid by the farmer to whom they sell, the farmer is in his turn paid by the artisan and the merchant to whom he sells, and each of them gets paid for his work" (*CG* 127). Weulersse remarks that here there is not merely mutual dependency between the different classes; there is actually equal dependency, which has important social implications (*La Physiocratie sous les Ministères*, 230).

He agrees with Baudeau and Le Trosne that Condillac analyses the role of capital in production with "far less precision" than the physiocrats (ibid., 231). But Weulersse emphasises passages in *Commerce and Government,* such as "all citizens are, each by reason of his work, co-proprietors in the wealth of the society," to suggest remarkably that Condillac even comes close to a labour theory of value (ibid., 232).

The respect of Jevons, Menger, Walras, Gide and Rist, Morand, Weulersse, Hutchison, Allais and Hayek for the economics of *Commerce and Government* in the 200 years since its publication underlines that French political economy failed to take advantage of an important opportunity in 1776 and 1777.

In the development of British classical economics, Malthus and Ricardo enriched the economics of Smith. They strongly criticised several of his conclusions, but accepted his analysis as the starting point for their own. British political economy strengthened and developed as Malthus's theory of population and Ricardo's theory of value and distribution were integrated with the economics of *The Wealth of Nations* to culminate in the last great work of British classical economics, the *Principles of Political Economy* (1848) of John Stuart Mill. Classical French political economy would have become equally great if the *économistes* had been prepared to absorb the best of Condillac's economics instead of dogmatically condemning it.

Those concerned with the administration of economic policy in France would also have benefited from a familiarity with Condillac comparable to the familiarity with Smith of almost all who governed Britain in the nineteenth century. The continuing Colbertian dominance in official French economics might have been less pronounced if French political economists and administrators had been more aware of Condillac.

English language readers who come upon *Commerce and Government* for the first time will find, with Allais, that the case for competitive market economics has rarely been presented more powerfully, and that there is continuing relevance in Condillac's account of the difficulties that those who seek to liberalise economies still encounter.

## — 3 The Editions of *Commerce and Government*

THE INITIAL EDITION of *Commerce and Government* was published in Paris in 1776 by Jombert & Cellot in both a single-volume (vi + 586 pp.) and a two-volume (273 + 180 pp.) edition. On the title page, the place of publication of both editions is described as "Amsterdam and one also finds it at Paris." This is a typical convention of the period, and, as explained in Chapter 1, in many of the books actually published in Paris a principal and generally fictitious foreign place of publication is also stated on the title page so that the censors only needed to permit the sale within France of a book originally published outside the country. The 1767 edition of Quesnay's *Physiocratie* even claims publication in Peking, and as with *Commerce and Government*, Du Pont adds the words "and one also finds it at Paris."

The single-volume edition of *Commerce and Government* was published first: five errata are listed on page vi, and the latter three are corrected in what must therefore be the subsequent two-volume printing. The initial single-volume edition concludes with the statement "END OF THE SECOND PART. The third part of this work has not been written, the author will work on it if the first two parts create a demand." By the time the two-volume edition was printed, Condillac had removed that statement and simply has "THE END" at the foot of the final page.

In 1795 the 1776 text was republished in Paris by Letellier & Maradan as a single volume (380 pp.), virtually without amendment. A further erratum from 1776 is corrected, but still not all five, and there are a few one- or two-word changes. The failure to correct all the announced errata from the 1776 edition suggests that this is not a superior text: it is one produced by a Paris bookseller because there was sufficient demand to justify a new printing. A photographic reprint of the 1795 edition with an eleven-page introduction by G. Romeyer-Dherbey was published by Slatkine (Paris and Geneva) in 1980.

In 1798 a twenty-three-volume edition of the *Oeuvres de Condillac* "Reviewed and corrected by the Author, printed from his autograph manuscripts" was published in Paris by Houel, with *Commerce and Government* (559 pp.) as its fourth volume.

Condillac had made his elder brother, the abbé de Mably, his literary executor, but Mably died in 1785, five years after Condillac. It is stated in the introduction to the first volume of the 1798 *Oeuvres* that a wooden case containing Mably's and Condillac's papers was opened in June 1796 (*prairial an IV*) by order of the Minister of the Interior and the Director-General of Public Instruction so that a complete edition of Condillac's works could be prepared. The letter from Citizen Bénézech, the Minister of the Interior, to Citizen Commendeur, the bailiff who was present when the case was opened, reads in part:

> as these works are among the number of those which are most useful for education, I desire that the edition of these works which is going to be made should be the most complete possible. I know that you have had in your custody and under seal for more than ten years, a wooden box containing several volumes of the works of Condillac, where this author has written a large number of marginal corrections and added several notebooks written in his own hand. I invite you, Citizen, to pass this box to the general administration of Public Instruction . . . so that these volumes which are deposited in it can be used to perfect the complete edition which will be made of works which are equally useful to the public. (Condillac, *Oeuvres de Condillac,* 1:x–xi)

Citizen Ginguené, the Director-General of Public Instruction, then wrote to Citizen Arnoux, one of the two subsequent editors (the other was Mousnier) of the 1798 *Oeuvres,* that the seals should be removed in his presence by a magistrate. When this was done, it was found that the contents of the wooden case included:

> Item, a bound volume entitled, *Le Commerce et le Gouvernement, considérés relativement l'un à l'autre;* the first three pages are glued and crossed through, as though they should be deleted; on the fifteenth page a note of seven lines is stuck on; in addition another of three sheets is inserted after the twenty-first page; at the fifty-fourth page, a note of 33 lines, at the fifty-fifth another of 35 lines; at the seventy-first a folio of writing paper

written to half way down the fourth page: at the ninetieth a note of eight
lines; at the 195th and 196th, two notes under-lined, forming the end of the
eighteenth chapter. There are in addition, in the volume, several marginal
notes and several corrections in the body of the text.

Item, ten stitched paper booklets, printed, in duodecimal, comprising
part of a work on Commerce, in which is glued a note of twenty-four
lines. (Ibid., vii–viii)

The long insertions and the page references (evidently to a copy of the
one-volume 1776 edition) correspond exactly to the extra material subsequently included in the 1798 edition, extending its total length by about
3 per cent.

The crossing through of the first three pages indicates that Condillac may
have intended to replace these with a new opening to the book, but none
has been found. The only change in the first three pages which has survived
is an important new footnote (*CG* 93 below). As for the "ten stitched paper
booklets, printed, in duodecimal, comprising part of a work on Commerce,"
there is the fascinating possibility that these could form an incomplete draft
of chapters for the Third Part of *Commerce and Government*, which Condillac had expressed a readiness to prepare for publication in 1776. He wrote
quickly and published extensively, and it would be interesting to know what
Mably's executors and Condillac's editors made of these ten printed booklets.
There are no incomplete publications in the twenty-three-volume *Oeuvres
de Condillac*, so it is understandable that the editors may not have wished
to include a large fragment which twentieth-century editors would have un-
hesitatingly included in an author's complete works. It would be fascinating
to have the opportunity to read them now, if the editors had not decided to
discard these unpublished pages by Condillac. They conveyed most of the
material from Mably's wooden box to the Bibliothèque Nationale after they
had completed their edition of the *Oeuvres de Condillac* in 1798, two years
after the box was opened. Sgard (*Corpus Condillac*, 160–63) provides an account of what is now in the Bibliothèque Nationale from *Commerce and Government*, and he says that what is there "appears to be incomplete": he makes
no reference to the ten printed stitched booklets.

In 1821–22 A. F. Théry produced a sixteen-volume edition of Condillac's

*Oeuvres* where *Commerce and Government* is again volume 4 (414 pp.), and he republished the text of the 1798 edition with Condillac's additional material.

The next significant edition of *Commerce and Government* was published by Eugène Daire in 1847. He produced a series of compilations with the general title *Collections des principaux économistes*, which included the celebrated volume containing the principal publications of the physiocrats. The volume *Mélanges d'économie politique* followed in 1847 with important books and essays by Hume, Forbonnais, Condorcet, Franklin and Condillac's *Commerce and Government* (243–448). Daire reverted to the 1776 text and therefore included none of the additional material from Condillac's papers which were included in the collected *Oeuvres de Condillac* of 1798 and 1821–22.

Like the principal academic journals in the twentieth century, Daire's collections were in every significant library, so most subsequent citations to *Commerce and Government* have been to this 1847 edition. That was the case with Marx in *Capital* in 1867, with Menger in *Grundsätze der Volkswirthschaftslehre* in 1871, with Morand in *La Théorie psychologique de la valeur jusqu'en 1776* in 1912 and with Weulersse in *La Physiocratie sous les ministères de Turgot et de Necker* published posthumously in 1950.

The final significant edition of *Commerce and Government* is by Georges Le Roy in his three-volume *Oeuvres philosophiques de Condillac* which the Presses Universitaires de France published from 1947 to 1951. Le Roy included it in volume 2 published in 1948 (241–367), and his is now the definitive French language edition.

Le Roy uses the 1798 edition as his principal text, but he publishes almost every variation from the 1776 edition. He identifies the places where passages of the 1798 text did not appear in 1776, and he gives most words and all the passages published in 1776 but not 1798. Le Roy thus invites his readers to take the 1798 text as their starting point, but to be at the same time aware of what was there in 1776.

We follow Le Roy in offering both texts to our readers, but we have preferred to take the 1776 text as our starting point. This is because it is the sole text Condillac actually published. According to Sgard (*Corpus Condillac*, 163), most of the additional material in Mably's wooden box which is now in the Bibliothèque Nationale is in Condillac's hand, but not all of it. Two amendments in the 1798 *Oeuvres* may reflect that they were inserted after the Revolution.

In 1776, thirteen years before the Revolution, Condillac says that "The right to coin money can only belong to the sovereign." In the 1798 edition, nine years after the Revolution and eighteen years after Condillac's death, the reader is told that the sovereign is "the king in a monarchy, and in a republic the nation or the body which represents it" (*CG* 272 below). In 1776 in Condillac's lifetime, the cry of the people who rise in revolt because they believe the export of grain is denying them bread is described as "seditious [*séditieux*]." In 1798 what was seditious in the monarchy is no longer seditious, and the word is deleted (*CG* 301 below), a change Le Roy has overlooked. The 1795 edition still has *séditieux*, so those who produced it were not tempted to the "political correctness" which may have crept into the 1798 edition. These are slight changes, but it is likely that they were inspired by the editors of the 1798 edition, and if they permitted themselves these amendments, they may have made others.

The second reason for preferring the 1776 text as the foundation for the present edition is that, while the principal additions of 1798 are clearly by Condillac and correspond almost exactly in length to what was found in Mably's wooden case, he did not have the opportunity to approve them in print. The original 1776 book has the verve and momentum of an author who is writing an important book, full of discoveries and clarifications, to win over the enlightened public. Some of the passages he added in 1798 are those of a distinguished philosopher responding to technical criticism. The first chapter has a long additional passage (*CG* 103–5 below) which includes an account of the need to solve a system of knowns and unknowns. The tempo is slowed. There are other new passages which clarify the argument without slowing the exposition.

We believe that readers will prefer to read the book as Condillac initially wrote it, but to be aware of the additional material from the final years of his life. We have therefore made the 1776 text the starting point of this first English language edition. We offer a complete translation of the 1776 text, and add in parentheses or at the end of chapters a translation of the new passages added in 1798 and an account of what was deleted then.

A Note on French Currency, Monetary Values, and Weights and Measures[100]

### FRENCH CURRENCY AND MONETARY VALUES

Condillac most often refers to livres: francs were synonymous with livres in his time. There were 20 sols or sous to the livre, and each sou was made up of 12 deniers.

Condillac also refers to écus, coins stamped with a shield covered with fleur-de-lys. Their denomination was generally of 3 livres (the écu blanc or louis d'argent introduced in 1641), or 6 livres (an écu d'armes introduced in 1727). Condillac refers to occasions when the face value of the écu blanc (the number of livres and sous it represented) was varied from month to month.

Condillac's account of the development of coinage refers to coins made from gold, silver and copper. When the franc was introduced in 1360 it was a gold coin worth 20 sols. The first silver francs were coined in the reign of Henri III (1574–89), while silver sous were introduced in the reign of Philippe Auguste (1180–1223).

Several provinces had their own coinage with different values. The principal versions were the livre tournois of the Tours region and the livre parisis of the Paris region. Both of these were made up of 20 silver sous, but there were 12 copper denier to the sou tournois and 15 identically valued denier to the heavier sou parisis, so the sou parisis and the livre parisis were worth more. Their separate use was terminated by edict in 1667.

From the mid-seventeenth century, legal contracts were based on the livre tournois, with its 20 sous to the livre and 12 denier to the sou, as a money of account, while silver coins were legally accepted by weight rather than by face value, which was frequently altered. The article "Livre" in *Palgrave's Dictionary of Political Economy* remarks on "the complete distinction

---

100. A variety of detailed articles in *Larousse* (1866–79), which quote extensively from the *Encyclopédie* and other sources, provide a general source of information on the history of French currency and weights and measures.

between money of account and the money in actual circulation" (Lodge, "Livre," 617) in the France of the Ancien Régime.

The monarchy determined the weight of silver required to settle a debt in livres tournois through decrees which determined the number of livres to a silver marc of 244.75 grammes (8 troy ounces). A piece of silver of precisely that weight had been lodged in Paris in ancient times, and exact copies were subsequently lodged in the other mints. Thus in 1715, the year after Condillac's birth, it was decreed that the silver marc would be worth 40 livres in place of 27, devaluing the livre from 3.375 to a troy ounce of silver to 5 livres to the ounce. In 1718 an edict for which John Law was responsible devalued the livre further from 5 to 7.5 to an ounce of silver and in 1720 to 10 livres to the ounce in February and to 15 in July. After the fall of Law the value of the livre in fine silver was gradually raised until it reached 6.39 livres to the ounce (51 livres 2 sous and 3 deniers to the marc) in 1726, and it remained at that value until the Revolution (Labrousse et al., Histoire économique, chs. 3 and 4). Thus between 1715 and 1726 the livre was devalued from 5 to an ounce of silver to 6.39 (with a fall to 15 to the ounce during Law's monetary experiments). The damage to commerce and to economic activity in general from disruptions to the value of the currency such as these are the subject of Chapter 9 in the Second Part of *Commerce and Government* (272–76 below).

From 1726 until the Revolution silver remained stable at 6.39 livres to the ounce. Debts for which there were legal contracts made out in livres tournois could be met by weighing silver coins of any denomination, estimating the fine silver they contained and discharging a debt of 1000 livres with about 156 ounces of fine silver. Smaller day-to-day transactions would in contrast be settled with currently minted coin with face values which remained stable after 1726.

There was a parallel gold currency, and the standard on which this was based was the gold marc, also of 8 troy ounces. The principal gold coin was the louis d'or, named after the sovereign and introduced in 1641 under Louis XIII. The state determined how many louis would be coined from 8 ounces of gold of 11/12 fineness (22 carats when fine gold has 24), and the number of livre tournois each louis would represent. Thus in 1715 it was decreed that 8 ounces of gold would be minted into 30 louis, each to make payments of 15.5 livres. An ounce of gold which was minted into 3.75 louis therefore sufficed to make payments of 58.13 livres. In the currency reforms of 1726 which survived until 1785, 3.75 louis were coined from an ounce of gold, and each louis had a face value of 24 livres, so an ounce of gold coins made payments of 90 livres against 58.13 in 1715. Hence between 1715 and 1726, there was devaluation of the livre tournois in relation to both gold and silver, after which its value was maintained in relation to both metals. In 1785 gold was slightly revalued, with the result that an ounce of gold coins made payments of 96 livres in place of 90, and at the same time commanded equivalently more silver because the silver value of the livre remained unaltered.

In the years before 1785, silver had a higher value in relation to gold inside France than in the world at large with the result that the currency which circulated in France was predominantly silver, while despite all prohibitions there was a tendency for gold to be exported. It has been suggested that the 1785 revaluation of gold reversed this tendency, and in the following years, about two-thirds of the currency minted in France was gold, while only one-third was silver. Gold circulated predominantly in the North and East and silver in the regions closer to Spain from which it mainly entered France (Dermigny, "La France").

A comparison of French with British monetary values is complex as conditions were very different in the two countries, but a few inferences can be drawn. Writing of the France of 1787, Arthur Young estimated that 1,800,000 livres tournois had a similar purchasing power to 78,750 pounds sterling (Young, *Travels*, 1:52). On that basis, the purchasing power commanded by 23 livres in France will have been close to that of a pound sterling in Britain. Since the gold louis commanded a value of 24 livres in 1785, its purchasing power on the basis suggested by Young will have been near to that of the 21-shilling gold guinea, and it has been shown that the gold content of these French and English coins was quite close after adjustment for the lower proportion of gold and higher proportion of base alloy in the French louis than in the British guinea (Law, "Louis d'or"). As the 24-livre French louis was equivalent to four 6-livre écus (Sir James Steuart [*An Inquiry*, Book 3, ch. 7] refers to these as "great crowns"), the late eighteenth century écu corresponded, within a few pence, to the 5-shilling British crown.

An alternative modern comparison produces a similar order of magnitude of the comparative purchasing power of the French and British currencies. Mathias and O'Brien ("Taxation") publish data on the average price of corn in England and France in the 1780s when one pound sterling purchased the same quantity of corn in England as 20 to 22 livres in France.

## FRENCH WEIGHTS AND MEASURES

The muid, to which Condillac refers, was an ancient measure of volume. The number of boisseaux to a muid depended on what was being measured. The muid of salt, for example, contained 192 boisseaux whereas the muid of oats contained 288 boisseaux. The muid of Paris was made up of 12 setiers, a measure frequently referred to by Condillac to describe quantities of grain, each of 12 boisseaux.

There were 2,304 litrons to the muid of Paris, and a litron was an ancient measure of capacity which amounted to 36 cubic inches (the modern litre has 61 cubic inches). The setier varied regionally; the setier of Paris, also known as the grain setier, was equivalent to 12 boisseaux. Muids of 12 setiers and 144 boisseaux were equivalent to 1,373 litres in modern decimal measures. The English bushel, a larger quantity than the French boisseau, also varied regionally in the eighteenth century, though less than the boisseau. Arthur Young remarked that, "in France the infinite perplexity of the measures exceeds all comprehension" (*Travels*, 1:315).

The arpent, a land measure, was also subject to regional variation and could be anywhere between 20 and 50 ares, where the are is now measured as 100 square metres. For comparison, the English acre is 4047 square metres (4840 square yards), so there were approximately 40 ares to the acre.

# COMMERCE AND GOVERNMENT

# LE COMMERCE

## ET

# LE GOUVERNEMENT,

*Confidérés relativement l'un à l'autre.*

## OUVRAGE ÉLÉMENTAIRE,

*Par M. l'Abbé DE CONDILLAC, de
l'Académie Françoife, & Membre de la
Société Royale d'Agriculture d'Orléans.*

---

*Vis confili expers mole ruit fuâ :
Vim temperatam Di quoque provehunt.
In majus.....*

---

*Cardinal* 🙢 *D. Rochechou*

## A AMSTERDAM;
*Et fe trouve à PARIS,*

**Chez JOMBERT & CELLOT**, Libraires,
rue Dauphine.

---

## M. DCC. LXXVI.

# COMMERCE

*and*

# GOVERNMENT

*Considered in their mutual relationship*

AN ELEMENTARY WORK

*by the Abbé DE CONDILLAC of
the Académie Française & Member of the
Royal Society of Agriculture of Orléans*

---

*Vis concili expers mole ruit sua:
Vim temperatam Di quoque provehunt
In majus . . .*

[Brute strength, if wisdom guide it not
by its own weight to earth is pressed,
but thought restrained, the gods exalt
its weakness into power]

Horace, *Odes,* iii.4

(trans. by Robert Wilmott)

# TABLE OF THE CHAPTERS
# CONTAINED IN THIS VOLUME

*End of the Table of Contents*

# THE AIM OF THIS WORK

EACH SCIENCE requires a special language, because each science has ideas which are unique to it. It seems that we should begin by forming this language; but we begin by speaking and writing and the language remains to be created. That is the position of Economic Science, the subject of this very work. It is, among other matters, the need which I propose to meet.*

This work is in three parts. In the first part, on commerce, I produce basic ideas which I determine according to assumptions, and I develop the principles of economic science. In the second part, I make other assumptions to judge the influence which commerce and government must have on each other. In the third part, I consider them both according to the facts in order to rest as much on experience as on reasoning.

I shall often make very ordinary remarks. But if I had to record them to speak on other matters with more precision, I should not be ashamed to say them. Geniuses who only make new statements, if there are such geniuses, should not write to instruct. The main point is to make oneself clear, and I only wish to produce a useful work.

---

*Footnote added in 1798:* Since the first edition of this work I have shown in my *Logic* that the art of dealing well with a science comes down to the art of creating its language well. Also, when I said that the language of Economic Science needed to be created, the public, for whom this science was still often no more than an indecipherable code, had no difficulty in believing this: because it thought, justly, that a language that is not understood is a badly constructed language.

# FIRST PART

*Elementary Propositions on Commerce,*
*Determined According to the Assumptions or*
*Principles of Economic Science*

# 1  The Basis of the Value of Things

LET US ASSUME a small tribe which has just been established, which has brought in its first harvest, and which, since it is isolated, can only subsist on the product of the land it cultivates.

Let us also assume that after setting aside the necessary seed corn, they have a hundred muids left; and that with this quantity, they can wait for a second crop without fear of scarcity.

Carrying on with our assumption, for this amount to remove all fear of scarcity, it must be enough not only for their needs, but also to relieve their fears. Now, that can only be found in a certain degree of abundance. Indeed, when people judge in line with their apprehensions, what would suffice at a pinch is not enough; and they only believe they have enough in what is to a certain extent abundant.

The quantity which remains for our tribe, once the seed corn has been deducted, therefore makes, for this year, what we call abundance. Consequently if they have some muids more, they are in surplus and they would be in dearth if they had some less.

If a people could judge, exactly, the relationship between the quantity of corn it has, with the amount needed for its consumption, this known relationship would cause it always to know, with the same precision, whether it was in abundance, surplus, or dearth.

But it cannot judge this relationship precisely: because it has no way of informing itself exactly, either of the amount of corn it has, or of what it will consume. It is all the less able to do so, as it could not store the corn without waste, and the exact amount of this waste is by its nature unpredictable. If it estimates it then it is only roughly, and on the experience of several years.

However, in whatever way it judges the relationship, it is always true to say that the tribe believes that it is in abundance, when it thinks it has a sufficient amount of grain to set aside all fear of running out of it; that it believes it is in surplus, when it thinks it has more than enough to meet all its fears; and that it believes itself in dearth, when it thinks it only has a quantity which is inadequate to set aside its fears.

It is therefore in the opinion that is held of the quantities, rather than in the quantities themselves, that abundance, surplus or dearth are found: but they only rest on opinion because the amounts are assumed.

If, instead of a hundred muids, our tribe, after deducting seed corn, had two hundred, it would have a hundred which would be of no use for its consumption between one crop and another; and if it took no care over storing this surplus grain, the corn would ferment and go bad, and what was left of it would be useless for the following years.

Several consecutive years of a large harvest would do nothing but embarrass our tribe with a useless surplus, and it would soon happen that they sowed less land.

But harvests which are inadequate for the needs of the tribe will create awareness of the need to store the corn when there is a surplus. A way to do this will be sought, and when it is found, the corn that is useless in years of surplus will become useful in years of dearth. The hundred muids which the tribe has not consumed, and which it has known how to store, will make up the shortfall in several years when all that is left for its consumption, after seed corn has been deducted, is sixty or eighty muids.

Properly speaking there will no longer be a corn surplus, once it is known how to preserve it, because what is not consumed in one year can be consumed in another.

If our tribe was surrounded by other tribes, cultivators like itself, it would not have the same need to keep corn in granaries; because, by giving the surplus that it had in some other commodity, it could obtain for itself surplus corn from another tribe. But we have assumed it to be completely isolated.

We have two kinds of needs. One set follows from our makeup: we are created to need food, or to be unable to live without nourishment.

The other kind follows from our customs. Something which we could do without, because our constitution does not make it a need for us, becomes necessary by custom, and sometimes as necessary as if we had been constituted to need it.

I call *natural* the needs which follow from our constitution, and *artificial* those which we owe to habit formed by the use of things.

A wandering horde lives on the fruits which the land produces naturally: on the fish it catches, on the animals it kills hunting; and when the area it covers no longer provides its subsistence, it moves elsewhere. In this form of life we only see natural needs.

Our tribe can no longer wander. It has created for itself the need to live in its chosen place. It has made itself a need of the abundance which it finds in the fields it cultivates, and the bounty of the fruits it owes to its labour. It is not satisfied with hunting the animals which can provide its food and clothing, it raises them, and tries to increase their number to meet its consumption.

There you have a type of life in which we notice artificial needs, that is to say, needs which arise from the habit we have formed of satisfying natural needs by chosen methods.

You can see that these first artificial needs separate themselves as little as may be from natural ones. But you can also foresee that the tribe will form others which will move ever further from natural needs. That is what will happen when our tribe, having made progress in the arts, wants to satisfy its natural needs through more multifarious and refined ways. There will even come a time when the artificial needs, by dint of moving away from nature, will end up changing it completely and corrupting it.

The first needs which our tribe creates for itself are of the essence of the social order, and this would cease if these needs themselves ended. So one is thus justified in considering them as natural. Because if they are not so for the wandering savage, they become so for man in society, for whom they are absolutely necessary. That is why I shall from now on call *natural* not only the needs which follow from our makeup, but also those which are a consequence of the constitution of civil societies; and I shall understand by *artificial* those which are not essential to the social order, and without which, in consequence, civil societies could continue to exist.

We say that a thing is useful when it supplies some of our needs; and that it is useless when it meets none of them, or when we can do nothing with it. Its utility is therefore founded on the need we have for it.

Following this utility, we esteem it more or less, that is to say we judge whether it is more or less adapted to the uses to which we want to put it. Now this estimation is what we call *value*. To say that a thing has value is to say that it is, or that we think it is, good for some purpose.

The value of things is thus founded on their utility, or, which comes to the same, on the need we have of them, or, which again comes back to the same, on the use we can make of them.

As our tribe creates new needs for itself, it will learn to use for its tasks things of which it made nothing previously. It will therefore give in one time period value to things to which it gave none in another.

In abundance, need is felt less because people do not fear being without. For the opposite reason, people feel need more in scarcity and in dearth.

Now, because the value of things is based on need, it is natural that a more strongly felt need gives things a greater value, and that a less pressing need gives them less value. The value of things therefore grows with scarcity and decreases with abundance.

Value can even diminish in abundance to vanishing point. For instance, a surplus good will be without value every time one can do nothing with it, since then it would be completely useless.

Such would be a surplus in corn, if one considered it with reference to the year in which it does not contribute to the quantity needed for consumption. But if one considers it with reference to the following years, when the harvest may not be adequate, the surplus will have a value, because one judges that it could be part of the quantity required for the need one will have of it.

This need is distant. For that reason it does not give a good the same value as a present need. The latter makes one feel that the good is absolutely necessary now, and the other simply makes one judge that it could become so. One flatters oneself that it will not become necessary; and with that prejudice, as one is led not to foresee the need, one is also led to give less value to the good.

Greater or lesser value, the utility being the same, would be based simply on the degree of scarcity or of abundance, if this degree could always be known precisely; and then one would have the true value of each good.

But this degree can never be known. It is therefore chiefly on the estimation that we have of it that greater or lesser value is based.

If one assumes that a tenth of the corn needed for the tribe's consumption is lacking, nine-tenths would only have the value of ten if one estimated the scarcity accurately, and if one saw for certain that it really was only of a tenth.

That is just what one does not do. Just as people are complacent in abundance, so they are fearful in scarcity. In place of the tenth which is the short-fall, they judge that there are two-tenths, three-tenths or more deficient. They believe themselves to be at the point where corn will be completely unavailable; and the shortfall of a tenth will produce the same terror as if it were of a third or a half.

Once opinion has exaggerated the dearth, it is natural that those who have corn think to keep it for themselves; in fear of running out, they will set aside more of it than they need. It will therefore happen that the dearth will be really total, or near enough, for some of the tribe. In this state of affairs it is clear that the value of corn will grow in proportion to the exaggerated opinion of the dearth.

If the value of things is based on their utility, their greater or lesser value is thus based, the utility staying the same, on their scarcity or their abundance, or rather on the opinion we have of their scarcity and their abundance.

I say "the utility staying the same" because one has enough appreciation that, in supposing them equally rare or equally abundant, one judges them of more or less value, depending on whether one judges them more or less useful.

There are things which are so common that although they are very necessary, they seem to have no value. Such is water, it is found everywhere, people say, "It costs nothing to get it for oneself, and the value which it can gain through transport is not its value but only the value of the carriage costs."

It would be amazing if one paid carriage costs to get oneself something valueless.

A good does not have a value because it has a price, as people suppose, but it has a price because it has a value.

I say therefore that, even on the banks of a river, water has value, but the smallest possible, because there it is infinitely surplus to our needs. In an arid place by contrast it has a huge value, which one assesses according to how far away it is and the difficulty of getting hold of it. In such a case a thirsty traveller would give a hundred louis for a glass of water, and that glass of water would be worth a hundred louis. For value is not so much in the object as in how we esteem it, and this estimation is relative to our needs: it grows and diminishes, just as our need itself grows and diminishes.

As one judges that things have no value when one has assumed they cost nothing, one judges that they cost nothing when they cost no money. We have much difficulty in seeing the light. Let us try to put some precision in our ideas.

Even if one gives no money to obtain a thing it has a cost if it costs work.

Now what is work?

It is an action, or series of actions, with the aim to gain from them. One can act without working: that is the case with idle men who act without making anything. To work is therefore to act to obtain a thing one needs. A day labourer whom I employ in my garden works to gain the wage I have promised him; and one must state that his work begins with the first blow of the spade: because if it did not begin with the first, one could not say where it began.

Following these preliminary reflections, I say that when I am far from the river, water costs me the action of going to get it; action which is work, since it is accomplished to get me something I need; and when I am at the river edge, water costs me the action of leaning over to get it; I agree that the action is very little work: it is even less than the first blow of the spade. But then again does not the water have only the smallest possible value at that time?

The water therefore has the value of the effort I make to get it. If I do not go to get it myself, I will pay for the work of the man who brings it to me; it is then valued at the wage I will give; and consequently the carriage costs give it a value. I give it this value myself, since I judge that it is worth these carriage costs.

You would be astounded if I said that air has a value; and yet I must say so, if I reason consistently. But what does it cost me? It costs me every effort I make to breathe it, to change it, to renew it. I open my window, I go out. Now each of these actions is work, very light work in truth, since the air, even more abundant than water, can only have a minute value.

I can say the same of light, of those rays which the sun spreads so profusely on the surface of the land: for it certainly costs us an effort or money to turn it to all our uses.

Those whom I contest consider it a great error to base value on utility, and they say that a thing cannot have value unless it has a certain degree of scarcity. *A certain degree of scarcity!* Now that I do not understand. I can conceive that a thing is scarce, when we *judge* that we do not have as much of it as we need for our use; that it is abundant, when we *judge* that we have all we need of it, and that it is in surplus, when we *judge* that we possess it beyond our needs. Finally I can conceive that a thing of which one makes nothing, and of which nothing can be made, has no value, and that on the other hand a thing has value when it has utility; and that if it did not have a value by its utility alone, it would not have a greater value in scarcity, and a lesser in abundance.

But one is led to regard value as an absolute quality, which is inherent in things independently of the judgements we bring to bear, and this confused notion is the source of bad reasoning. We must therefore remember that, although things only have a value because they have qualities which make them fitted to our use, they would have no value for us if we did not judge that they do indeed have these qualities. Their value therefore lies principally in the judgement we have of their utility; and they only have more or less value because we judge them more or less useful, or that, with the same utility, we judge them scarcer or more abundant. I have only rested so firmly on this point because it will provide the basis of this whole work.

[*In the 1798 edition, the final sentence of Chapter 1 is omitted, and the following passage is added:*
Value being based on the opinion we hold of the utility of things, and the utility of things itself resting on the need we have of them, we must distinguish a natural value which only assumes natural needs, and an artificial value which only assumes artificial needs. Corn, for example, has a natural value among our tribe, because we assume that all the citizens have naturally the same need of it. But diamonds, if their use should be introduced among them, would only have an artificial value, since such a need, useless at least to society, could only be that of some individuals.

Natural value is directly the same for all, because it is the value of things absolutely essential to the support of society. On the other hand, artificial value, which is very great for some people, would not be in itself worthless for the others; but, because wealthy people will only get goods of an artificial value in so far as they give in exchange goods of natural value, it is a consequence that artificial value becomes, at least indirectly, a real value for everybody. So it is that things which are useless to the vast number of people end up being of general utility when they are considered the equivalent of something essential to all.

Value, of whatever kind, natural or artificial, thus exists principally in the opinions we hold of the utility of things; and one should not say with the *économiste* writers, that it *consists in the exchange relationship of one thing and another:* that would be to suppose, with them, that the exchange preceded the value; this would reverse the order of ideas. Indeed, I should not make any exchange with you, if I did not judge that the article you were handing over had a value; and you would make no exchange with me, if you did not judge likewise that what I was selling you has a value. The *économiste* writers have, if I may use a saying, thus put the cart before the horse.

This misconception seems a very small matter since it comes down to taking the second idea for the first. But it took no more to spread confusion. So the right value for an exchange relationship is a vague notion that people could not determine; and one may reckon that in dealing with economic science along these lines one will not be understood at all wherever value counts for something, that is, almost everywhere.

The object of a science is properly a problem which, like every problem to resolve, has as givens [*données*] knowns and unknowns. In Economic Science, the knowns are the means which we understand to be appropriate for obtaining abundance in certain forms, the unknowns are the means we still need to discover to obtain abundance in every way; and it is clear that, if the problem can be resolved, it is for the knowns to make the unknowns known to us.

This very complex problem comprises a large number of others each of which will give us new difficulties if we do not analyse them methodically; and we shall find ourselves, as has happened to all governments, falling into gross errors with each solution we think it right to proffer.

But the order that analysis prescribes is, firstly, to concern ourselves with the knowns, because, if we do not begin by determining them, it will be impossible to determine the value of the unknowns. Secondly, it requires us to look, among the knowns, for that which must be the principal one; because, if the principal known is not determined, one will not determine the others. Therefore let us look for it.

Among the means of obtaining abundance, I see first the cultivation of the land. But, if agriculture seems to begin before trade, it is certain that it cannot improve itself except in so far as trade establishes itself and spreads. Perfected agriculture, that is to say, agriculture which is bound to procure the greatest abundance, thus assumes trade. Trade assumes exchanges, or, as is basically the same thing, purchases and sales: the purchases and sales assume that things have a price and the price assumes that they have a value.

So there are the knowns; however confused they still are, I can at least see clearly in what order they initially present themselves; and that order, which I had to start by revealing, shows me the value of things as the first idea which needs to be determined and developed. From that point, the further forward I go, the more clearly I see my goal; because, from one chapter to the next, I shall always clear some unknowns, and one problem solved will bring forward the solution of a new problem. I may have carried out this plan badly: but it is none the less true that you will only deal properly with Economic Science in so far as you use my language, or correct it following my method, which is the only one.

This chapter will act as a basis for this work, which is why I have drawn it out perhaps to excess. However, I must allow myself another observation: it is essential.

In the current prejudice that definitions are the sole principles which can spread enlightenment, people think that they understand a word when they have seen what is called the definition; and, because they suppose that I myself am also making definitions, they will think they understand, for example, the word *value*, as soon as they have read what I say about it, at the very moment that I begin to analyse it. They will therefore rush to make objections which they would not have made if they had waited until the analysis was completed. That is what happened to those writers who thought they were refuting me, and who did not understand me at all.

If, in making definitions, one has the advantage of saying everything one wishes to say in just one proposition, it is that one is not saying everything necessary, and often one would be better to remain silent. Analysis does not pride itself on such brevity; as its aim is to develop an idea which must be grasped from different viewpoints, it can only succeed in so far as it has the word scrutinised in all the senses which show up all the concomitant ideas. We shall require several more chapters before we have finished analysing the word *value*, or at least before we have removed from it all the vague ideas that are attached to it, and which often make the language of Economic Science unintelligible.]

# 2  The Basis of the Price of Things

I HAVE A surplus of corn and I am without wine: you, on the other hand, have a surplus of wine and are without corn. The surplus corn, which is useless to me, is thus needed by you; and I myself should need the wine which is surplus and useless for you. In this position we think of making an exchange: I offer you corn for wine, and you offer me wine for corn.

If my surplus is what is needed for your consumption, and yours is what is needed for mine, by exchanging one for the other, we both make an advantageous exchange, because we both give up something that is useless to us for something which we need. In this case, I reckon that my corn has the same value for you as your wine has for me, and you reckon that your wine has the same value for me as my corn has for you.

But if my surplus meets your consumption, and your surplus is inadequate for mine, then I will not give all my surplus for yours: because what I would yield to you would be worth more to you than what you would yield to me would be worth to me.

I would not give you all my surplus corn therefore; I would want to hold some of it back, so as to obtain for myself elsewhere the quantity of wine which you cannot yield to me, and which I need.

You, on your side, have to be sure to get all the corn necessary for your consumption with your wine surplus. You will therefore refuse to leave me all that surplus, if the corn I can yield to you is not sufficient.

In this haggling, you will offer me as little wine as you can for a lot of corn; and as for me, I will offer you as little corn as I can for a lot of wine.

However, necessity will force us to strike a bargain; because you need corn, and I need wine.

So, as you neither want nor are able to give me all the wine I need, I shall resolve to consume less of it; and you, on your side, will take the road of cutting back on the consumption of corn you had counted on making. That way our paths will come closer. I shall offer you a little more corn, you will offer me a little more wine; and, after several reciprocal offers, we shall settle. We shall agree for example to exchange a cask of wine for a septier of corn.

When we make each other reciprocal offers, we are dealing: when we agree, the deal is made. So we reckon that to you a septier of corn is worth what a cask of wine is worth to me.

This reckoning that we make of the corn vis-à-vis the wine, and of the wine vis-à-vis the corn, is what we call *price*. Thus your cask of wine is for me the price of my septier of corn, and my septier of corn is for you the price of your cask of wine.

So we know what the value of the corn and the wine is between you and me, because we have calculated the values which follow from the need we have of each; a need which is known to us. We know too that both have a value for other people, because we know that other people need them. But, because this need can be greater or less than we think, we cannot judge exactly the value which other people give them, until they themselves have informed us. Now that is what they will teach us by the exchanges they make with us or between themselves. When everyone in general is agreed to give so much wine for so much corn, then the corn vis-à-vis the wine and the wine vis-à-vis the corn will each have a value, which will be generally known by all. Now, this relative value, widely known in exchanges, is the basis of the price of things. Price is therefore only the estimated value of a good vis-à-vis the estimated value of another; estimated, I say, in general by all those who exchange the goods.

In exchange, goods do not have an absolute price; they only have a price in relation to the estimation we make of them when we conclude a deal, and they are the reciprocal prices of each other.

In the first place, *the price of things is relative to the estimation we make of them;* or rather it is only the estimation we make of one vis-à-vis another. And that is not surprising, since, in their origin, *price* and *estimation* are perfect synonyms, and the idea which the first originally signified is identical with the idea which the second expresses today.

In the second place, *they make each other's prices reciprocally.* My corn is the price of your wine, and your wine is the price of my corn; because the deal concluded between us is an agreement by which we estimate that my corn has the same value for you as your wine has for me.

We must not confuse these words *price* and *value* and use them indiscriminately for each other.

As soon as we need a good, it has a value; it has a value by virtue of that need alone, and before there is any question of making an exchange.

On the other hand, it is only in our exchanges that it has a price, because we only estimate it in comparison with another good, in so far as we need to exchange it; and its price, as I have said, is the estimation we make of its value, when, in exchange, we compare it with the value of another good.

Price therefore assumes value; that is why one is so strongly driven to confuse these two words. It is true that there are occasions when one can use them indifferently for each other. However, they express two ideas which it is important not to confuse, if we do not want to obscure the remaining development of the argument.

# 3 Of Price Variations

WE HAVE JUST seen that price is based on value. Now as value varies, so price must therefore vary. There are many causes of this variation.

First of all it is clear that abundance and scarcity make price vary, like value, and they make it vary by reason of the greater or lesser need.

Secondly, it is also possible for the price of things to vary, even in the case where the tribe has the same abundance and the same needs.

Let us suppose that after the harvest I have all the surplus grain in my barns, and that, on the other hand, the surplus wine is divided among the cellars of twelve people, all of whom need my grain.

With this assumption, these twelve people come to me to exchange wine for corn; and because last year I gave a septier for a cask, they each offer me a cask for a septier. But in the previous year I was only dealing with one person, and I was forced to give more corn: now that I can deal with a dozen people, and I do not need all the wine they wish to off-load, I announce that I will only give corn to those who will give me a larger quantity of wine. By that action I make them vie with each other to make me more favourable offers. As a result, my grain will be at a higher price for them, and their wine will be less costly for me.

If one made the assumption that the surplus corn was distributed among the barns of a dozen people, and that, on the other hand, all the surplus wine was shut up in the cellars of one person, then the price would no longer be the same as with the first assumption: because the price of corn would fall, and that of wine would rise.

When several people need to exchange a foodstuff, this competition lowers its price; and the absence of competition raises the price of the foodstuff they wish to dispose of. Now as competition is greater, or less, or non-existent, now on the one hand, now on the other, so it comes that prices rise and fall in turn.

From this variation, it follows that there is no absolute price. Indeed, every time we talk of high and low price, it is that we are comparing two things whose exchange is in question: for example, wine will be at a high price in comparison with corn, if we give little of it for a large quantity of corn, and corn will be at a low price. In the opposite case, the price of corn will be high, and that of wine will be low.

# 4  Of Markets or Places Where Those Who Need to Make Exchanges Congregate

THOSE WHO have exchanges to make seek each other out, and they scour the tribe: it is the first idea that occurs to each of them. But they will not be slow to perceive the inconvenience of this practice. Firstly, they will often not meet each other; because the person to whose house they have come will have gone to another's, or even to that of the man who has come to look for him. They would lose a lot of time in these errands.

Secondly, they could still meet and resolve nothing. After much haggling, they would separate and begin their errands again, each hoping to make a more profitable exchange with another person. By following this practice, it would therefore be very difficult for them to agree on the respective price of foodstuffs.

Sooner or later experience will teach them these disadvantages. Then they will look for a convenient place to meet near enough to the centre of the tribe, each on his side, on appointed days, and to which they will bring the produce they intend to exchange. This gathering and the place where it happens are called a *market* [*marché*], because dealings [*marchés*] are proposed and concluded there.

So in the market one sets out all the foodstuffs intended for exchange; each person can see them, and can compare the amount of one with that of another. Following that, they make each other offers.

If there is a lot of corn and little wine, people will offer a smaller quantity of wine for a larger one of corn; and if there is little corn and a lot of wine, they will offer a smaller amount of corn for a larger amount of wine.

By thus comparing foodstuffs, following the quantity of them to be found in the market, people see near enough in what ratio to make the exchanges, and then they are not far from striking a deal. So as soon as some are agreed on the ratio to follow in their exchanges, others take that ratio as a rule, and the respective prices of the foodstuffs are determined for that day. It will be said, for example, that the price of a cask of wine is a septier of corn, and that the price of a septier of corn is a cask of wine.

I only consider quantity because I want to simplify. You can easily enough understand that quality must make a difference in the price of produce. It just needs to be noticed that as quality is less easily assessed than quantity, the deals are more difficult to make; and that in such a case, opinion will doubtless carry much weight. But a deal will eventually be struck, and whatever the quality of the goods, they will have a fixed price for that day.

If the price of corn has been high compared with that of wine, more of it will be brought to the following market, because people will count on a more favourable exchange, and conversely, they will bring less wine.

In this market, the proportion between corn and wine will therefore not be the same as in the previous one. There will be much corn and little wine; and just as the large quantity will lower the price of the one, the small quantity will raise the price of the other.

So prices will vary from market to market.

Doubtless it would be an advantage for the tribe if produce always had a determined and fixed price: because exchanges could be made without discussion, promptly and without loss. But that is not possible, because there cannot always be the same proportion between the foodstuffs, whether one considers them in the warehouses where the owners store them or in the markets to which they are carried.

If the variations are slight, they will hardly be felt. In that case they will have no disadvantages, or they would produce such small ones that it would be pointless to prevent them. It might even be impossible to anticipate them, and dangerous to try. Besides, we shall see that government deals a blow to agriculture and to commerce each time it tries to fix the price of foodstuffs.

If the variations are large and sudden, great drawbacks arise: because the excessively high price of a foodstuff will place those who need it under the compulsion to make disadvantageous exchanges, or to suffer for not having been able to obtain it.

These large and sudden variations will still arise when a crop has completely failed. One will be able to guard against that by making provision for years of scarcity during years of surplus, and that is what will be done. Experience will enlighten the tribe on this matter.

These variations will also occur in markets when too much of one foodstuff is taken there and too little of another: but this disadvantage will not often recur, if everyone is free to bring what he wishes to the market, and in the quantity he chooses. That is still a matter on which experience will throw light. By observing prices in a sequence of markets, and the causes of their variation, people will learn the type and quantity of foodstuffs they should take there to be able to exchange them profitably, or with the least possible disadvantage. The different foodstuffs exposed at the market will then keep the same proportions between themselves, or near enough, and consequently prices will vary little.

They will vary all the less since, when the settlers have learnt by experience what is consumed of each thing, they will grow it in that proportion; and they will only bring to the market as much or near enough as they expect to be able to exchange. They will act in this respect according to the observations they have made.

One sees therefore that in general prices will regulate themselves according to the respective quantities of the goods on offer for exchange.

You can see too that prices can only regulate themselves in markets, because it is only there that the assembled citizens can, by comparing the interest they have in making exchanges, judge the worth of things in relation to their needs. They can only do it there, because it is only in markets that all the goods to be exchanged are in evidence: it is only in markets that one can judge the relative abundance or scarcity of one against another; the relationship which determines their respective prices.

That is how prices constantly adjust, in the case where everyone has, as I said, freedom to bring to the market what he pleases, and in the quantity he chooses. We shall deal elsewhere with the disadvantages which will arise from a lack of freedom.

# 5 What Is Meant by Trade

W E C A L L *trade* the exchange that is made when a person gives us one good for another which he receives; and we call *merchandise* [*marchandises*] the goods on offer for exchange, because one only exchanges them by creating a market, or by agreeing, after some haggling, to give so much of one for so much of the other.

Now we have observed that two goods that are exchanged create each other's price. They are therefore each at the same time price and merchandise; or rather they take one or other of these names, following the relationships in which we consider them.

When the good is considered as price, the man who gives it is called *buyer:* when it is considered as merchandise, the man who delivers it is called *seller;* and since in different lights it can be regarded as price and as merchandise, it follows that those who make exchanges can be considered with respect to one another both as seller and as buyer. When I give you a septier of corn for a cask of wine, it is I who buy the wine, it is you who sell it, and my septier is the price of your cask. When you give me a cask of wine for a septier of corn, it is you who buy the corn, it is I who sell it, and your cask is the price of my septier. In all that, there is nothing but exchanges, and however one expresses them, the ideas are always the same. But the expressions vary, because we are obliged to consider the same things in different respects.

Commerce presumes two things: surplus production on the one hand, and on the other consumption to be made.

*Surplus production,* because I can only exchange a surplus.

*Consumption to be made,* because I can only exchange it with someone who needs to consume it.

Up till now our tribe is composed only of settlers, that is of men who cultivate the soil. Now these settlers can be considered as producers and as consumers: as producers, because it is their wants which made the land bring forth all sorts of foodstuffs; as consumers, because it is they who consume the different products.

According to the assumptions we have made, exchanges up to now have been made directly between the settlers; commerce has thus been conducted immediately between producers and consumers.

But it is not always possible for the settlers who come to market to sell their merchandise at a favourable price. They will therefore on occasion be compelled to take it back again. That is an inconvenience which they would avoid if they could dispose of it somewhere, and give it to someone who could seize the opportunity to exchange it profitably in their absence. With this prospect, they would willingly give up a part.

Those who have their dwellings in the neighbourhood of the market will thus have an interest in drawing merchandise into their hands. Consequently, they will build storehouses where it can be kept, and they will offer to sell it on behalf of others, in exchange for an agreed commission.

These commission agents, which is what one calls those who undertake a thing on behalf of others, are between the producers and consumers; it is through them that exchanges are made, but it is not for them. They just find a profit in the deal, and it is their due: because the settlers find an advantage in exchanging their produce, without being forced to deal directly with each other.

I assume that the person who entrusts a septier of corn promises to give a bushel of corn if the commission agent obtains for him a cask of wine in exchange; and that the agent, well-placed to seize the right moment, gets a cask plus ten pints for this septier. He will have gained both from the seller of corn and from the buyer.

On the one hand, the tribe feels the need of these agents, and on the other, there is an advantage in being one. You can judge therefore that they will set up business, and perhaps in excessive numbers. But, because the more of them there are, the less profit they will make, their numbers will gradually adjust to the tribe's needs.

An agent is only the recipient of a good which is not his. But because he makes profits, one day he will be able to buy himself the merchandise that was previously entrusted to him. Then he will buy the goods; he will have them at his risk and hazard, and he will sell them again for his own account. There we have what one calls a *merchant*.

Before there were agents and merchants, one could scarcely sell except at a market, and only on the day that the market was held. Since we have agents and merchants, one can sell every day and everywhere, and as exchanges have become easier, they are more frequent.

The settlers thus have a greater number of outlets to move their surplus among themselves; and the tribe experiences every day how advantageous it is to have agents and merchants.

In truth the agents and merchants will make profits at the expense of the tribe: but, by their intervention, the tribe itself will make profits it could not have made without them. For any surplus, which is useless and without value when it cannot be exchanged, becomes useful when it can be exchanged and acquires a value.

This surplus, as I have remarked, is the only negotiable good; since one only sells what one can do without. It is true that I could certainly sell a good that I need; but since I would only do it to obtain another that I needed even more, it is clear that I regard it as useless for me, compared with the one I acquire. It is again true that I could even sell the corn needed for my consumption; but I should only sell it because, being sure to be able to re-place it, I find an advantage in selling on the one hand to buy back on the other. In a word, whatever assumption one makes, in going back from seller to seller, one must always reach an original one who only sells and only can sell his surplus. That is why I say that the surplus is the sole thing that ex-ists in trade.*

When the settlers deal directly among themselves they exchange their own surplus. But when the merchants themselves trade is it likewise their surplus that they exchange? And can one say that the merchandise they have in their warehouses is also surplus for them? Doubtless not: merchants are exchanging the farmers' surplus. They are like channels of communication between producers and consumers by which trade circulates; and through their intervention, the settlers most widely separated from each other com-

---

*It is not that I think that each settler only ever sells his surplus; but I think that everything that is sold is surplus for some one of them. For example, if there was a great dearth in Spain, I do not doubt that France would sell there some of the grain necessary for her own consumption: but she would replace it with what she bought in the North, and she would only replace it because there was a nation in the North where there was a surplus of corn.

municate between themselves. Such is the utility of the trade carried on by the merchants.

There are different types of commerce, and it is important not to confuse them.

Either we exchange produce such as nature has given us, and I call that exchange *trade in produce.*

Or we exchange these products when we have made them take forms which adapt them for various uses, and I call that exchange *trade in manufactures,* or of hand-made goods.

The settler engages in trade in produce when he sells the surplus of his crop; and the artisans or manufacturers engage in trade in manufactures when they sell the articles they have made.

But when trade is conducted through the intervention of merchants I call that *commission trade* because the merchants set themselves up as agents between the producers on one side and the consumers on the other. Considered as merchants they are neither farmers nor manufacturers; they merely resell what they have bought.

One distinguishes the retail merchant and the wholesaler, whom it is easy not to confuse; the name alone shows the difference well enough. It is not so easy to mark what distinguishes the trading merchant from the transacting merchant. Both of them are engaged in commission trade; but common usage seems to confuse them.

I shall call a merchant [*marchand*] a *trader* [*trafiquant*] when, through a sequence of exchanges made in several countries, he seems to trade in everything. For example, a French merchant is a trader when he carries merchandise to England; then in England, where he leaves it, he takes another good which he carries elsewhere; and after several exchanges he comes back to France, to which he brings foreign merchandise. One understands that he can, without travelling, carry on this trade through factors or commission merchants.

The trader [*trafiquant*] is called an *international dealer* [*négociant*] when, having made of commerce a speculative matter, he watches all its branches, brings together its circumstances, and calculates their advantages and drawbacks in the purchases and sales to be made, and, through his connections, he seems to dispose of the tradable effects of many nations.

All these types are included under the name of *merchants* [*commerçants*]. Besides, since they only differ in degree, you may understand that it will often be impossible to distinguish the merchant [*marchand*] from the international trader [*trafiquant*] and the trader from the dealer [*négociant*]. That is why one can often use indiscriminately for each other the words *commerce, trading, dealing.* One must just remember that merchants, of whatever type they are, only carry out commission trade, a trade that I shall sometimes call *dealing.*

WE HAVE SEEN that trade, which consists in the exchange of one article for another, is carried on chiefly by merchants, traders and dealers. Let us now try to understand the utility which society draws from all these men who have set up as agents between producers and consumers; and to that end, let us look at the source of wealth and the course it follows.

Wealth consists in an abundance of things which have a value, or, which comes to the same, in an abundance of things that are useful because we need them, or finally, which is again the same, in an abundance of things which are used for our food, for our clothing, for our housing, for our comforts, for our pleasures, for our enjoyment, in a word for our use.

Now, it is the earth alone which produces all these things. It is therefore the sole source of all wealth.

Naturally prolific, it produces by itself and without any work on our part. Savages, for instance, live off the fecundity of lands which they do not cultivate. But they need for their consumption a vast extent of land. Each savage can consume the product of a hundred arpents. Then again it is hard to imagine that he will always find plenty in that space.

It is that the earth, left to its own natural fecundity, produces everything indiscriminately. It is especially fecund in things which are useless to us and of which we can make no use.

If we make ourselves masters of her fecundity, and obstruct certain products to encourage other products, the land will become fertile. Because if we call land which produces plentifully and all at hazard *fecund*, we call land which produces plenty and to our wishes *fertile*.

It is only by observation and work that we will succeed in curtailing certain products and enabling other products to grow. We must discover how the land produces, if we want to multiply exclusively things for our use and eradicate all the rest.

The collection of observations to this end makes the theory of a science called *agriculture*, or cultivation of the fields; and the work of the settler who daily follows these observations constitutes the practice of this science. I shall call this practice *cultivation*.

The settler thus multiplies things which are for our use, which have a value, and the abundance of which makes what we call wealth. It is he who digs the ground, who opens the spring, who makes it spurt forth; it is to him that we owe abundance.

What then do we owe to merchants? If, as everyone supposes, one always exchanges a product of a uniform value against another product of the same value, one multiplies the exchanges in vain; it is clear that afterwards, as before, there will always be the same accumulation of values or of wealth.

But it is false that in exchanges one gives equal value for equal value. On the contrary, each of the contracting parties always gives a lesser value for a greater value. People would recognise that fact if they thought precisely, and you can already understand it from what I have said.

A woman whom I know, having bought a piece of land, counted out the money to pay for it, and said: "However, I am very happy to have a plot of land for that." There was very true reasoning in that artlessness. One can see that she attached little value to the money which she kept in her strongbox, and that, in consequence, she was giving a lesser value for a greater one. From another standpoint, the man who was selling the land was in the same position and he was saying: "I have sold it well." In fact he had sold it for thirty or thirty-five deniers. Thus he too reckoned on having given less for more. There is the position of all those who make exchanges.

Indeed, if one always exchanged equal value for equal value, there would be no gain to be made for either of the contracting parties. Now, both of them make a gain, or ought to make one. Why? The fact is that with things only having value in relation to our needs, what is greater for one person is less for another, and vice versa. [*Passage added here in 1798 is printed at the end of the chapter.*]

The error into which people fall on this subject comes [above all: 1798] from the way one talks of things which are traded, as though they had an absolute value; and that as a result people reckon that it is a matter of justice, that those who make exchanges give each other equal value for equal value. Far from noting that two contracting parties give each other less for more, people think, without much reflection, that that cannot be; and it seems that for one person always to give less, the other would have to be stupid enough always to give more, which one cannot suppose.

It is not the things necessary for our consumption that we are considered to put on sale: it is our surplus, as I have noted several times. We want to give up something which is useless to us to get ourselves something which we need: we want to give less for more.

The surplus of the settlers: there you have what supplies all the basis for commerce. The surplus is wealth, so long as they can find an outlet for it; because they procure for themselves something that has value for them, and they hand over something which has value for others.

If they were unable to make exchanges, their surplus would stay with them, and it would have no value for them. Indeed, surplus grain, which I store in my barns without being able to exchange it, no more represents wealth to me than the grain which I have not yet pulled from the ground. So I will sow less next year, and I shall be none the poorer for having a smaller crop.

Now merchants are the channels of communication through which the surplus runs. From places where it has no value it passes into places where it gains value, and wherever it settles it becomes wealth.

The merchant therefore in a way makes something out of nothing. He does not till, but he brings about tillage. He induces the settler to draw an ever greater surplus from the land and he always makes new wealth from it. Through the meeting of the settler and the trader abundance spreads all the further, as consumption grows in proportion to the products, and reciprocally products increase with consumption.

A spring which disappears into rocks and sand is not wealth for me; but it becomes such, if I build an aqueduct to draw it to my meadows. This spring represents the surplus products for which we are indebted to the settlers, and the aqueduct represents the merchants.

[*Additional passage from 1798 edition referred to on page 120*
The advantage is reciprocal, and there you have no doubt what made them say that they gave each other equal value for equal value. But they have lacked consistency: since, precisely from the fact that the advantage is reciprocal, they should have concluded that each gives less for more.

People have said, you are confusing the value of things with the motive that leads to their exchange. Probably, and with reason, indeed value is the sole motive which can persuade me to act. What other could I have?

Value depends, they add, on the particular estimation each person makes of goods and consequently it will for ever vary. So it varies: is there anything which has an invariable value? I say therefore that in individual exchanges value is the particular estimation each person makes of goods; and I add that it is the general estimation that society itself makes of them, if we consider it in the markets where all end up agreeing on a measure to settle the respective value of goods, that is, the value they are given when they are considered against other goods.

But we must not confuse, as people are always doing, this measure of value with value itself. Properly speaking it is only the price which has been regulated in the markets by the rivalry of the sellers and buyers. For example, there will be general agreement that a barrel of wine is worth a muid of corn, which means that the one is the price of the other. So, if I want a muid of corn I must give a barrel of wine, and you will conclude, with reason, that it is not my particular judgement that fixes the price of corn; but it is none the less true that it fixes its value, and it alone fixes it. Because, once more, in such an exchange it is for me alone to judge the value the corn has for me; it only has one following my own estimation; and, although the market price sets the law for me, it is clear that I only give a barrel for a muid because I judge that the muid is worth more to me than the barrel. I should never end if I wanted to reply to all the objections of certain writers who, because one does not follow them, seem to want, from pique, not to understand what one is saying to them.]

# 7 How Needs, in Multiplying, Give Birth to the Arts, and How the Arts Increase the Mass of Wealth

JUST AS I have distinguished natural needs and artificial needs, I shall also distinguish two kinds of necessary things; the first of primary need, which I shall refer back to natural needs; and the others of secondary need, which I shall refer back to artificial needs.

Such fruits as the land produces through fecundity alone are of prime necessity for a savage, because he needs them as a consequence of his makeup; and our wines, our brandies would be of secondary need for him, if, in trading with us, he acquired a taste for these drinks.

For our tribe, settled in the fields which it cultivates, corn is a thing of prime need, because it is necessary to it, as a result of the formation of a society which would not subsist without this aid. We must however place, among things of secondary need, all those which it could do without, while not ceasing to be a settled, agrarian society.

Observe the tribe while it is limited to things of prime need. This is the state where, without being poor, it has the least wealth. I say, *without being poor*, because there is only poverty where essential needs are not met, and it is not being poor to lack a type of wealth of which one has not acquired a need, and which one does not even know.

Therefore it is not in a state of poverty, it is rather in a state of *lacking*. Please allow me this word: that of *privation* would not convey my thought. For we deprive ourselves of those things which we have, or which we might have, and with which we are familiar; whereas we do not have those which we lack, often we do not even know of their existence.

In this state it is enough for our tribe not to be exposed to a lack of food, to shelter itself from the force of the elements, and to have the means of defence against its enemies. Its food, its clothing, its dwellings, its weapons are all rough and lack artistry. It only uses the commonest objects for its various tasks, and so it is sure not to lack them.

While lacking a host of things we appreciate, it is plentifully supplied with all those which it needs.

Nothing is expensive in the tribe. Just as in all the goods it uses there is nothing too choice, so there is also nothing too rare.

Currency would be useless to it, and it has none. Each person exchanges his surplus, and no one perceives a need to use metals, or anything else to that end.

Let us move to a time when it begins to enjoy goods of secondary need, and when these goods are none the less still of a kind to be able to be common to all. Then the tribe introduces higher quality into its food, its clothing, its dwellings, its weapons; it has more needs, more wealth. However, there are no poor people among it; since I still only include in the goods of secondary need common goods which all can partake of more or less, and of which no one is entirely deprived.

In this position it is impossible for each person to provide by himself for all his needs. The farmer, busy in the fields, would not have the time free to make himself a coat, to build a house, to forge weapons, and he would not have the aptitude because these jobs require knowledge and a skill he does not possess.

Several groups will therefore form. Besides that of the farmers there will be tailors, architects, armourers. The three latter groups could not subsist on their own. It is the first group that will provide for their subsistence, and it will in addition provide the raw material for the arts.

When I distinguish four classes it is because we must choose a number. The tribe may and even must have many more. They will multiply in proportion as the arts come into being, and make progress.

All the groups, each busy with its own tasks, come together in competition to increase the mass of wealth, or the abundance of goods which have value. Because, if we have seen that primary wealth consists uniquely in the products of the land, we have also seen that these products only have value, and their abundance is only wealth, in so far as they are useful, or as they meet some of our needs.

It is the farmer who provides all the primary material. But such primary material, as would be useless and without value in his hands, becomes useful and obtains value when the artisan has found the way to make it serve the needs of society.

With each skill that begins, with each advance it makes, the farmer thus acquires new wealth, because he finds value in a product which previously had none.

This product, given value by the artisan, gives a fresh spur to commerce for which it is a new stock in trade; and it becomes a new source of wealth for the farmer because, as each product acquires value, he makes new consumption for himself.

Thus it is that all, farmers, merchants, artisans, come together to increase the mass of wealth.

If one compares the state of deprivation our tribe is in, when, without artisans, without merchants, it is confined to goods of prime need, with the state of plenty in which it finds itself, when, through the hard work of artisans and merchants, it enjoys goods of secondary need, that is, of a host of things that habit turns into needs for it; one will understand that the work of artisans and merchants is as much a source of wealth for it as the very work of the farmers.

Indeed, if on the one hand we have seen that the land is the source of products, and hence of wealth; we see on the other hand that industry gives value to a number of products, which otherwise would have none. It is therefore proved that in the final analysis industry is also a source of wealth. We shall expand on this matter some day soon. It has been much obscured by some writers.

# 8  Of Wages

A MERCHANT has made some advances. They consist in the price he gave for the things he wants to sell again, in carriage costs, in the costs of the warehouse, and in the day-to-day expenses of keeping the merchandise.

Now, not only does he have to be reimbursed for all these advances, but he also has to find a gain in carrying on his trade.

This gain is rightly what we call a wage [*salaire*]. One conceives that it must be made and portioned out turn by turn on all the goods he has for sale; and that it must be enough for his subsistence, that is to say to obtain for him the use of things of primary and secondary need.

But to what extent should the merchants enjoy these things? That is a matter which will regulate itself unaided, given that competition will force the merchants to live more or less economically; and since this competition will apply to all equally, we will know, in accordance with the general custom, the pleasures to which each of them can lay claim. They will calculate for themselves what wage they need for the pleasures which custom allows them, to obtain these for their families, to raise their children; and because they would have very little foresight if they were content with gaining the means to live from one day to the next, they will also calculate what they need to cope with accidents and, if possible, to improve their condition. They will try to bring all these gains into their wage. Those who would like to buy will try to beat down these gains; and they will beat them down all the more easily as an ever-increasing number of merchants will be eager to sell. The wage will be regulated on the one hand by the sellers' rivalry, and by the buyers' competition on the other.

The artisan's wage will be self-regulated in the same way. Suppose that there are only six tailors in the tribe and they cannot meet the demand for clothes, they will themselves fix their wage, or the price of their labour, and that price will be high.

That is a disadvantage, and they will fall into another when the lure of gain has multiplied the tailors beyond the tribe's needs. Then they will all find themselves reduced to lesser gains, those who have no custom will offer to work for the lowest price, and will force those who have custom to work also for a smaller wage. There will even be those who do not have enough to live on, and who will be forced to find another trade. The number of tailors will thus gradually come into line with the demand for them; and that is the moment when their wage will be regulated as it should be.

But there are trades which call for more intelligence, and trades which call for more skill; it takes more time to become skilful at them; one must bring more effort and more care to them. Therefore those who distinguish themselves at them will be authorised to demand better wages, and one will be forced to give these to them; because, as they will be few in number, they will have fewer competitors. People will get used to seeing them with a greater abundance of things of primary and secondary need; and in consequence custom will give them rights to this abundance. As they have greater and rarer talents, it is fair that they also make greater gains.

So it is that, when wages are regulated, they in their turn regulate consumption, to which everyone has a claim according to his status; and then one knows what are the primary and secondary needs which belong to each class. All the citizens do not share the same pleasures equally, but all have subsistence from their work; and though there are some richer people among them, no one is poor. There you have what happens in civil society, where order establishes itself freely, according to the particular and combined interests of all the citizens. Note that I say *freely*.

If I have only spoken, in this chapter, of the wage due to the artisan and the merchant, it is that by showing how prices regulate themselves in the market place, I have given a sufficient explanation of how the farmer's wage is regulated. It will do to note here that all the citizens [apart from those of the landowners who do nothing: *1798*] are given a wage with regard to each other. If the artisan and the merchant are paid by the farmer to whom they sell, the farmer is in his turn paid by the artisan and the merchant to whom he sells, and each of them gets paid for his work.

# 9 Of Wealth from Land and Movable Wealth

WE SEPARATE the land's production into food and prime materials. The foodstuffs are the produce which meets our subsistence and that of the animals we raise. Raw materials are the products which can take different forms, and hence be adapted to various uses.

Products considered as food or as raw materials are called landed wealth, because they are the product of the land's soil.

Raw materials, fashioned, manufactured, worked up, are called movable wealth; because the shapes they are given turn them into movable goods which serve our needs.

If there were no landed wealth, there would be no movable wealth; or, which comes to the same thing, if there were no raw materials, there would be no worked-up materials.

So landed wealth constitutes wealth of the first order, or wealth without which there would be no other wealth.

Movable wealth is only of the second order, as it presupposes landed wealth. But it is none the less wealth. The forms which convey utility to raw materials give them a value.

To speak with precision, the settler produces nothing; he simply prepares the earth to produce.

The artisan in contrast produces value, since there is value in the forms he gives the prime material. Indeed, production is giving new shapes to matter; since the earth does not make anything different when it produces.

But since the land left to itself would often leave us without the most essential products, we can regard all that he gathers in the fields he has cultivated as being the settler's product.

I shall therefore say that the settler produces landed wealth, and the artisan produces movable wealth. If the first did not work, we should lack products; and if the second did not work, we should lack movable goods.

We have seen that value, based on need, grows in scarcity and diminishes in abundance.

Works of art therefore have greater value when they are of a kind that can only be made by a small number of artisans, since then they are rarer; and they have less value when they are of a kind that can be made by many artisans, as then they are more common.

Their value is the actual value of the prime material plus the value of their form.

The form's value can only be the value of the work which produces it. It is the wage owed to the craftsman.

If we paid this wage in products, we would give the craftsman as many as he had the right to consume, during the whole period of his work.

When the work is complete, the value of its form is thus equal to the value of the products which the craftsman is deemed to have consumed.

These products no longer exist. But if one considers they have been replaced by others, one can judge that the quantity of landed wealth is the same, in normal years.

Landed wealth only replaces itself to the extent that it destroys itself. Produced to be consumed, it only replaces itself by reason of consumption; and the quantity consumed is set by need, a need which has limits.

Movable wealth does more than replace itself, it accumulates. Since it is intended to obtain for us all the pleasures which we have made a matter of habit, it multiplies like our artificial needs, and they can multiply without limit. In addition movable wealth is in general of a lasting material which often keeps almost without waste.

Value builds up through the artisan's work, but he has consumed equivalent values in products; and so it follows that movable wealth only multiplies with the aid of landed wealth.

The settler produces more than he consumes. It is with his surplus that he gives subsistence to those who do not till the land. But, as we have said, he does not pile up value on value; he only replaces products, at the rate that they are destroyed; and, through his work [landed: *1798*] wealth and the products are always in proportion to the amount of them consumed. The artisan, in contrast, adds to the mass of wealth values equivalent to the value of the products he has consumed, and by his work movable wealth accumulates.

When the land is covered with products of every kind, there is no other matter than that which existed before: there are only new forms, and it is in these forms that the whole wealth of nature consists. Natural riches are therefore only different transformations.

In these transformations we find the products that nature has prepared for our subsistence, and the products she has prepared to be the raw material for the arts.

Now the arts make this raw material take different forms which are more or less useful. They thus make it suitable for new uses; they give it a new value.

Consequently, just as there is natural wealth, so there is artificial wealth: and both are equally true wealth, since the transformations of art produce values as do the transformations of nature.

It would often be easier to make a new language than to give precision to an existing language. Either the terms were originally badly chosen, or people forget both the original sense of the words and the analogy which has caused them to pass from one sense to another. If the main idea fits, which is not always the case, people add additional meanings or remove meanings, and we end up by not understanding each other any more. As we are drawn to use the same words, every time we think we see some resemblance between ideas, we imperceptibly multiply their meanings; and, because it would be difficult or even absurd to keep on analysing to explain what we want to say, it seems quicker to follow usage blindly, that is to say, to speak badly following each other's example; and we seem to limit the art of speech to the mechanical art of pronouncing words.

We think to remedy this abuse by definitions, as though it were possible to make known all the meanings of a word by a definition. So everyone defines in his own way: we dispute, we divide, we subdivide, we distinguish; and the more we write the more we confuse all notions.

I am making these observations on encountering landed wealth and movable wealth, terms which do not seem to me to have been well chosen, and ones from which people make ideas which lack clarity.

To refer to etymology, the term *landed* [*foncières*] comes from the way one has perceived wealth as pertaining to the land [*fonds*] which has produced it, or as being the land itself; and the name *movable* [*mobilières*] comes from our having seen wealth as mobile or transportable.

We wanted to make two classes of wealth: therefore we had to distinguish them; and yet we have chosen names which confuse them with each other.

Indeed, if a field is landed wealth, what will the corn it produces be? Will it be landed wealth before the harvest, because it adheres to the ground and is not yet transportable? And will it become movable wealth after the harvest, because it has been carried to a barn, and from there it can be carried to the market?

But a house, in which class should we place it? It is not landed wealth, because it is not a product of the ground on which it is raised; and it is only in fairyland that it can be movable wealth. There is something to trouble the legal experts.

People have seemed to see the defect of these categories, and looked for others. But because we have become used to the word *movable*, we have said that all wealth is movable or fixed, that is to say, portable effects or *fixed* effects. So a house has become a fixture.

Yet, because we cannot include in the class of immovables all that one would like to include, people have made up for that by a definition, and they have said, *An immovable good is land, or what stands for it.*

Or what stands for it! There's a definition for you, and that is how people make them. But how do we decide, for instance, if notes drawn on tax farmers represent land or not? Also we have seen more than one lawsuit where the judges did not know if an effect was a movable or an immovable.

Without bothering about etymology, I shall put all the products of nature in the class of immovables, or landed wealth, and I shall put all the products of the arts in that of movables, or mobile wealth. That is to say, in using the customary terms I shall hold to the distinction I have made of wealth into natural wealth and artificial wealth. So, just as a field is landed wealth, so shall the corn be, even when it has been carried into barns: a house on the other hand will be movable wealth, and we shall place in the same category all public paper, although these effects, being for the most part products of an art which tends to destruction, are normally the wealth of a people that is ruining itself. I anticipate that this distinction will not do for the legal experts, whose language will always be chaos; but it will do for my purposes. Need I warn that by products one must understand natural products every time the word is used on its own.]

# 10 Through What Types of Labour Wealth Is Produced, Distributed and Preserved

WE HAVE JUST seen two kinds of work. One kind brings produce into being, the other gives raw materials the forms which make them fitted to various uses, and, for this reason, to have a value.

If the farmer works with intelligence and persistence, he multiplies his products and improves their types.

If the artisan works with the same intelligence and the same assiduity, he multiplies his works, and he gives more value to the forms which he gives to the raw materials.

The farmer and the artisan thus enrich themselves in proportion as they work more, and to better effect.

The farmer thrives because he produces more than he can consume.

The artisan grows rich, in giving shape to prime materials, because he produces value equivalent to all the consumption he can make.

People will doubtless say that the farmer and the artisan have expenses to pay, and I agree that the expenses could reduce them to a wretched state. But to simplify, I assume them to be free from every tax. I shall deal elsewhere with subsidies due to the state.

All tasks are not equally easy.

In the easiest, people have more competitors, and are reduced to lower wages. So they consume less, or even only consume the absolutely essential. If this essential were never lacking, they would be rich in relation to their estate in life. But how is one to ensure oneself subsistence, if one does not earn more than subsistence? If in the days when one is working, one uses up all one's wage, how is one to subsist in the days when one is not working?

In more difficult work people have fewer competitors, and they obtain higher wages. Therefore they can consume more. They will be better fed, better dressed, better housed. Then if they want to save or cut back on their consumption they will have the extra, and will be rich in the real sense of the word.

When writing one is constantly pulled up short, and precisely by the words that are in everyone's mouth; because it is often those words whose sense is the least fixed. Thus I say that people are not rich in absolute terms; but they are in relation to their estate; and in their estate they are rich with regard to the neighbourhood and the times they live in. If Crassus came back today with his ideas of wealth, he would find very few rich men among us.

Men, who only earned the absolutely essential from day to day, would live harshly, and would not be rich, even in relation to their estate. They would always be in a strained and precarious situation.

To be rich in relation to one's estate, one does not just have to be able to make savings on one's consumption, one must also not have to make greater savings than one's equals. It must be the case that by working as much and as well as them, one can obtain the same pleasures for oneself.

At the birth of each art, a new type of work brings a new type of wealth, and our wealth multiplies and varies as our needs do.

Liberal arts follow on from the mechanical arts. The latter are more essential, and yet the former are more highly esteemed. That is, if ever a thing is thought to be useful, it has great value whenever it is rare. Now good artists are infinitely scarcer than good artisans. With higher wages they can therefore consume more and acquire more wealth.

So it is that farmers, artisans and artists come to divide the riches they produce.

The merchants make the riches circulate. If the riches could not leave the places where they were in surplus, they would necessarily lose their price; but, merely through the offer the merchants make to take them to places where they are deficient, they maintain the same value for them everywhere. The merchants produce nothing; they transport from producer to consumer; and they find in the wage given for their work a larger portion if they have fewer rivals, and a smaller one if they have more rivals.

But if they are to be produced in plenty and to circulate freely, riches require a power which protects the farmer, the artisan, the artist and the merchant.

This power is called *sovereign*. It protects, because it maintains order internally and externally. It maintains it internally through the laws it passes and enforces; it maintains it externally through the fear or the respect it inspires in the foes who threaten the state.

A grandee protects a simple individual because he advances him, because he wants to bring him some benefit, without considering that he hurts other individuals, or even worrying about harming them. The sovereign power must not protect in this fashion. It is important to note and not forget that its protection is confined to the maintenance of order, and that it would disturb such order if it had partialities.

This power has work to do. It has tasks as legislative power, as executive power, as armed power for the defence of the state; and I should add as priestly power; for, although in all nations the priesthood is not joined to the imperium, they must come together in maintaining order, as if they were one and the same power.

The work of the sovereign power is owed a recompense [*salaire*]. With this claim it participates in sharing the wealth it does not produce; and its share is large, because it is due to the services it renders, and these services demand rare talents. It is under its protection that all the arts flourish, and that wealth is preserved and multiplied.

When one considers the labours which produce wealth, those which make it circulate, and those which keep the order appropriate to preserve and multiply it, one can see that all are needed, and it would be difficult to say which is the most useful. Are they not all equally so, as each has need of the other? Indeed, on which could one cut back?

I agree that in times of disorder great wealth becomes the recompense of work that is often more harmful than useful. But in my assumptions we are not at that point. I assume that all is in order, because that must be one's starting point. Disorder will come only too soon.

Now, when everything is in order, all work is useful. It is true that these labours divide up wealth unequally but that is fair since they require talents that are scarcer or more common. So no one has cause to complain and everyone stays in his place. To keep the citizens in perfect equality you would have to forbid any division, ignore talent, put all their property in common, and condemn them for the most part to live in idleness.

# ⌁ 11　The Origin of Towns

WE HAVE MARKED out three classes of citizens in our tribe: farmers, artisans and merchants.

I assume that until now the first class has had the ownership of all the land. It will not keep it, at least not entirely; and there will come a time when the farmers will cultivate most of the land for a small number of citizens who will have appropriated it.

If we consider that, from generation to generation, a father's lands are divided among his children, we will reckon that they are often divided to the point where the different portions are no longer adequate for the subsistence of those who have inherited them. The owners of these portions will be obliged to sell them, and they will plan to earn their living in some other way.

Thousands of other faster-working forces will bring about this revolution. Sometimes a lazy or wasteful farmer will be forced to sell his fields to a more careful or less wasteful farmer, who will go on making acquisitions.

On other occasions, a rich owner who has no children will leave all his possessions to another owner who is as rich or richer than him.

Finally merchants who have become wealthy by business and saving will, in all probability, gradually buy up a part of the land; and one can say the same for those artisans who have made large gains and considerable savings. But it is pointless to go into further detail on this subject.

The great owners will manage their estates themselves, or have them managed.

In the first case they will take some of the work upon themselves; they will at least keep an eye on the cultivators, and they will find in the gains they make the price or wage for their work.

In the second case they must give up this wage to the manager, and they will give up part of their income. That is what they will do whenever they have more land than they can cultivate themselves.

[*1798 addition:* This manager will account to the owner for income as for expenditure. But, because this method of exploitation has great drawbacks

[ 135 ]

for absent or distant owners, they will sooner or later give it up, and en-trust their lands to cultivators, who are in a position to make the advances and see to the expenses of cultivation, and will guarantee the proprietors a definite income.]

This manager is a farmer who takes a plot on a lease. He is owed a wage which is regulated like any other. He needs his subsistence, his family's, something for a rainy day, and a gain he can put aside to improve his condition. He will fix his own wage according to custom. He will hardly ever come to demand more than that; and he will be satisfied whenever his condition is no worse than other farmers'. That sort of person is more fairminded than people think: and they would be even more so if they were less harassed, and besides competition forces integrity upon them.

Experience teaches this farmer the quantity and quality of the products on which he may reasonably count in normal years, and he estimates these according to the markets' current prices. He takes from this product all the advances he is obliged to make annually, the taxes due to the state, his wage; and, for the surplus, he promises to give the owner a certain number of ounces of silver.*

As this custom becomes established, the landowners who have farmed out their lands gradually move further from them, to gather near the markets, where they are better placed to satisfy their needs. This assemblage attracts artisans and merchants of every kind to settle in this place, and a town forms. The rest of the countryside is sown with farms: at intervals there are villages, peopled by farmers whose lands are adjacent; by the day-labourers who work for them for a wage, and by the artisans whom the ploughman needs daily: farriers, wheelwrights, etc. If our tribe is prolific, and occupies an extensive and fertile country, it can form towns, or at least boroughs, wherever it holds markets. There will then be a transformation in the way of living.

When the tribe lived on its fields, each one lived on his own products, or on those which his neighbours gave him in exchange; and it was unusual for anyone to think of going far to find another type of product.

---

*Footnote added in 1798:* Sharecroppers [*métayers*] are farmers who do not make the same advances. But these distinctions are useless for my purpose. For me it is enough that there are farmers.

It is not the same when the owners, gathered in towns, inform each other of the products of the different cantons where they have lived. Then it is natural for them all to want to enjoy all these products. It follows that they establish new needs for themselves, and they consume more than they did before.

The agreeable nature of this way of living will increase affluence in the towns. Consumption will grow proportionately; and it will happen that the farmers, more confident of selling their crops, will take greater pains with agriculture. There will therefore be less fallow land, and products will multiply.

[*1798 addition:* However we must note that the towns will not help to make agriculture flourish except in so far as they exist, at certain intervals, throughout the land which our tribe occupies. We shall see elsewhere that large towns cause the ruin of remote provinces.]

When the product of the lands has increased, the landowners will increase their incomes at the renewal of the leases. As they become richer, they will seek to obtain new commodities. Their consumption, at the same time greater and more varied, will stimulate industry on a larger scale; and, it follows that agriculture, the arts and commerce will flourish all the more, as the new needs created will offer fresh gains to the ploughman, the artisan and the merchant.

During this transformation, production and consumption will balance themselves continuously; and, depending on the proportion between them, they will cause the price of everything to rise and fall in turn. If consumption is greater, everything will become more expensive; if on the other hand production is greater, all will be cheaper. But these fluctuations will have few drawbacks; because the complete freedom trade enjoys will soon bring production and consumption into line, and will give each thing the price that it ought to have. You may already be persuaded by what I have said on competition; and I shall give fresh proof when I deal with the true price of things.

## 12 Of the Right of Ownership

WHEN, AFTER THE formation of our tribe, the land had been divided, each settler could say: "This field is mine, and mine alone." Such is the origin of the right of property.

At the time of the harvest each settler could again say: "If this field was mine in its fallow state, because it came to me in the division of land, today when it is cultivated it is mine on more than one ground, since its cultivation is my work. It is mine with all its product, because its product is at the same time the product of my labour."

Ownership of the land is thus based at one and the same time on the division which has been made, and on the work which makes it fertile.

When later on some settlers acquired more land than they could farm themselves, they had no less good a reason to regard all these lands as their own. Their ownership of them was guaranteed by the releasing of them by those to whom they had belonged. Received custom, or laws passed to that end, further guaranteed the lands to them. Now these customs and these laws are the most recent basis of the right of property. It is even usual to go back no further.

But if they continued to have the ownership of all the lands, they could no longer have complete ownership of all the product; since this product was in part the result of the work of the men they employed to cultivate the fields. Their farm hands and day-labourers thus became co-owners of this product.

In this co-ownership, the settler has the lion's share, because he provides the stock of land, because he makes the advances, and because he works himself. He does not have to plough; it is enough that he supervises the labourers. His vigilance is his main work.

The wage which is contracted with his farm hands and hired labour, and which is regulated by custom, represents the share they have in the produce as co-owners. This wage is the sum total of their ownership, and, when it has been paid, all the product of the fields belongs to the settler.

Once he has retired to a city, the settler no longer supervises the cultivation of his lands himself. So he gives up, from his product, a part of his ownership to the farmer who manages them [who cultivates them: *1798*], and that part is the farmer's wage. The latter gathers the harvest; he gives up the agreed portion to the settler [who properly speaking is now only the owner: *1798*], and he acquires a right of ownership to all the rest.

In this order, we see one man who provides the ground, that is the settler [owner: *1798*], an entrepreneur who assumes the task of overseeing the cultivation, that is the farmer, and farm workers or hired men who carry out the work.

We shall find the same situation in large undertakings of every kind. Does one want to set up a manufacturing enterprise? A rich man or a company provides the capital, an entrepreneur directs the business, and the workmen toil under his orders.

By that one sees how in each profession the citizens divide into separate classes; and how each of them finds, in his wage, the part which he has, as co-owner, of the enterprise's return.

But one does not have to work in an enterprise to become a co-owner of the product. It is enough to be working for the entrepreneur. The shoemaker, for example, becomes a co-owner of the land's product when he works for a settler, and he becomes the co-owner of the returns of a manufacturing business when he works for a manufacturer. So it is that all the citizens are by reason of their work co-owners of society's riches; and that is right since each of them contributes to producing them by reason of his work.

All this ownership is sacred. One could not without injustice deprive the manufacturer of his business or the worker of his wage. Therefore one should not be able to force the settler to sell his grain below its worth, just as one should not be able to force those who need the grain to pay more than it is worth. These truths are so simple that perhaps one does not notice them and you may be astonished that I have commented on them. You will, however, need to remember them.

We have seen how the settler [become simply a landowner: *1798*] retains ownership of the lands he no longer cultivates himself. But we ask if he is limited to having a life interest, or if he is authorised to have the right to dispose of his lands even after his death.

My reply is that when I clear a field, the product of the investment I make can only be mine. I have the sole right to enjoy it: why then, at the time of my death, can I not hand over the enjoyment of it? And how should I hand that over, if I do not have the disposition of the ground?

I have drained the marshes, I have raised the dykes which protect my lands from flooding, I have directed water to the meadows which it makes fertile; I have sown the plantations whose product belongs to me, and which however I shall not enjoy; in a word, I have given these worthless lands a value which is mine as long as it lasts, and over which, for that reason, I hold rights against the time when I shall be no more. Take back these lands in the waste state in which I found them, and leave them to me cultivated and productive. You cannot separate the two things. Therefore agree that I have the right to alienate them equally.

If the man who clears a field acquires the right to dispose of it after his death, he conveys the field with that right to the person to whom he bequeaths it; and from one generation to the next, each owner enjoys the same right. What man would concern himself with the ways of giving a plot of land a value which it would not have in his lifetime, if he were not free to bequeath it in favour of those whom he wishes to enjoy it? Do you say that a love of doing good would make him? But why take from the citizen a motive which will be more efficacious: the interest he takes in his children or in people he loves?

We have dealt with value, price, riches; the arts have multiplied; trade has spread out. Now the need is felt to mark more exactly the value of every good, and money is discovered. That will be the subject of the following chapters.

# 13 Of Metals Considered as Merchandise

GOLD, SILVER AND copper are the first metals men knew. They were often found on the earth's surface without having been sought. Rain, floods, a thousand chances brought them to light; several rivers bear them along.

Besides, these metals are easily recognised in their pure, unadulterated state or when their purity is at least little altered. That always happens with gold, often with silver, and often enough with copper, though less frequently. Nature offers them endowed with all their properties.

It is not the same with iron. Although it is to be found almost everywhere, people have all the more difficulty in recognising it, as it normally appears in the guise of earth which is bereft of all metallic properties, and to which one needs to have learnt to restore them. So of all metals it is iron which seems to have been the last known.

Nowadays iron is in use for all mechanical arts. They all owe their progress to the use of this metal, and many even their birth. For centuries it was unknown even to organised nations, which used copper in its place. As for the tools of barbarians, they were and still are made of wood, stone, bone, and sometimes of gold or silver.

I assume that our tribe is familiar with gold, silver, copper and iron, that it has learnt the skill to work on them, and that it uses them in various ways.

Making this assumption, these metals are a commodity which has value for the tribe in relation to its needs; value which rises or falls, depending on whether they are scarcer or more plentiful, or rather following the view the tribe has of their scarcity or their abundance.

When they are still in their raw state, or as nature offers them, they have one value. They have another when they have been refined or purified from all extraneous matter. Finally, they have an ultimate value, when work has made out of them tools, weapons, vessels, utensils of all sorts; and this ultimate value grows in proportion as these articles are better conceived, better worked up, and offered for sale by a smaller number of workmen.

Metals considered as raw material have thus one value; and they have another when they are considered as worked up material. In the first case, one values the metal alone; in the second, one values the metal and the work.

Metals are essential merchandise. So there must be men in the tribe whose work it is to seek for them and refine them; and others will be needed to work on them, since one needs the articles of which they are the raw material.

In the early days our tribe had little refinement, and dressed in roughly sewn skins: it had seats made of wood, stone or turf; and its vessels were made of shells, stones or pieces of hollowed wood, or of earth, first cropped and then dried in the sun, or cooked in a fire.

Each settler could make, for his own need, all these utensils whose raw material was to hand, and the making of which was neither lengthy nor troublesome.

If some people, harder working, made a larger quantity than they needed, these surplus utensils, when carried to the market, had as little value for those to whom they were offered for sale as for those who would offer to sell them. Since I assume that each settler obtained all the utensils he needed for himself, it is clear that those put up for sale were a surplus for which the tribe had no use. But if there were some settlers who did not have the time to make enough for their needs, then these utensils would become merchandise, whose value would be in proportion to their quantity compared with the amount needed by the settlers who wanted to buy them.

These utensils, roughly made, would thus count for little in trade; and they will only become a real object of trade when, worked with more skill, they are more suitable and more durable. Then they will have all the greater value, as the number of settlers who lack either the time or the skill to make them will be larger.

The entrepreneurs who undertake this work are what we have called artisans. They will grow in number according to the needs of the tribe, and competition will regulate the price of their works; the greater the number of artisans, the more they will be forced to undercut each other when they deliver the goods, and each will give them at the lowest price possible.

All the utensils I have just mentioned are made by all and sundry, from a material I assume to be plentiful; which is worth little in itself, and the work involved alone determines almost all the price.

The case is not the same for works of metal. Metals are scarce. It takes time and effort to find them. Then they have to be refined. Lastly they have to be worked up.

No sooner are they known than they become an object of trade, and people expect to be able to use them for various purposes. Not only are they merchandise when they leave the artisan's hands; they are so already, when they have just been drawn from the mine.

If we did not know the uses to which metals are adapted, they would be quite useless, and one would not seek them out. They would be left among the stones and earth, where they would stay without value.

But as soon as their utility is known, they are sought after; and people seek them out all the more because, being somewhat rare, they become an object of curiosity. So they acquire a new value, and this value is proportional to the number of the curious.

Considered as rare and as objects of curiosity, they soon come to be used for ornament, and this new use gives them another new price.

From all that has been said, we must conclude that metals are only merchandise because we make varied use of them, hunt them out through curiosity, and use them for ornament. Now it is because they are a commodity that they have become money. Let us see the transformation they have made in commerce.

WHEN IN EARLIER chapters I posited measures, it was only to speak more precisely about the relative value of the goods being exchanged. It appears that at the origin of society the tribes had none; nowadays several tribes still do not have any. It is the case that whenever people are not concerned to look closely, they are happy to estimate the quantity of goods at a glance.

Let us move to the time when, in the absence of merchants, the settlers were exchanging their surplus foodstuffs among themselves; and let us look at two settlers, one who has a surplus of corn and lacks a certain quantity of wine, the other who has a surplus of wine, and lacks a certain quantity of corn. To simplify, I assume that they are each furnished with everything else they need.

With this assumption, it is clear that the man who has corn to deliver would not look closely at the size, or the number, of his sacks. Since this corn would have no value for him if it was left on his hands, he considers it well paid for when, by an exchange, he gets for himself all the wine he needs.

The man who has a surplus of wine reasons in the same way. So they exchange without measuring; indeed, it is enough for them to judge on sight, the one the amount of wine he needs, the other the amount of corn.

It is not the same when the settlers make their exchanges through the medium of merchants. Since the latter want to make a profit at one and the same time from the person from whom they buy and the person to whom they sell, they are concerned to judge the quantity of goods more precisely. So they will think of ways to ascertain what they have gained each time they buy and resell.

Now, when instead of judging goods in a rough and ready fashion they have got used to measuring them, one will assume that their value is treated like their quantity, for which there is a fixed measure. We will be all the more likely to assume it, as values will seem to vary like measures. So people will come to make misconceptions. They will speak of value and price without thinking what they are saying: they will forget that the notions they make of them can only be relative; and they will assume that they are absolute.

It is the merchants who will above all have occasioned this misunderstanding: as they were concerned to estimate goods more accurately, they seemed to give them an absolute value. "This measure is worth so much," they said, and people no longer saw an idea of relativity in this language.

Besides, they were not in the same position as the settlers who, in the days when they traded directly, attached no value to the surplus, except in so far as they could provide themselves with the goods they needed by giving it up.

The surplus with which the merchants trade had belonged to the settlers who gave it up to them. But for the merchants it is not a surplus; it is a useful good they expect to profit from. And so they appreciate it to the full; and the more they claim to appreciate it, the more they seem to give it an absolute value. Metals, used as money, will especially create this illusion.

Iron disintegrates: exposure to the air, however little humidity there is in it, gradually decomposes it. Copper destroys itself too. Only gold and silver keep without corruption.

Each of these metals has a value, which stems from its scarcity, its adaptability and its *lasting qualities*. Gold is more valuable than silver, silver than copper, and copper than iron.

It has probably always been impossible to calculate exactly the relative and proportional value of these metals; all the more so because this proportion must vary each time some of them become scarcer or more plentiful. They were estimated roughly, sometimes more, sometimes less, according to the quantity of them appearing in trade. A metal had more value when there was little of it on sale, and when people wished to buy a lot. It had less value in the opposite case. We shall deal with their respective value elsewhere.

As soon as it was appreciated that metals have a value, it was found useful to give a piece of metal in exchange for what one was buying; and as this custom took hold, metals became the common measure of all values. Then a merchant was no longer forced to cart wine or some other foodstuff to the settler who had corn to sell. He gave him a piece of metal, and this settler bought everything he needed with the same metal.

Iron was the least suitable for this use. As it corrodes day by day, the person who received it in exchange would make a loss each day. Besides, one is only accustomed to make use of metals as a common measure, because they make commerce easier. Now iron would facilitate it less than the other metals since, as it is the least valuable, we would have to cart it about in greater quantities.

Copper, which keeps better and which is more valuable, would deserve its preference. Every nation uses it; however, since its value is still very limited, it is only useful when one buys low-price goods retail.

So it was gold and silver which were bound especially to be chosen for use as a common measure. They are indestructible; they have great value. The value is found in due proportion in each part; and so one can find, in each part, depending on whether it is larger or smaller, a measure of any sort of value.

So it is not following a convention that gold and silver have been introduced into commerce as a convenient means for exchanges; it is not by whim that they have been given a value. They have, like all other merchandise, a value based on our needs; and because this value, larger or smaller according to the amount of metal, does not perish, they have, for that reason alone, become the measure of all others, and the most convenient.

We have seen that trade increases the amount of wealth, because by facilitating and multiplying exchanges it gives value to those goods which had none. We see here that trade must increase this quantity of wealth still further when it has, in gold and silver considered as merchandise, a common measure of all values, since exchanges are then made easy and multiply ever more.

But this measure had to be fixed and determined. However, it is probable that, in the early days, people judged volume by sight, and weight by hand. This uncertain regime doubtless caused damage and complaints. The need to avoid them was felt: people set about it, and scales were invented to weigh metals. So an ounce of silver, for instance, was the price of a septier of corn or of a cask of wine.

This innovation succeeded in confusing all ideas on the value of things. When people believed they were seeing price in a measure which, like an ounce of gold or silver, was always the same, they did not doubt that they had an absolute value, and no longer entertained other than confused ideas on this subject.

All the same there was a great advantage in being able to determine the weight of each piece of gold and silver; because if previously what we call *price* was a vague estimate without precision, you can understand that people must have found in these metals, weighed and cut up, the more exact price of all other merchandise, or a surer measure of their value.

It is as merchandise that gold and silver circulated, when the buyer and the seller were reduced to weighing the quantity they needed to hand over as the price of other merchandise. This practice, which was general, still carries on in China and elsewhere.

However, it was inconvenient always to have to carry scales, and that was not the only drawback: one also had to make sure of the degree of purity of the metals, a degree which affects the value.

Public authority came to the help of trade; it had the gold and silver circulating assayed: it determined what one calls the standard, that is the degree of purity. It then made separate portions which it weighed; and it stamped on each a mark which attested the standard and the weight.

Here we have money. One knows its value at a glance. It prevents fraud, it injects confidence into trade and consequently makes trade still easier.

Gold and silver coin would not have been suitable for the small purchases one makes daily: one would have had to cut it up into tiny pieces which could scarcely have been handled. That is why copper coin was introduced. Copper coin even seems to have been the first in use; it sufficed on its own, when the tribes only had things of small value to exchange.

In becoming coin, metals have not ceased to be merchandise; they have an extra imprint and a new denomination; but they are still what they were, and they would not have a value as coinage if they did not continue to have value as merchandise. This observation is not as pointless as it might seem, because people would say, in the common reasoning on money, that it is not merchandise, and yet they do not have much to say about what it is.

Gold and silver coinage reveals that there are things of high price in trade. It is therefore a proof of wealth. But it is not so by virtue of its quantity: because commerce can make do with less as with more. If it were eight times more plentiful, it would have eight times less value, and one would have to carry a mark to market instead of an ounce. If it were eight times scarcer, it would have eight times more value, and one would only have to carry an ounce instead of a mark. It is therefore a proof of wealth by the mere fact that it is used. It is that in having a great value on its own, it proves that there are articles in trade which also have great value. But if it became as common as copper, it would lose its value; and then, in exchanges, it could serve as a measure of value for the nations which seem to us the poorest. When we deal with the circulation of silver we shall see how one judges its abundance and its scarcity.

Used as coin, gold and silver had a new use and new utility. These metals thus acquired fresh value. An abundance of gold and silver is thus an abundance of articles which have value, and consequently it is wealth.

But whatever value one places on gold and silver, the first and main wealth is not at all in the plentifulness of these metals. This wealth is only in the abundance of products which are consumed. However, because with gold and silver one can lack for nothing, one soon comes to regard these metals as the sole wealth, or at least as the principal wealth: that is an error. But it would also be an error to say that an abundance of gold and silver is not true wealth. We must confine ourselves to distinguishing two types of wealth.

I shall note in finishing this chapter that those who consider coin as representative signs of the value of things express themselves too inexactly; because they seem to regard them as arbitrarily chosen signs, which only have value by convention. If they had noticed that metals were merchandise before they became money, and that they have continued to be merchandise, they would have recognised that they are only suited to be the common measure of all values because they have value in themselves, and independently of all convention.

# 15 That Silver, Used as a Measure of Value, Has Brought Misunderstanding About the Value of Things

WE HAVE NOTICED that when trade comes about through the exchange of goods in surplus, everyone gives something which had no value for him, because he has no use for it, for something which does have a value for him, because he can use it, and that, consequently, everyone gives less for more. Now that is how it would have been natural to work out value in every case, if one had always traded through barter and without minted coin.

But once money had been accepted as the common measure of value, it was just as natural to reckon that one was giving equal value for equal value in exchanges, all the goods one exchanged were each considered equal in value to an identical quantity of money.

It was seen that through the medium of money one could determine, with some precision, a respective value between two quantities of a different nature, for example between a quantity of corn and a measure of wine. From then on, in these respective values, only the quantity of money which was the measure of them was noticed: every other consideration was removed; and because this quantity was the same, it was reckoned that in exchanges one gave equal value for equal value.

However, when I give you a quantity of corn, valued at ten ounces of silver, to get from you a quantity of wine at the same price, it is not certain that this exchange is equally advantageous for you and for me, although these two quantities seem to be the equivalent of each other.

In fact, if the corn which I have given you is absolutely essential to me, and if the wine you have given me is surplus to your needs, the advantage will be on your side and the disadvantage on mine.

Therefore, it is not enough to compare quantity in money with quantity in money, to work out who gains, you or I. There is another consideration which must come into the calculation; that is to know whether we are both exchanging a surplus for a necessary good. In such a case, the advantage is the same for both parties, and we each give less for more; in every other case it cannot be equal, and one of us gives more for less.

We have noticed that, in exchanges, goods are reciprocally the price of each other. We shall note here that if money is the measure of the value of the goods one buys, the value of the goods one buys is reciprocally the measure of the value of money. For example, to suppose that with six ounces of silver one can buy a muid of corn, is that not to suppose that a muid of corn is the measure of the value of six ounces of silver?

So when money has been taken as the common measure of all value, it is solely, as we have seen, because of all tradable goods it is the most suitable for this purpose; and that does not infer that it cannot itself have, as a measure, the value of the goods against which it is exchanged. On the contrary, it is clear that the value of what one buys is always the measure of the value of the money one gives.

But once people have taken money as a common measure, they soon come to see it as an absolute measure: that is to say, as a measure that is a measure by itself, independently of any connection, or as a good which, by its nature, measures all others, and is not measured by any of them. This misapprehension could not fail to spread much confusion. It has also made us see an equal value in the goods we exchange, and we have made a principle of commerce out of this equal value.

However, if what I am offering you was equal for you in value, or, which comes to the same, in utility, to what you are offering me; and if what you are offering me was equal for me to what I am offering you, we should each of us stay with what we have; and we should not make any exchange. When we make an exchange, then you and I judge that we each receive more than we give, or that we give less for more.

Let us remember the time when Europeans began trading in America, where, for things to which we attach little value, they received other goods to which we attach the greatest value.

Following our line of argument, you will agree that they gave less for more when they gave a knife, a sword, or a mirror for an ingot of silver or gold. But we cannot deny that the American also gave less for more when he gave, for example, an ingot of gold for a knife: because he was giving something to which people attached little value in his country because it was useless, in exchange for something to which they attached value, because it was useful.

So people said that the Americans did not know the price of gold and silver. They spoke as though these metals must have an absolute value. People did not think that they only possess value in relation to man's uses, and that in consequence they have no value for a tribe that has no use for them.

Inequality of value following the customs and opinions of peoples: that· is what has created trade and what supports it; because it is what produces the situation that in exchanges each person has the advantage of giving less for more.

However, because we are not inclined to believe that money can be overplentiful, however much of it one has, we will find it difficult to understand that, when we give money for something we buy, we have the advantage of giving less for more, especially if the good is what we call expensive. So let us see how money can be considered as a necessary good, or as a surplus good.

All your property is in land, and you have produce of all kinds, more than you can consume. It is clear that, in giving up the produce which is surplus to your consumption, you are giving up something which is useless to you; and however little utility you find in what you receive in exchange, you will have given less for more.

I only have rents, and all my income is in money. Now I cannot live off this money, as you can with your produce. On its own it is thus useless to me, and it would always be so if I could not exchange it with you or with someone else. When I hand it over, I therefore abandon something which is useless to me for something I need, and I give less for more. But we find ourselves in very different situations; because in the product of your lands, it is only the produce surplus to your consumption that is useless to you; while in the product of my rents, if I do not manage to exchange it, all is useless to me, since there is nothing for my consumption.

So money, which is useless on its own, because with money alone one could not subsist, only becomes useful because, having been chosen as a common measure of all value, it is accepted as the price of the goods one buys.

Now, the amount of money which I need to supply me with everything necessary for my subsistence is for me the equivalent of the foodstuffs you are obliged to set aside for your subsistence. If I give up that money for things that are useless for my consumption, I should make an unfavourable exchange; I should be giving an essential good for a useless good, I should be giving more for less.

But the money I have left, when I have set aside all that I need for my subsistence, is a surplus for me; just as the produce which you do not need to consume is a surplus for you.

Now, the more confident I am of being able to subsist in accordance with the needs I have created for myself, the less this money surplus is of value for me. So I shall not scrutinise it too closely; and even when I give some of it for frivolities I should like to enjoy, I shall believe I am giving less for more.

It will be the same for you when, after you have made ample provision of products of every kind, nothing can be lacking for your subsistence. Then what you have left is a surplus which you will give happily for a frivolity which seems worthless.

It will follow from this that the value of essential goods will always be estimated more accurately than the value of superfluous goods; and that these values will never be in proportion to each other. The price of essential goods will be very low compared with the price of superfluous goods, because everyone is concerned to estimate them as exactly as possible. In contrast, the price of superfluous goods will be very high compared with the price of necessary goods, because the very people who buy them are not concerned to estimate them with precision. But in the end, at whatever price one buys them, or however dear they appear, the person who purchases them with surplus money is always considered to give less for more.

# 16  Of the Circulation of Money

EACH YEAR, at appointed times, farmers bring the entire price of their leases into the towns: each market day, they sell some produce, and so they carry back to their village, in small amounts, the sums they have paid the landowners.

In the course of the year, the merchant receives in individual sales the price of the goods he bought wholesale; and the artisan, who bought his raw materials wholesale, sells them retail, when he has worked on them. So it is that day by day sales reimburse in small sums the large sums which have been used for payments or purchases in gross; and, when this reimbursement has been made, people pay out or buy again with large sums to have themselves reimbursed by new retail sales.

Money is thus constantly moving around, to be collected later as into reservoirs, from which it spreads through a mass of small channels which bring it back into the first reservoirs; whence it spreads out again, and to which it returns again. This continual movement, which collects it to distribute it, and distributes it to gather it up again, is what we call *circulation*.

Do I need to point out that this circulation assumes that, at each movement the money makes, there is an exchange; and that when it moves without causing an exchange, there is no circulation? For example, the money which comes from taxes has gone through many hands before it reaches the Sovereign's treasury. But that is not circulation, that is only transport, and often very costly transport. It is important that, through circulating, money changes itself in some way into all the goods which are needed to support life and strength in the body politic. Thus money from taxation only begins to circulate when the sovereign exchanges it for products or works.

All the money in commerce circulates from the reservoirs to the channels, and from the channels to the reservoirs. If any obstacle holds up this circulation, commerce languishes.

I say *all the money in commerce,* and I do not say all that is in the state. There is always a certain amount which does not circulate at all, for example what one puts aside to have a standby in case of misfortune or to improve one's position someday: such also are the savings of misers, who cut back on their needs.

That money does not circulate at all at present. But it is not very important whether there is more or less in circulation; the main point is that it should circulate freely.

We have seen that money is only a measure of value because it possesses value itself; that if it is scarce, it has greater value; and that it has a smaller value if it is plentiful.

If there is twice the amount of money in commerce, we will give for a good two ounces of this metal instead of one; and if there is half the quantity of money, we will only give half an ounce instead of a whole ounce. In the first case, an owner who would put out his land to farm for fifty ounces, would let it for a hundred; and in the second he would let it for twenty-five. But with a hundred ounces he will only do what he did with fifty; just as with fifty he will only do what he did with twenty-five. So he would be deceiving himself if he thought himself richer in one of these cases than in the other. His income is always the same, whether the coin is smaller or greater. Whether one counts it at a hundred ounces, or fifty, or twenty-five, nothing is changed; since with these various ways of counting, one can only ever make the same consumption.

So one sees that it is fairly unimportant whether there is plenty of money, and that it would even be a good thing if there were less. Indeed commerce would be carried on more conveniently. Would it not be dreadfully awkward if silver were as common as iron.

All products come from cultivated land. So one can consider farmers as the first reservoirs of all the money that circulates.

They spread some on the lands for the expenses of cultivation, another part, at different times, is carried bit by bit to the towns, where the farmers buy worked materials which they cannot find in their villages. Finally, a last portion is carried to the towns, in large sums, for the payment of the leases.

The landowners therefore form other reservoirs, from which money spreads among the artisans who work for them; among the merchants from whom they buy, and among the farmers who come to the town to sell their foodstuffs.

The merchant, who plans to make bulk purchases, becomes in his turn a reservoir as he sells his goods; and it is the same with the artisan, who needs to build up a stock in order to be able to supply himself with raw materials.

I agree that the merchant and the artisan can buy on credit, to pay later at different dates. But whether they pay when they buy, or only pay later, they must necessarily keep back a proportion of what they sell each day, if they do not want to fail to meet their undertakings. They therefore have to accumulate.

It would be beneficial for the use of credit to become established, since then a merchant and an artisan, without money, could keep an inventory, the one of merchandise, the other of raw materials; and, consequently, a larger number of actively occupied men would join together in advancing trade. For that to happen good faith must bring confidence. This is especially what happens in republics which have, shall we say, habits of simplicity and frugality.

The merchant and the artisan can do nothing without money, or at least without credit. The same does not hold true of the farmers. If they need the one or the other for the goods they buy in the town, they do not have the same need in providing for the expenses of cultivation; because they can pay all the country-dwellers who work for them with the grain they harvest, with the drinks they make, with the animals they raise. Custom sets the wages they owe, and the foodstuffs they hand over are valued at the market's prices.

So one spends no money in the country, or one spends little; and as one can only earn on the one side what someone spends on the other, it must be the case that those who work for the farmers earn little money, or earn none at all. Money thus circulates less in the countryside than elsewhere.

The consequence is, in the last analysis, that the towns form large reservoirs which money enters and from which it issues by a self-sustaining movement, or one which constantly renews itself.

Let us suppose that half our tribe lives in the town, where we have seen that the landowners consume more than they did in their villages, and where, in consequence, they will consume more than half the product of the land.

To settle our ideas, let us value the produce of all the land at two thousand ounces of silver. On this assumption, since the inhabitants of the town consume more than half of all products, they will need more than a thousand ounces of silver to buy everything necessary for their subsistence. I make the assumption that they need twelve hundred, and I say that if this sum is enough for them, it will be enough to support commerce throughout the tribe. That is, it will pass to the farmers to return to the landowners; and as this cycle will only finish to begin again, it will always be with the same quantity of money that exchanges are made in the town and in the country. From that fact one could speculate that the amount of money that commerce needs depends mainly on the amount of consumption in the towns; or that this amount of money is almost equal to the value of the products that the towns consume.

It is at least certain that it could not be equal in value to the product of all the lands. Indeed, although we have evaluated this product at two thousand ounces of silver, it would not be enough to give our tribe these two thousand ounces to give it a value in silver equal to the product of all its lands. Silver would lose all the more of its value as it became more available: the two thousand ounces would only be worth twelve hundred. So it is in vain that one would put a larger amount of silver into trade. Whatever this quantity was, it could only ever have a value roughly equal to the value of the products consumed in the towns.

Indeed, as the wealth of the countryside is in products, the wealth of the towns is in silver. Now, if in the towns, where we assume that at the end of each year consumption had been paid for with twelve hundred ounces, we suddenly spread out another eight hundred, it is clear that the silver will lose its value in proportion to its increased plentifulness. So people will pay twenty ounces, or near enough, for what they used to pay twelve; and consequently the two thousand will only have the value of twelve hundred, or near enough. I say *near enough* since these proportions do not fix themselves by exact, geometric calculations.

The amount of silver needed for trade must also vary according to circumstances.

Let us assume that the payment of leases and that of everything on credit takes place once a year; and that to liquidate them, the debtors need a thousand ounces of silver; there would have to be, in relation to these payments, a thousand ounces of silver in circulation.

But if these payments were made half-yearly, half this amount would be enough, because five hundred ounces, paid twice, equal a thousand paid once. One can see that if these payments were made in four equal terms, two hundred and fifty ounces would suffice.

To make the calculation easier I am omitting the small, daily disbursements which are made in ready money. But people will no doubt say that I am establishing nothing precise about the quantity of money in circulation.* I would reply that my sole purpose is to show that internal trade can be conducted, and it is, following the customs of countries, with less money in circulation as with more; and it is not otiose to comment on it, in these days when people imagine that a state is only rich in proportion as it has more money.

Often little money is needed in trade, and credit takes its place. Established in different countries, the traders or dealers send each other goods which command a higher price in the places to which they are carried, and in continuing to sell the goods they stock, each for his own account, they all sell for each other's accounts the goods they have received. By this means they can make an extensive trade without requiring silver to circulate between them. Because in valuing the merchandise entrusted to them, according to the current price, they will only have to pay for whatever some have supplied beyond that; yet again one can meet obligations towards them by sending them other merchandise. So it is that the largest enterprises are often those where silver circulates in the least quantity.

But money is needed for daily expenses: it is needed to pay the wages of artisans who live by work from day to day. It is needed for the small merchants who only buy and sell retail and who need their capital to come back to them continuously.

It is in small channels that circulation takes place more perceptibly and more rapidly. But the faster it is, the more the same pieces of coin pass and pass again frequently through the same hands; and as, in such a case, one coin

---

*It is estimated that the money which circulates in the states of Europe is in general equal to at least half the product of the land, and at most to two-thirds, [R. Cantillon, *Essai sur la nature du commerce en général* (Paris, 1755), Book 2, Chapter 3]. I have drawn the basis of this chapter from this work, and several observations of which I have made use in other chapters. It is one of the best works I know on this subject: but I am far from knowing them all.

takes the place of many, it is clear that this smaller trade can carry on with a quantity of coin which gets less as the circulation speeds up. So, in small channels one needs little money because it circulates rapidly; and in large ones even less is needed, as often it hardly circulates at all.

We may conclude that it is impossible to say anything with confidence about the precise amount of money circulating which is, or which should be, in commerce. I might have put it far too high when I supposed it roughly equal to the value of the products which are consumed annually in the towns. Since at the beginning of January each citizen certainly does not have all the money he will need in the course of the year; but because, as he is spending it, he is earning it, one can appreciate that, at the year's end, the same coins have come back many times into the towns, just as they left them a good many times.

The circulation of money would be very slow if one always had to change it at great expense in the distant places where one might need it. Therefore it would matter to be able to make it pass in some way over very great distances. This is what one achieves by means of exchange which we are going to deal with.

# 17 Of Exchange

WHY HAVE THE operations of exchange which are simple in themselves become matters so difficult to understand in every language? Was it impossible then for bankers to explain themselves more clearly? I have not studied their language at all: but in my intention to cast some light on this branch of commerce, I only need to study the exchange market: it will explain itself, if I make precise enough notions of it.

I want to send a hundred thousand francs to Bordeaux. If I were obliged to send them by road, it would cost me expenses, and I should have to run some risks. But in Paris there are some Bordeaux people who themselves need to bring money from Bordeaux; and there are businessmen to whom this city owes money, because they have sent it merchandise.

I search for and find a man from Bordeaux who has fifty thousand francs in Bordeaux which he would like to have at Paris. There is no more involved than to exchange the fifty thousand francs which are in Paris against the fifty thousand francs which are at Bordeaux. Now there we both have the same advantage, because both of us avoid all expenses and all risks. And so I count out for him fifty thousand francs in Paris, and he gives me a letter, drawn on the person who has his funds at Bordeaux, by which he says to pay the bearer fifty thousand francs to my order. So there you have half my sum which I have arranged to send to Bordeaux. The other half will go there in the same fashion, because I find businessmen who are owed that amount in Bordeaux, and who will give me similar letters for fifty thousand francs that I disburse to them.

By means of these letters, we thus exchange sums which are remote from each other. That is why we have called them *bills* [lit. letters] *of exchange*.

In all the towns of the kingdom there are people who are in the same position as I, and in all of them there is also the facility of bills of exchange, because the business, which they carry out among themselves, is always putting them in a state of debt with regard to each other. One must just note that this facility is more often found in mercantile towns or in those of easy access.

But if every time one needed a bill of exchange one had to go from door to door to find the businessman who could give it, this would certainly be a great nuisance. So here we have something which has summoned up the energy of some individuals, and gradually produced a class of men whom one calls *exchange brokers*, because with the bills they give, one exchanges two sums that are at a distance from each other.

I imagine one from among many ways in which this class of men could have formed. I postulate a rich individual who has lands in different provinces, and who, not knowing how to gather his revenue, gives his agent the task of seeing to it. The latter seeks in Paris for merchants who bring various goods from these provinces, and who, in consequence, need to make money go there. He gives them bills of exchange drawn on these provinces: the merchants pay him in person in Paris; and once he has established a connection with them, his master's revenues arrive each year with the same ease.

The master, who has no idea how this is done, admires the genius of his agent. He never ceases praising him to his acquaintances. So all the rich men apply to this man, and he amazes them all equally.

Here he is an exchange broker: with a connection that is constantly extending, he is in a position to find money everywhere, and people come to him from all parts. So he no longer needs to serve a master. He takes a house in which he sets up his exchange office, and from the table on which he counts out the money, which one calls *banque*, he takes the name banker [*banquier*]. If he were alone, he would be able to raise his wage to the skies, but, happily for the public, his fortune, which is a proof of what he earns, gives him rivals, and bankers multiply.

The profit that a banker made in his business was originally called *agio*, a term which has become odious, and which today marks an excessive, usurious profit made in a bank.

A profit is doubtless due to bankers. Sometimes they are forced to transport money on the roads; they run up expenses in maintaining their connections; in a word, they give their time and their attention.

We imagine their wage will adjust, like all others, through competition. But one finds in exchange a multitude of circumstances of which the public is ignorant; and a banker, who has acquired the art of winning trust, can abuse it all the more because he carries out banking in some sense exclusively. Let us observe exchange between the different towns of a kingdom: we shall afterwards look at it from nation to nation.

In commerce, the person who accepts goods on the understanding that he will pay for them in an agreed period, recognises in writing that he will pay such a sum; and this recognizance, in the hands of the person to whom he has made it, is called *credit* [*créance:* lit. belief], because it is a title on which one must believe one will be paid. Thus credit is opposed to debt [*dette*], as creditor [*créancier*] is to debtor [*débiteur*].

I assume that the merchants of Paris have a hundred thousand francs of credits on Bordeaux, and that the merchants of Bordeaux have credits on Paris for the same amount: all these credits would disappear by a simple reversal of the sides; that is to say, when at Bordeaux the merchants who owe in Paris pay those whom Paris owes; and in Paris the merchants who owe in Bordeaux pay those whom Bordeaux owes.

If Paris owes a hundred thousand francs at Nantes, Nantes a hundred thousand francs at Bordeaux, Bordeaux a hundred thousand francs at Lyons, and Lyons a hundred thousand francs at Paris; it will be enough to wipe out all these debts if Paris sends to Nantes a hundred thousand francs of bills of exchange on Lyons; because with these bills Nantes will pay Bordeaux, and Bordeaux will pay Lyons. In such a case the merchants can effect the exchange among themselves, without the intervention of any banker, and the operation is simplicity itself.

But I, who am not involved in business and who am not at all conversant with what goes on in commercial centres, I am obliged to apply to a banker when I want to send money to a province. Now this banker might only have to pay the cost of travelling from his home to the residences of some Paris merchants, and yet it would be open to him to take advantage of my ignorance, and to demand far too great a payment from me. This abuse could happen if there were only one banker in Paris. But there are many, many honest ones, and competition forces them all to be honest.

Every bill of exchange assumes a debt on the part of the person on whom it is drawn. Bordeaux, for instance, can only give one on Paris, because Paris owes at Bordeaux. Now it is these reciprocal debts or credits between towns which regulate all the operations of exchange.

The debts between two towns can be equal on either side: Lyons can owe a hundred thousand francs in Paris, and Paris can owe the same sum at Lyons.

The debts can also be unequal: Lyons can owe three hundred thousand francs in Paris, and Paris can owe four hundred thousand at Lyons.

In the case of equality of debts on the one hand and on the other, if we only look at that consideration, it is certain that two merchants, one in Paris needing a hundred thousand francs in Lyons, and the other, who is at Lyons, needing a hundred thousand francs at Paris, must make that exchange, equal sum for equal sum. For both of them find like benefit in giving a hundred thousand francs for a hundred thousand francs; and since this exchange does not put the one to more expense than the other, neither of the two has the right to demand more than the hundred thousand francs.

When the exchange is made from one town to another, equal sum for equal sum, one says that it is at par.

Take note that I say *sum* and not *value:* because the two words are not synonymous. When in Paris I give you a hundred thousand francs to receive a hundred thousand francs at Lyons, the sums are equal; and yet, so far as I am concerned, I give a lesser value for a greater one if it is more advantageous for me to have a hundred thousand francs at Lyons than at Paris. It is the same for you: you give me a lesser value for a greater one if you find an advantage in having this money in Paris rather than at Lyons. We must recapitulate what we have said about exchanges.

In the case where the debts between two towns are unequal: when Paris, for example, owes four hundred thousand livres at Lyons, and Lyons only owes three hundred thousand in Paris, one will be able to settle three hundred thousand with bills of exchange, but there will remain a hundred thousand francs [*sic*] which will have to be transported from Paris to Lyons.

In settling the three hundred thousand francs of respective debt with bills of exchange, the merchants can make the exchange at par between themselves, that is to say, equal sum for equal sum.

A hundred thousand francs remain to be paid. The merchants of Paris apply to a banker who, having no funds at Lyons, is obliged to have the sum transported there, and to whom, consequently, one will owe the costs of transport in addition to a payment. Now I assume that one has agreed to give him 4 per cent for the whole transaction; one will thus pay out to him one hundred and four thousand francs in Paris and he will give bills on Lyons for a hundred thousand.

In this example, the exchange rises above par, because the merchants give in Paris a larger sum than the one that they can receive at Lyons.

The merchants of Lyons have credits on Paris. They are therefore not in the position of sending money there: rather they need it to come back to them.

If in this situation someone offers to give them ninety-eight thousand francs for a hundred thousand francs of bills of exchange on Paris, they will accept the offer; because it will only cost them two thousand livres to have their money at Lyons, instead of the four thousand their correspondents would have paid the banker.

When one gives a smaller sum to receive a greater one, it is said that the exchange is below par.

From these explanations we can see that exchange, like trade, is no more on one side than a purchase, and on the other than a sale; that in this transaction money is the sole good that is being bought and is on sale, and that the bankers are only money merchants. It is essential that we only see in things what is there, if we wish to speak with clarity and precision.

As soon as money exchange is a purchase, we can consider, as the price of the exchange, the sum that I give in Paris for a sum that must be given to me at Lyons. So it is called the *rate* [lit.: price] *of exchange*.

The exchange would regulate itself, as I have just explained, if one always knew exactly the state of the reciprocal debts between two towns: but that is not possible, especially when the exchange is made between two towns which, like Paris and Lyons, carry on a substantial trade with each other.

If, for example, one knows that Paris is in debt, one does not know by how much, either because the amount may vary from one day to the next; or because the dealers, who gather at the place of exchange, cannot be informed at once of the variations; or finally, because some have an interest in exaggerating the debt, whereas others have an interest in reducing it.

The one set of people exaggerate it because, as they want to sell bills of exchange on Lyons, they would like to take the rate of exchange to 4 per cent above par; the other group talks it down, as they want to buy bills of exchange on Lyons, and do not want to pay more than 2 per cent above par.

So here we have haggling: but in the end the parties will come together, and the rate of exchange will be fixed, for that day and subsequent ones until the first assembly, at 3 per cent.

There are thus three ways to consider the rate of exchange. It is at par, it is above par, it is below par.

When it is at par one gives like sum for like sum, and you will perhaps be astonished to hear that one identical sum is the price of an equal sum; that a hundred francs is the price of a hundred francs. You will say, there is no price at all, since one is adding nothing to one side or the other.

But one must remember that the price of a thing is relative to the need of the person who receives it in exchange: it is according to this need that he estimates it; and in proportion as his need is greater or smaller, he will give a higher or a lower price. That being so, the hundred francs you receive in Paris are for you the price of the hundred francs you enable me to draw at Lyons; because you yourself reckon that this money has a greater value for you in Paris, where you can use it, than at Lyons, where you do not need it. If the sums are equal, the values are not; and as we have remarked, one must not confuse sum and value.

For the same reason, when the exchange is below par and I give you, for example, ninety-six livres in Paris to receive a hundred at Lyons, these ninety-six livres are for you in Paris the price of a hundred at Lyons. They form the price, I say, just as much as the one hundred and four when the exchange is above par.

So you can conceive how in exchange you and I each give a lesser value for a greater one, whatever relationship the sums otherwise have to each other. Let me repeat again that value is uniquely based on the utility which things have with regard to those who exchange them.

But if, to make our money pass from Paris to Lyons or from Lyons to Paris, we had to deal with a man for whom it was a matter of indifference whether he had his money in the one or the other of these towns, it is clear that then these values would be, with regard to this man, like sums of money: a hundred and four livres would have for him a greater value than a hundred, and a hundred a greater value than ninety-six. There you have precisely the situation in which the bankers are placed, and that is why they gain doubly in practising exchange dealings. They gain from you, who wish to send money from Paris to Lyons, and they gain from me, who wishes to bring it from Lyons to Paris.

Whether the exchange rises above par or drops below it, there can always be profit for the banker, to whom it is a matter of indifference whether his money is in one town rather than another. As he does not find himself in the same circumstances as the merchants, he has no other interest than to acquire a greater sum of money for a lesser one, and this greater sum always has a greater value for him.

But, you will say, if in exchange deals a dealer always gave a smaller value for a greater value, he would always gain, and yet he would end up ruining himself if he always gave a larger sum of money for a smaller one.

That is true: but that objection is a sophistry which causes me to say that a dealer always gives in exchange a larger sum of money for a smaller one, and that this larger sum always represents a smaller value.

I say then that he gives a sum of money, sometimes larger, sometimes smaller, and that this sum, whatever it is, is always a smaller value for him, because he himself judges that what he is given in exchange has more utility for him. That is a truth which everyone may have experienced.

For the rest, since, in its course, exchange necessarily experiences alternate rises and falls, it is clear that merchants, turn by turn, will give sometimes a larger sum of money for a smaller, sometimes a smaller one for a larger: and it might be that after a certain time the result was the same for both parties, or near enough, as if they had always made the exchanges at par.

We have noticed that one cannot know exactly the state of reciprocal debts between several towns. One can only see that they owe more than they are owed when the exchange is above par; and that when it is below, they are owed more than they owe. Yet this rule is not absolutely without exception: because many circumstances can cause the rate of exchange to vary independently of the state of the debts.

If, when at Lyons the exchange is below par, and one only pays ninety-eight livres to receive a hundred in Paris, several people ask at the same time for five to six hundred thousand francs of bills of exchange on Paris, this demand would raise the price of exchange, so that to buy a hundred francs which are in Paris, you would have to pay a hundred instead of ninety-eight in Lyons, or even a hundred and two, a hundred and three. What is happening is something we have already noticed in markets, where prices rise and fall following the proportion in which the goods for sale relates to the demand for them. If, in the place of exchange, one offers more bills of exchange than are wanted, they will be at a lower price; and they will be at a higher one if one asks for more of them than are on offer.

The bankers' rivalry can sometimes alone make the rate of exchange vary.

I postulate that in a town a rich banker, who has won trust, wishes to be the sole banker; he has a certain way to elbow aside every rival. He only needs suddenly to lower the rate of exchange and sell his bills of exchange at a loss. He will lose, if necessary, fifteen to twenty thousand francs, but he will have put off those who wanted to carry on this business with him; and when he is the only one, he will know for certain how to recover what he lost and more. If in that town there were several accredited bankers, they would be able to get together at their common expense to carry out what I had one person doing. It is certain that in general dealers think of reducing, as far as possible, the number of their rivals. Now bankers have all the more room to do this, as they have persuaded people that banking is a very arcane matter, because indeed their jargon is very difficult to understand. In the very commercial centres, the greatest praise one can think of giving a merchant is to say, "He understands the exchange market." One can see that ignorance delivers the merchants into the bankers' discretion.

Many factors, such as those I have just pointed out, can cause the price of exchange to vary, but as they are all chance, it is pointless to linger on them. It is enough to remember that, outside the case where they operate, the exchange, according to whether it is above or below par, causes one to judge whether a town owes or whether it is owed money.

Exchange rates rise and fall in turn in all the towns which have some mutual commerce. Now these successive rises and falls in which it manifests itself in turn from town to town is what I call the *course of exchange*, and here we now have all the mystery of this type of business.

A banker watches the course of exchange himself and through his correspondents. He knows not only that it is rising in such and such a town and falling in another; he also knows by how much it is rising above par and by how much it is falling below par.

Given the actual state of exchange, he can foresee, from what his experience teaches him about the ebb and flow of trade, that where the exchange is high, it will not take long to fall; while where it is low, it will soon rise.

I even add that he will often be able to judge it with certainty: because if he is well informed by his correspondents, he will know which are the towns which must make large dispatches of merchandise within a few months. He will thus work out that in such a place, where the exchange is high now because it is indebted, the exchange will be low in some months' time, because it will have acquired credits. That if Lyons, for example, is owing in Paris, the exchange will be high there, and you will have to pay a hundred and three livres to have a bill for a hundred on Paris. But within six months it will be low if Lyons acquires credits on Paris.

Now, once a banker knows in advance the rises and falls of exchange in the chief trading towns, it will be easy for him to make his arrangements from far away to turn these to his advantage. He will seize the opportunity and, making his money or his credit move swiftly from place to place, he will gain in each in a short time, 2, 3 or 4 per cent, or more. Let me give one example.

I postulate two bankers who have credit, the one established in Paris, the other at Lyons.

The Lyons banker, who sees that the exchange is at 3 per cent above par because Lyons owes Paris more than five hundred thousand francs, knows that a great dispatch of goods is being prepared for that capital, and that, in three months, Paris itself will owe more than five hundred thousand francs at Lyons.

In this situation, this banker will take every opportunity to draw on his correspondent in Paris; and to have the advantage, he will be satisfied, if need be, to gain on each bill of exchange 2½ per cent.

Three months later, when Paris owes at Lyons, and the exchange there has risen to 3 per cent above par, his correspondent will carry out the same manoeuvre. So it is that, in a few months, they will each have made a gain of 2½ or 3 per cent by drawing bills on each other.

Note that to have drawn these bills of exchange they did not run down their assets; because, when the Paris banker paid a hundred thousand francs, the Lyons banker received them; and in his turn the Paris banker received them when the Lyons banker paid them. Beyond the gain on exchange, they therefore also have the product of these hundred thousand francs which they continue to put to use.

The fact is that a bill of exchange is bought with ready money and is paid on account. You give a hundred thousand francs today to have access to a hundred thousand in a month. The Lyons banker thus has the enjoyment for a month of the product of the hundred thousand francs you have counted out to him; and the Paris banker has the enjoyment at the same time of the product of the hundred thousand which he will only pay you in a month's time.

Such are the great speculations we admire because we are drawn to admiration when we understand nothing of what is occurring. We all resemble that master I mentioned who was amazed at his agent's intelligence.

The principles which we have given for exchange between the different towns of a kingdom are the same for exchange from nation to nation. But one uses a different language, because the monies have neither the same values, nor the same denominations. A banker will say to you: "The rate of exchange in Paris for London is sixty sous for twenty-nine, thirty-one, thirty-two pence sterling," and in this language you cannot judge at all if the exchange is at par, above or below, because you do not know what a penny sterling is worth.

Yet again he will say to you that the rate of exchange in Paris for Amsterdam is three livres for fifty-four guilders of Holland, or for sixty. In a word, he will always speak to you in a language you do not understand. You would understand him if he said to you: "The sum which you want to send to London contains so many ounces of silver. Today the exchange is at par. Here is a bill with which you will receive the same quantity of ounces at London in English coin, and they will count out to you so many pounds sterling." That is how he himself evaluates the different countries' monies. Because he well knows that from Paris to London or to Amsterdam, as from Paris to Lyons, the exchange is at par when one gives a hundred ounces for a hundred ounces, that it is above par when one gives more, and that it is below when one gives less.

I do not know why bankers affect an obscure language. But it is certain that this language prevents us seeing clearly into their operations; and that it cuts down the number of their rivals, because it leads one to believe that banking is a very difficult science. In my powerlessness to know all the means they deploy to make huge profits, I shall only speak of those which I perceive in the nature of the business.

Let us say that in Paris I am asked to transfer a thousand ounces of silver to Amsterdam, when the exchange is 6 per cent above par; and then let us suppose it is at 4 per cent above par in Paris for London, and at 2 per cent below par in London for Amsterdam. In such a situation one can see that there is a much greater profit in drawing first of all on London, in order to draw next from London on Amsterdam, rather than to draw directly from Paris on Amsterdam.

A banker's skill therefore sometimes consists in taking a roundabout rather than a direct route.

A person brings to my establishment a thousand ounces of silver that Paris owes in London, and only 4 per cent is paid for the transfer. But because I have credit in England, instead of sending this sum there, I send bills of exchange. So I gain, at one and the same time, both the 4 per cent the person has initially paid me and the interest that a thousand ounces of silver brings in France. As long as my credit can make this debt last, I shall repeat the same operation, and I shall be able to make it worth two, three, four thousand ounces of silver profit or more to me.

Interest in Holland is lower than in France, and the dealers of that republic have often much more silver than they can use in trade. If I am accredited among them, people will seek me out to have bills of exchange on Amsterdam. I will draw as many as I am requested: the money I have received will stay in my hands more or less long term: I shall pay interest in Holland at 2½ or 3 per cent, and I shall draw it in France at 5 to 6 per cent. In that way, I shall continually draw profit from sums that are not mine. The richer I become, the more I shall be trusted and the more I shall find profit in my business. I shall carry on banking almost on my own.

There you have a slight idea of the profits that one can make in exchange dealing. You can see that if the art of drawing profit from the land had made as much progress as that of putting money to use, our cultivators would not be as poor as they are.

## ⁓ 18 Of Lending at Interest

A FARMER, who takes land on a lease, exchanges his work for a part of the product, and gives the other part to the landowner, and that is in the order of things.

Now would the borrower be in the same position as the farmer? Or does money have a yield of which the borrower owes the lender a part?

A septier of corn can produce twenty, thirty or more according to the goodness of the soil and the hard work of the cultivator.

Indubitably money does not reproduce itself in the same manner. But it is not with corn that we should compare it: it is with land, which does not reproduce itself any more than money.

Now in commerce, money yields a return according to the effort of the person who borrows it, just as the land yields one according to the hard work of the farmer.

Indeed, an entrepreneur can only maintain his trade in so far as the money, with which he makes advances, comes back continuously to him with a return in which he finds his subsistence and that of the workers he employs, that is to say, a wage for them and a wage for him.

If he were alone, he would make the most of the demand people had for the articles he sells, and he would bring this return to the highest point.

But as soon as many entrepreneurs carry on the same trade, forced to undercut each other, they make do with a smaller wage and those whom they employ are reduced to smaller gains. Thus competition regulates the return they can reasonably draw from the advances they have made; advances which are for them what the expenses of cultivation are for the farmers.

If commerce could only be carried on by entrepreneurs who were rich enough to provide the capital for it, a small number would carry it on exclusively. Less under pressure from competition to sell at a discount, they would put their wage at a rate that would be all the higher because they would be less pushed to sell their goods, and because it would be easy for them to get together to wait for the moment when they could take advantage of the citizens' needs. Then their wage could be taken to 100 per cent or more.

But if in contrast commerce is carried on by entrepreneurs to whom people have given advances from their stock, they will be under pressure to sell in order to be able to pay out as their obligation falls due. It will therefore not be in their power to await, from one day to the next, the moment when people will have the greatest need of their goods, and competition will force them all the more to make do with a smaller wage because, being more numerous and for the most part under pressure to make money, it will be harder for them to take concerted action. One cannot doubt that it is desirable for commerce to be carried on by such entrepreneurs.

Now I assume that, having subtracted all the expenses of commerce, there is a general net residue, to form the wage of each entrepreneur, of 15 to 20 per cent.

How will a man manage who has no property, and yet who could with hard work carry on some branch of commerce? He has only two openings. Someone must lend him a stock of merchandise, or someone must lend him the money to buy it, and it is clear that these two possibilities come down to the same thing.

He approaches a rich businessman who says to him: "I am going to advance you what I should have given you for one hundred ounces of silver if you had been able to pay me in ready money, and in a year you will give me one hundred and ten ounces for it."

He accepts this offer, in which he sees a profit of 5 to 10 per cent for himself out of the 15 to 20 per cent that one may customarily earn when one owns one's own capital.

No one will condemn this transaction, which is freely made and is at one and the same time advantageous to both contracting parties, and which, by multiplying the number of merchants, increases competition, an absolute necessity if trade is to benefit the state.

No one will deny the rich businessman the right to demand interest for advances which he runs the risk of losing. He counts, as a matter of fact, on the honesty and the hard work of those to whom he has made them; but he can be deceived: he is sometimes: it is necessary for those who pay him to compensate him for the losses he makes with the others. Would it be fair to condemn him to make advances on which he would often lose, without his ever being able to compensate himself? He would certainly never make the advances.

Besides, you cannot deny that a merchant who advances a stock of merchandise has a right to reserve to himself a share in the profits which this stock must produce; he who before advancing the stock had the sole right to the profits.

Now we have just noted that to advance an entrepreneur a stock of merchandise, or to advance him the money he needs to buy that stock is the same thing. If one is in the right to demand interest in the first case, one then has the same right in the other case.

It is a fact that the interest-bearing loan sustains commerce. It has besides been shown that it increases the number of merchants; that in increasing them, it increases competition; that in increasing competition, it makes commerce more profitable to the state. The loan at interest is therefore equitable, and must be allowed.

I know that the casuists condemn it when it is made in money; but I also know that they do not condemn it when it is made in goods. They allow a businessman to lend at 10 per cent, say, merchandise to the value of a thousand ounces of silver; but they do not allow him to lend, at the same interest rate, the thousand ounces in kind.

When I say that the casuists allow the loan of goods at 10 per cent I do not wish to accuse them of using this language, "to lend at 10 per cent": they would be contradicting themselves too palpably. I mean to say that they allow a businessman to sell for 10 per cent more the goods that he advances for a year. One can see that the contradiction is less palpable.

Our legislators, if that were possible, reason even worse than the casuists. They condemn the loan at interest, and they allow it. They condemn it without knowing why, and they allow it because they are forced to. Their laws, the outcome of ignorance and prejudice, are useless if they are not observed; and if they are observed they damage trade.

The error into which the casuists and the legislators fall comes uniquely from the confused notions they have formed. In effect, they do not blame the exchange market, and they blame the loan at interest. But why should money have a price in one that it does not have in the other? The loan and the borrowing, are they anything other than an exchange? If, in the exchange market, one exchanges sums of money where the loan or the sum borrowed are separated in place, cannot one exchange sums of money which are separated in time? And because these distances are not of the same kind, must one conclude that the exchange in the one case is not an exchange in the other? So one does not see that to lend at interest is to sell; that to borrow at interest is to buy; that the money one lends is the goods which are sold; that the money one must give back is the price which is paid; and that the interest is the profit to the seller. Certainly, if one had only seen in the loan at interest, goods, sale and profit, one would not have condemned it; but one has only seen the words *loan, interest, money;* and without reflecting too much on what they mean, one has judged that they should not go together.

Interest at 10 per cent is only an assumption that I make, because I needed to make one. It can be higher, as it can be lower: it is a matter on which the legislator must not reach any decision if he does not want to harm liberty. Custom, which regulates this interest, will cause it to vary, according to circumstances, and the variations must be allowed. Observe how it must of necessity rise and fall in turn.

It will be high, however plentiful money may be, if there are many people wanting to borrow, and if there are few who want to lend.

If those who have money, or who own most of it, need it themselves to support enterprises in which they are engaged, they will only be able to lend by abandoning their enterprises, and it follows that they will only lend when they are assured of a profit equal to, or larger than, the one that they would have made. One will therefore have to give them a lot of interest.

But, even at a time when money is scarce, the rate of interest will be low if money is mainly in the hands of a large number of economical landowners who seek to place it.

Interest rises and falls in turn, in the proportion that the money that people wish to borrow is to the money on offer for loan. Now this proportion can vary all the time.

In a time when rich landowners make very great outlays of every kind, one will borrow more; firstly because the landowners will themselves often be forced to contract loans; and secondly, because to provide for all the consumption they make, a larger number of entrepreneurs will be established, or of men who for the most part need to borrow. That is one of the reasons why interest is higher in France than in Holland.

On the other hand, in a period when more economical landowners spend less, there will be fewer borrowers: for instead of their having to contract loans themselves, they will have money to lend; and since they will consume less, they will reduce the number of entrepreneurs and, consequently, of borrowers. There you have one of the reasons why interest is lower in Holland than in France.

If a new kind of consumption gives rise to a new branch of commerce, entrepreneurs will not fail to multiply in proportion as they believe they can promise themselves much greater profits; and the interest on money will go up because the number of borrowers will be greater.*

If this branch of trade collapses the money will come back to those who lent it, they will seek to place it a second time, and the interest rate will go down, because the number of lenders will have grown.

If entrepreneurs carry on their business with as much careful management as hard work, they will bit by bit become owners of the sums they borrowed. So they will have to be removed from the number of borrowers and added to the number of lenders when they have gained more than the money they need to carry on their commercial activities.†

Finally, laws will increase the number of lenders when they permit interest-bearing loans. Today, in contrast, they tend to reduce the number.

But it is pointless to seek to provide an exhaustive account of all the factors which cause variation in the ratio of the demand for money to borrow to that on offer for loan: I have said enough to show that interest rates must sometimes be higher, sometimes lower.

Just as prices settle themselves in the market place, following the haggling of sellers and buyers, so the rate of interest, or the price of money, is fixed in the places of trade following the haggling of borrowers and lenders. The government recognises that it is not its function to make laws to fix the price of goods which are sold in the market; why then should it think it ought to fix the rate of interest or the price of money?

---

*Is it really true, I have been asked, that growth of commerce raises the interest rate? I reply that it necessarily makes it rise if it increases the number of borrowers. Now that is what can happen and what I assume.

†There you have a case where the growth of commerce causes the rate of interest to fall.

To make a wise law on this subject, it would need to grasp the ratio of the quantity of money available to lend to the demand for borrowing. But since this ratio forever varies it will not grasp it, or it will only hold it for a moment and by chance; it will therefore need to keep on making new regulations without ever being sure it is doing good: or if it persists in wanting to enforce those it has made, because it does not know how to make others, it will only disturb commerce. People will escape these regulations in secret markets; and the interest rate, which it claimed the right to fix, will rise all the more, as the lenders, having the law against them, will lend with less security.

In contrast, in commercial centres, interest will always regulate itself well, without interference, because it is there that the offers of lenders and the demands of borrowers make apparent the ratio of money to lend to money to borrow.

Not only can interest rates vary from one day to another, they also vary according to the type of trade. That is what we still have to examine.

A merchant who has borrowed to raise the stock for a shop has to earn, over and above his subsistence, the wherewithal to pay the interest he owes. If he has formed a large concern, which he directs with hard work, his outlay to maintain it will be small beer compared with the profits he can make. He will therefore be all the more in a position to pay what he owes: one will therefore run fewer risks in lending to him; one will therefore lend to him with more confidence, and, consequently, at lower interest rates.

But if, with a trade that produces little, he barely earns his subsistence, then what he needs for his subsistence is a high proportion of what he earns. There is therefore no longer the same security in lending to him. Now it is natural that the interest which lenders demand increases in proportion as their confidence falls.

In Paris, the retailers from the Halles pay five sols interest a week for an écu of three livres. This interest puts up the price of the fish they sell in the streets; but the people prefer to buy from them than to go to the Halles to stock up.

On a yearly basis this interest comes to more than 430 per cent. However exorbitant it is, the government puts up with it, because it is profitable for the retailers to be able to carry on their trade at this price, or perhaps again because it cannot stop it.

However, the price that the lender places on his money, and the profit that the retailer makes, are out of all proportion. That is why this interest is hateful; and it becomes all the more open to abuse as the loans are made secretly.

It is not the same with loans made to entrepreneurs who carry on a large-scale business. The interest demanded, proportional to the profits they make, is regulated by custom; because money in the commercial centres has a current price, just as corn has one in the markets. People deal openly, or at least do not hide themselves, and a person sells his money as one would sell any other good.

It is only in the commercial centres that one can learn what rate of interest one may draw from one's money. Every loan which conforms to that rate of interest is honest because it is in line.

If you ask me what is usury nowadays, I say that there is none in the loans of which I have just spoken, and which adjust themselves to the price that the dealers themselves have placed on the money, and have placed freely.

But the loans made to the retailers of the Halles are usurious, because they are without rules and underhand, and the greed of the lender rides rough-shod over the need of the borrower.

In general, every loan between merchants and dealers is usurious when the interest that is extracted is higher than the rate which has been publicly fixed in the commercial centres. But when loans are made to individuals who do not carry out any trade or business, by what rule can one judge the interest one may extract from one's money? The law. It is here, I think, that the government can without inconvenience set interest. It even ought to do it, and it would be an act beneficial to the state if it made borrowing more difficult. Let it only allow loans at the lowest rate of interest to owners of lands; fathers of families would have less scope to ruin themselves, and money would flow back into trade. Let it tax usury, or let it cover with a still more stigmatising note every loan, even at 1 per cent, made to a son who borrows without his family's consent. Let it forbid underhand loans; or, if it cannot prevent them, let it give help itself to the entrepreneurs who are in the lowest class of merchants. In a word, while leaving the freedom to borrow in commercial centres, let it check it wherever it can degenerate into abuse. Doubtless it would not be easy to carry out this design but it would be useful to concern itself with it.

[*A revised conclusion to the chapter in place of the above final paragraph* When one considers the loans in these two extremes, it is easy to understand where usury lies: it will not be as easy to determine where it begins, if one considers in this interval the different prices money can have. Because, in commercial centres, this price is fixed between dealers who know each other to be solvent, would that be a reason to lend at the same price to a merchant whose affairs are in disorder? If so, no one will lend to him, and he will be utterly ruined. It seems that in such a case the risks one runs allow one to demand a higher price than that of the market place. Now what is this price? It is bound to vary according to the degree of confidence that the borrower's honesty and hard work inspire. It is therefore impossible to predetermine it, and the government must leave well alone.

If trade were perfectly free, secrecy, which is the hallmark of a dishonest action, would be the true character of usury, and the fear of being found out would be the biggest restraint on it. Nowadays, when the law forbids an interest rate that it ought to allow, secrecy means nothing, since one only hides from a law which is held in contempt. People avoid it openly, they are even forced to. Usurious loans, as defined by this law, are authorised by practice which regards them as legitimate, and they are well known in all sorts of loans: people no longer fear opprobrium, and they end up demanding interest publicly.

But is it only the price of money that can be usurious? Cannot the price of every other good be equally so? Is not a merchant a usurer when he abuses my trust or my need in order to gain from me more than he should? Doubtless he is, and he is so with impunity. Now why does the government wish that it should only be the money merchants who cannot take interest, and why nevertheless, contradicting itself, does it allow it to the bankers? It would do better to tolerate in every instance what it cannot prevent.]

# 19 Of the Comparative Value of the Metals
## from Which Coins Are Made

COPPER, SILVER and gold which one uses in coinage have, like all merchandise, a value based on their utility; and that value increases or diminishes according to whether one reckons them to be scarcer or in greater abundance.

Let us suppose that in Europe there is a hundred times more copper than silver, and twenty times more silver than gold. With this assumption, where we only consider these metals with reference to quantity, it will take a hundred pounds of copper to make a value equivalent to a pound of silver, and twenty pounds of silver to make a value equal to a pound of gold. So one will express these relationships by saying that copper is to silver as a hundred is to one, and that silver is to gold as twenty is to one.

But if mines are found that are very plentiful in silver and especially in gold, these metals will no longer have the same relative value. Copper, for example, will be to silver as fifty is to one, and silver will be to gold as ten is to one.

In commerce there cannot always be an unchanged quantity of each of these metals. Their relative value must therefore vary from one time to another. However, it does not only vary by reason of the quantity, because if the quantity remains the same, there is another cause which can make these metals scarcer or more abundant.

Indeed, the use one makes of a metal may be more or less common. If one used copper in most of the utensils for which one uses earth, the metal would become scarcer; and instead of being to silver in the ratio of fifty to one, it could be in the ratio of thirty to one. On the other hand, if in our kitchens we came to use iron instead of copper pots, it would become more plentiful and would be to silver as eighty is to one.

It is then not only by the quantity that we judge the abundance or the rarity of a good: it is by the quantity considered in relation to the uses to which we put it. Now, it is clear that this relative quantity diminishes, in step with our using the good for a greater number of tasks; and that it increases as we use it for a smaller number.

We shall reason likewise about gold and silver. That when these metals are in the ratio of twenty to one, and the practice comes in of lavishing silver on movable goods and on clothes, silver will become scarcer, and could be in the ratio of ten to one with gold. But should one then come to prefer gold and silver on movable goods and on clothes, gold in its turn will become scarcer, and will be in the ratio of one to fifteen with silver.

Metals are thus rarer or more plentiful, depending on whether we use them for more or fewer purposes. In consequence we can only judge their relative value in so far as we can compare the uses we make of the one with those we make of the other.

But how are we to judge these uses and compare them? By the amount of each of these metals that people ask for in the market. Because one only buys goods in so far as one wants to use them. The relative value of these metals is therefore appraised in the markets. In truth it is not done so geometrically: it cannot be done with exact precision. But in the end the markets alone make the rule, and the government is obliged to follow it.

If this value must vary from time to time, such variations are never abrupt, since habits always change slowly. So in the long term, gold and silver keep the same value in relation to each other.

Between neighbouring peoples, trade tends to make the same goods equally plentiful in each one as in the others; and in consequence it gives them all the same value; it succeeds in this especially when they are, like gold and silver, transportable with ease and without hindrance. The position is that then they circulate among many nations as they would in a single nation; and they sell in all the markets as if they were selling in a single common market.

Let us assume that the states of Europe are all in the habit of forbidding the export and import of gold and silver, and that this prohibition has had its effect.

Let us assume again that there is the same quantity of gold in England as in France, but more silver in one of the kingdoms than in the other. Finally, let us assume that in Holland there is much more gold than anywhere else, and much less silver.

With these assumptions, where the quantity of gold relative to silver is different from one state to another, the relative value of these metals cannot be the same in the markets of the three nations. Gold, for example, will have one price in France, one in Holland, another in England.

But if one allows these metals to circulate freely among the peoples of Europe, then one will not value them according to the ratio they bear to each other in France, in Holland, or in England; but one will value them according to the relationship they bear to each other in all the nations taken together. Although unequally divided, they will be considered to be in the same quantity everywhere, because whatever surplus there is in gold, for instance, in a state today, can leave it and pass tomorrow into another. There you have the reason why in all the markets of Europe one judges the ratio of gold and silver as one would judge it in a single common market.

You can see how the relative value of gold and silver is estimated in the same way in several states, when these metals can pass freely from the one to the other. But when distant nations cannot have continuous trade between each other, and so to speak daily trade, then this value is reckoned differently in each, because it is fixed in markets which have not enough contact with each other, and from which, for that reason, one could not form a single common market. In Japan, for example, gold is to silver as one is to eight, while in Europe it is as one to fourteen and a half, or one to fifteen.

I have said that markets set the law for government. To understand this, let us assume that in all the markets of Europe, gold is to silver as one is to fourteen, and that none the less the government in France values these metals in the ratio of one to fifteen, and let us see what must ensue.

In France you will need fifteen ounces of silver to buy one ounce of gold; while abroad, you will pay for an ounce of gold with fourteen ounces of silver: on fifteen ounces of silver you will therefore gain an ounce each time that you carry silver abroad to change it against gold, and consequently silver will gradually slip out of the kingdom. When later the government wants to bring it back, it will again lose a fifteenth; since, for one ounce of gold, one would only give fourteen ounces of silver. Now it would avoid all these losses if it conformed to the price of the common market.

WE HAVE JUST seen how the price of gold and of silver settles itself at the same point in all the markets of several nations when these metals can pass continuously without obstacle from one to another. By reasoning according to the same principles, it will be easy for us to judge the true price of each thing.

I assume that, in a large country like France, the provinces are forbidden all trade with each other, and yet that there are some where the harvest is never adequate, others where, in ordinary years, it only furnishes what is needed for consumption, and others where there is almost always a surplus. This is what must happen.

Let us first consider a province where the harvests are never adequate. If we assume that internal trade enjoys complete freedom there, all its markets will communicate with each other; and, in consequence, foodstuffs will be sold in each separately, as though they all came to be sold in a common market. Because from one nearby place to another, it can be known in each what they sell for in all, it will not be possible to sell foodstuffs in one at a much higher price than in the others. In a similar way gold has the same price, near enough, in all the markets of Europe.

In this province the harvests are never adequate, that is what we have assumed; and, since we assume also that it has forbidden itself all external trade, it follows that the other provinces cannot make up what it lacks.

That being so, corn will be at an even higher price as there will be less of it, while more will be required; and because it is an imperative that the inhabitants reduce themselves to the number that the province can feed, it will infallibly lose population.

In a province where there is almost always surplus, supposing perfectly free internal commerce, corn will sell in all the markets at near enough the same price, because, as in the first province, it will sell as if it were being sold in a single common market.

We have assumed that this province too is forbidden all external trade.

Therefore it cannot export. Its corn therefore will be at all the lower a price, because it has more, and it needs less.

This surplus being at the expense of the cultivator who cannot sell a larger quantity of corn, and who nevertheless sells it at a lower price, he will cease to plough and sow a part of his fields.

He will even be compelled to do that, because with the feeble profit he makes on the corn he sells, he will be all the less able to enter into the great expenses of cultivation, as the day-labourer who, through the low price of bread, earns in one day his subsistence for two, will not want to work every day or will demand higher wages.

It is therefore bound to happen that crops in this province will diminish to place them in proportion with the population; just as in the other the population has fallen to place it in proportion with the crops.

Finally, let us consider a province where the crops in normal years produce exactly what is needed for consumption; and let us assume for it, as with the two others, completely free internal trade and no external trade.

Since in normal years this province only harvests exactly what it needs, there will be dearth in some years and surplus in others. The price of corn will therefore vary from year to year; but in normal years it will be lower than in the province where we have assumed that the harvest is never sufficient, and it will be higher than in the province where we have assumed that the harvest is almost always in surplus.

In this province, the land under the plough and the population will be able to keep themselves at the same levels, or near enough. The province will simply be exposed to great variations in prices, as we assume that no one will bring it cereals when it lacks them, and that it will not export them when it has too much.

In these three provinces we have three different price levels: in the first, a high price; in the third, a low price; and in the second, a moderate price.

Therefore it is not possible that any of these prices can be at the same time the true price of corn for all the provinces, that is to say, the price that they should all give for it.

Each province values corn according to the relationship it perceives, or believes it sees, between the quantity and the demand. If it judges that the quantity is insufficient, the price is high; if it judges that it is sufficient, the price is low.

I call *proportional* the prices which establish themselves on such relationships. By this we see that whatever the prices are, they are always proportional, since they are always founded on the view which people have of the quantity relative to the need. But the price which is current in one of our provinces, although proportional within it, would be disproportional in the others, and could not suit them.

The price of cereals is only so different in the three provinces because we have forbidden all trade between them. The price will thus no longer differ if we allow them the freedom to export reciprocally to each other.

Indeed, if they trade freely, the same will happen in the markets which are held in all three as happened in the markets which were held in each individually. They will communicate with each other, and the corn will sell in all at the same price as if it was being sold in a single common market. Then this price, the same for all three, and at the same time proportional for each, will be that which it is equally right for all three to give to the corn; and, consequently, it will be the true price for all three.

This price is the one which will be most beneficial to the province whose soil, by its nature, has a surplus product; because it will sell the grain it does not consume, and it will no longer be in the position of abandoning some of its cultivated land to bring its crops into balance with its consumption.

This price is just as beneficial to the province whose soil is naturally not very fertile; because it will buy the grain it lacks, and will no longer be in the situation of losing people to bring its population into balance with its harvests.

Finally, this price will be no less advantageous to the province whose soil only supplies, in normal years, just what is needed for its consumption. It will no longer be open to seeing its grain rise or fall excessively, suddenly and as if by shocks; because in surplus it will be able to sell at the price of the common market, and in dearth it will be able to buy at the same price. In a word, this price of corn, this true price, will make the surplus of one province flow constantly into another, and will spread abundance in all.

I say, *that it will spread abundance in all*. It is the case that a poor harvest will not be able to cause dearth even in the least fertile province, because this province receives the cereals which are surplus elsewhere since, through the freedom that trade enjoys, they will always be ready to enter it.

When I say that it buys at the same price as the others, it is that I consider the purchases in the common market, where the price is the same for all three; and I exclude the transport costs which it will have to pay on top. I do not say, like some writers, that transport costs are not part of the price of corn; because one would certainly not pay these costs if one did not judge that the corn was worth the incurring of them. But I set them aside, because to judge the true price, which must be the same for all the provinces, one must only consider the purchases and sales in the common market. I may add that this market is always held in the province where the corn is in surplus, or in the one which is placed to act as a depot for all. It is to that market that people come from all over to buy.

My line of argument on these three provinces could be extended to a larger number, to all those of France for example: and then one would see that free trade between them would establish a price, at one and the same time, the same for all and proportional in each, which in consequence would be the true price for France or the most beneficial for all her provinces.

One has no idea what is the true price of corn in Europe and one cannot know it. There is a price, in each nation, which is the true price for it; but it is so only for it. Each has its own price, and of all these prices none could be at one and the same time proportional in all the others; and consequently, none could be the true price for all equally.

If, in a time when the English and the French do not trade together at all, harvests are in surplus in England but are inadequate in France, two prices will prevail, both based on quantity in relation to need; and both different, since the quantity relative to the need is not the same in France and in England. Neither of these prices will therefore be at one and the same time proportional for both nations; neither will be equally beneficial for both; neither will be the true price for both.

But if the English and the French should trade with each other in complete and utter freedom, the corn that is surplus in England would pour into France; and because then the quantities in relation to need would be the same in each monarchy, a price would evolve which would be the same for both countries, and this would be the true price for both, as it would be equally beneficial to them.

One can see from that how important it is for all the nations of Europe to lift the obstacles which for the most part they place on export and import.

It is not possible for harvests to be equally bad in every country in the same year: no more is it possible that they should all be equally good in every country in the same year. Now uninhibited trade, which would make the surplus circulate, would produce the same effect as if the harvests were good everywhere, that is to say as if they were sufficient for consumption everywhere. Corn, with transport costs deducted, would have the same price in the whole of Europe: this price would be permanent and the most advantageous for all nations.

But when they forbid import and export, or when they place on them both duties which have the effect of a prohibition; when in allowing export they forbid import, or in allowing import they forbid export; finally, when in the guise of behaving differently in different circumstances, they forbid what they have allowed, they allow what they have forbidden, turn by turn, suddenly, without principles, without rules, because they have none, and can have none: then it is impossible for corn to have a price which is the same and the true price throughout Europe; it is impossible for it to bear any relation to the permanent price. And so one sees it rise to an excessive price in one nation, while it falls to a paltry price in another.

It is not that the true price can be exactly the same year in, year out; doubtless it must vary, but it would always maintain itself between two limits, which are little apart from each other: that is what must be explained.

We have remarked that crops could not be equally good or equally bad in the whole of Europe. But one can appreciate that there will sometimes be years when they are generally more plentiful, and that sometimes too there will be other years when they will generally be less so. The true price of corn will therefore sometimes rise and sometimes fall.

It will fall in the greatest general abundance in proportion as the amount of corn is greater than consumption; and in a lesser general abundance it will rise to the extent that the amount of grain approaches what is consumed.

I say that it *will rise in a lesser general abundance* and I do not say in a dearth, because it would be really extraordinary for there to be bad years throughout the whole of Europe. There can only be better years than others; and it is those better years that will cause the price of corn to fall.

In ordinary years, if all its provinces traded freely with each other, Europe should harvest as much grain as she consumes, because land under the plough should adjust to consumption. The price of corn should thus be permanently based on a like quantity relative to demand, and in consequence it would always be the same.

Now let us assume that corn was at twenty-four livres the septier: in great and widespread abundance it could fall to twenty-two, to twenty, or, if you like, to eighteen. But certainly general abundance will never be great enough to let it fall to a rockbottom price.

Likewise, in a lesser general abundance the price may rise to twenty-six, twenty-eight or thirty. But the scarcity will never be great enough all round to raise it to an excessive price. I even find it hard to believe that it could vary from eighteen to thirty since these limits seem to me very far apart.

In contrast, when the nations of Europe forbid each other trade by clear prohibitions or equivalent duties, one can imagine that the price of corn can vary, turn and turn about, now with one, now with another, to the point where it will be impossible to set a limit to the highest and the lowest price. The same people will see corn fall suddenly to ten livres or rise to fifty. Let us stop there on the fatal consequences of these variations.

When corn is at ten livres, the farmer sells more than when it is at fifty, because people consume more. But it is only at ten livres because there is far more of it than he can sell and this surplus is valueless for him. Yet he finds no compensation in the corn he does sell, since he sells it at a rockbottom price. So he has worked the land and he has drawn no profit. It may even be that he will not recoup the expenses of cultivation.

It is therefore not in his interests to sow as much land as he would have done.

Even if he wanted to, he could not. He is not in a position to make the outlay.

"He is not in a position," I say, "to make the outlay": firstly, because he has not gained enough on the sale of his corn; secondly, because the day-labourers who, as we have already noted, gain in one day enough to live on for two, work half as much. They will thus be scarcer and, being scarcer, they will cost more. Thus the expenses rise for the farmer as his profit falls.

So he has sown less, and consequently the crop will be smaller; and it will be reduced to very little if the year is a bad one.

The surplus of the previous harvest will make it up, you will say. My response is that if the cultivator had been able to sell it abroad, he would have drawn a greater profit from the sale of his cereals, because he would have sold them at a better price and in larger quantity. He would have been in a position to sow more land. He would have found it in his interest, and the harvest would have been more plentiful.

He could not store his surplus corn without expense and loss; and it is without expense and without loss that he would have kept the money he would have received from it. He would therefore be richer with that money than he is with the surplus corn left on his hands. The surest and least costly way to keep the corn is to keep it in money; since to keep the money is to keep the corn, as with money one can always buy it. Why force the farmer to build barns, to leave the plough to inspect his grain, and to pay farm hands to turn it over? If he is not rich enough to make these expenditures, his corn will germinate, it will be eaten by insects, and the surplus on which he had counted will no longer be found.

We also note that dearth always comes after abundance, and that when cereals have been at a rock-bottom price, they suddenly move to an excessive price. Now that price, burdensome to the people, does not recompense the cultivator for whom a bad crop leaves all the less corn to sell, as he only sowed a part of his land.

We have noted that when corn is at a rockbottom price, the day-labourers price themselves too high; we shall note here that when it is at an excessive price, they price themselves too low.

In the first case, as it takes little to earn the wherewithal to buy bread, several labourers spend days without working. On the other hand, in the second case, they all vie with each other for work, they want it every day, and they offer themselves on the cheap. Further, many offer themselves in vain. The cultivators, feeling the losses they have incurred, are not rich enough to employ all those who come forward.

In these times of variation, wages are thus necessarily too high or too low;

and that is true for all: because the craftsman, like the day-labourer, sells his labour on the cheap when bread is dear; and when bread is cheap, he offers his work to the highest bidder.

During this disorder everyone's fortunes are disturbed to a greater or lesser extent. Most people cut back on their needs. Rich men at least cut back on their extras. Many workers lack work, manufactures collapse, and one sees misery spread in the countryside and in the towns, which trade could have made to flourish.

If trade enjoyed complete and entire freedom, always and everywhere, the true price of grain would necessarily establish itself, and it would be permanent: then disorder would cease. Wages, which would proportion themselves to the permanent price of corn, would set all types of work at their true price. The cultivator would better judge the outlays he has to make, and he would be all the less afraid to involve himself in them, as he would be guaranteed to recover his expenses and his profit from his crops. I can say as much of the entrepreneurs in every kind of business. They will all employ a greater number of workers, because they will all have the means and all will be assured of the profit due to their work. So no more idle hands. People will be at work equally in the towns and the countryside: they will not be reduced to cutting back on essentials: they will on the contrary be able to acquire new pleasures for themselves, and commerce will be as flourishing as it can be.

You will perhaps ask by what one can recognise the true price. You will recognise it in that its fluctuation will be between two closely set points, and it is in this sense that I call it permanent. If it only varied, for instance, between twenty and twenty-four, it would be low at twenty, high at twenty-four, and middling at twenty-two. Every other price would be a false price, which would take the name of *dearness* when it rose above twenty-four; and which would take that of *cheapness* when it fell below twenty. This false price would be bound to cause disorders, because in cheapness the producer would be damaged, and the consumer would be damaged in dearness. Now the true price must be equally beneficial to everyone.

To be the sole seller is to create a monopoly. This word which has become odious should not always be. A great painter may sell his works alone, because he alone can create them.

He takes his wage to the highest point: it has no other regulation than the wealth of the admirers who are interested in his paintings.

Do you dream of being painted by him, because he makes perfect likenesses, and always in fine style? He will ask a hundred louis for a portrait, or even more, if at this price people request more than he can paint. His interest is to earn plenty, while making few portraits; to make few, so as to make them better, and that way to secure his reputation all the more.

This price may appear exorbitant. However, it is not: it is the true price. It is ruled by an agreement made freely between the painter and the sitter, and no one is hurt. Are you not rich enough to pay a hundred louis for your portrait? Do not have it made, you can do without it. Are you rich enough? It is for you to see whether you prefer to keep your hundred louis or to exchange them for your portrait.

This price, because it is the true price, is based on the quantity in relation to the need. Here the need is the dream you have of being painted; and the quantity is one, since we assume just one painter who catches likenesses to your taste. Therefore the greater your fancy, the more the painter will be entitled to demand a very large wage from you. Should your portrait cost you a thousand louis it would not be dear, that is to say, above the true price.

One must not reason about the pleasures one obtains through fancy, whim, fashion in the same way as about those which are of absolute necessity. If you were the only corn merchant, and you made me pay a hundred francs the septier, you would not be able to say that you had sold it to me in accordance with an agreement freely entered into between us; it would be clear that I have been forced by need, and that you have cruelly abused your position. There is a monopoly which becomes detestable, since it is unjust.

In trade in essential goods, the price, when it is the true one, is permanent; and it is by that, as we have already noted, that it is recognised.

In trade in inessentials, the price is not at all permanent: it cannot be, it varies like fashions. Today one article is in vogue, tomorrow another. Soon, in place of one competitor there are several. So, compelled to limit himself to lower wages, he sells at a lower price what he previously sold at a high price. We have seen snuff-boxes of papier mâché at two or three louis which nowadays are at twenty-four sols. Despite this variation they have always been at their true price. It is a fact that the price of fancy goods cannot settle, and that it can be very high in comparison with that of necessities.

Since in the trade in necessities the true price is a permanent price, it is clear that it cannot live with monopoly, which would make it rise sharply stroke upon stroke. But if the person who is the sole seller causes prices to rise, multiplying the sellers will be enough to make them fall.

Now sellers will multiply of their own accord when no obstacles are placed in the way. As every type of trade offers a profit, it is not to be feared that this will not happen. If one leaves it free to happen, it will happen, and the number of merchants will grow, so long as carrying on the trade concurrently, they find enough profit to subsist. If they were to multiply too much, as must sometimes happen, a portion will abandon a trade which is not profitable to them, and exactly the right number of merchants will remain. Once more one must not interfere: if there are monopolists, freedom will purge society of them.

Every seller wants to gain, and to gain as much as he can. There is not one who would not like to push aside all his rivals and sell alone if he could.

Every purchaser would like to buy at the lowest price, and he would wish that the sellers, vying with each other, would offer him goods at a discount.

However, each seller in one capacity is a buyer in another. If it matters to him to be without rivals, it matters to him that the sellers, from whom he buys, have plenty of them; and it is no less important to the latter that he is not alone.

From these contrary interests, it follows that the interest of all is not to sell at the highest price and buy at the lowest, but to sell and buy at the true price. This true price is thus the only one which reconciles the interests of all the members of society. Now it will only be able to establish itself when, in every branch of trade, there is the greatest possible number of merchants.

As we have noticed, it is only great artists, unique of their kind, who can make a monopoly without injustice. By virtue of their talents they have the privilege of selling alone.

But when it is a matter of trade in essentials, where, happily, rare talents are not needed, I understand by monopolists a small number of merchants who buy and sell exclusively; and I say that there is monopoly, and in consequence injustice and disorder, whenever this number is not as large as it might be.

Nowadays all the commerce in Europe is therefore carried on by monopolists. I do not wish to speak of the customs, tolls and exclusive privileges which impede internal trade from province to province: we shall deal with these abuses elsewhere. I am only referring to the obstacles placed in the way of commerce between nation and nation.

When in France we prohibit the import of English goods, we reduce the number of merchants who would have sold to us; and in consequence our native merchants become monopolists, who sell at a higher price than they would have done if they had been selling alongside English merchants.

When we forbid export to England, we reduce for the English the number of merchants who would have sold to them; and in consequence those who sell to them become monopolists, who make them pay for goods at a higher price than they would have done if they had sold alongside our merchants.

Let us apply this reasoning everywhere that the government forbids exporting and importing, and we shall recognise that the nations seem to have forgotten their true interests, in order to concern themselves merely with the ways of gaining the greatest profits for monopolist merchants.

Indeed, when we ban import we reduce the number of those who sell to us and buy everything at the highest price; when we ban export, we reduce the number of those who buy from us and we sell everything at the lowest price. That is to say that we are never at the true price. We are above it when we buy expensively, and below it when we sell cheaply. Certainly it is not the way to carry on a profitable trade. However, it was in the hope of buying cheaply and selling dearly that these prohibitions were conceived. The nations sought mutually to hurt each other, and they each hurt themselves. It is only competition between the greatest possible number of buyers and sellers which can place goods at their true price, that is to say, at that price which, being equally advantageous for every nation, cuts out excessive price and cheapness at one and the same time.

# ~ 22  Of the Circulation of Grain

WHEN ONE IS without the means to wait for a second crop, say one only has corn for nine months, one is threatened with running out of it if none arrives; and it becomes all the more expensive, as one has less hope of seeing any corn arrive.

This rise in price which causes the price to go above the true price becomes dearness. So one cries out at dearth, not because one is completely without corn, but because one is threatened with a lack of it, and those who cannot pay the price it stands at are already without.

This dearth, which would be real if there was indeed not enough corn, is only a dearth in people's minds, when corn, which is not lacking in the barns, is only missing from the markets. This is what happens when there is a monopoly. The monopolists hold back from putting it on sale so as to find a greater profit in a greater increase in price. Their greed alarms the people: the belief in dearth grows, and corn reaches an excessive price.

When the dearth is real, we can only look to foreigners for help: they must bring us all we need.

If it is only in opinion, it is enough for them to show us some corn. At the mere rumour that corn is coming, the merchants, who would like to profit from the moment when it is still at a high price, will hurry to put it on sale, and, consequently, they will soon cause the price to fall.

Even in surplus, there would be a high price and the appearance of dearth if those who have corn persist in keeping it in their barns, or only putting for sale an amount which would not meet daily consumption; and, in the greatest scarcity, there would be a low price, and the appearance of surplus, if they were forced to put all their corn on sale at the same time, or merely a quantity a little more than enough for a day's consumption.

In the first case, the people would suffer as in a real dearth; and in the second, the cultivators and merchants would be harmed.

It would be just as damaging to put on sale, all at the same time, a quantity of corn that ought to serve for several months' subsistence, or to put on sale on each occasion only an amount that is insufficient for subsistence from one market to the next.

Therefore corn should come out of the barns gradually. It is enough that one delivers the amount that is wanted, and that the sale is made in proportion to need.

But the farmers would like it to be scarce in the markets in order to sell the corn dear, and the people would like it to be over-plentiful, to buy it cheaply. However, in both cases there would be harm to one side or the other, and even to both at the same time.

It is true that when the farmer sells dear he makes a greater profit on what he sells: but he sells a smaller quantity, because he forces the people to live off chestnuts, potatoes, roots, etc. Thus he gets them used to consuming less corn; and by reducing consumption, he reduces sales for following years and, in consequence, his receipts. What if the people revolt and ransack the barns? The farmer who wants to sell dear is thus the victim of his own greed.

The people are no less misguided when they want to buy cheaply. It is true that they find there a fleeting advantage. But we have seen that cheapness is always followed by dearness, where the people lack bread and cannot even work to earn it.

The harm which the farmer and the people do to each other turn and turn about, by too high and too low a price, rebounds on them.

So it matters that corn is put on sale in neither too great a quantity, nor too small; since it is important that it should be neither too expensive, nor too cheap.

But, because it is being consumed constantly, it is important that there should always be on sale as much of it as people need to consume, and it is then that it will be at its true price.

Corn does not grow the same everywhere. Not an ear is produced in the towns, where there is the greatest consumption. They do not even know how it is grown elsewhere; and there you have the explanation why people commonly reason so badly about the corn trade.

Be that as it may, for corn always to be on sale and in adequate quantity everywhere, it is essential that, from the places where it is in surplus, it never stops pouring into the places where it is lacking, which can only happen through a movement which is prompt and never disturbed: I say *prompt* and *never disturbed*, since every day consumers have the same need of it. This movement is what I call the *circulation of grain*.

The flow occurs from near at hand to near at hand, or at a distance.

At close quarters, when people bring the corn to the markets, and it moves in succession from one to another.

These markets, which are so many outlets, cannot proliferate too much. There must be some on all sides, and they must be in the most convenient places for the sellers as for the buyers. They should be where they choose, without dues and without hindrance.

The flow takes place at a distance when in a province people send convoys of grain to another, or when it is carried abroad.

To have these outlets, roads, canals, navigable rivers and a merchant navy are needed, an absence of tolls, no customs, no kind of feudal rights.

There we have the route traced for circulation; let us see how it must be made.

The need to attend to cultivation does not always permit a farmer to sell his cereals even in the closest markets. Indeed, will he leave his fields on a day that is just right for ploughing, for sowing, for harvesting, with the risk that there will not be another day as suitable? Now if he cannot always take his corn to the nearby market in person, he is even less in a position to take it to distant markets.

So it is essential that merchants are established to buy from the farmer in order to sell on to the consumer.

These merchants are men whom experience has moulded. They will only succeed in their trade in so far as they busy themselves with it exclusively, and to the extent that they have acquired a body of knowledge which is only built up over time.

They must know about the quality of the cereals in order not to be deceived in their choice; they must have learned to transport them at the best possible cost; they must know how to calculate the wastage, the costs of transport, and all the risks to be incurred; they must be able to work out the source from which corn can come to the places to which they intend to carry it, and they must predict the time of arrival. Because it is only the merchants who show up first who are assured of being able to sell profitably.

They will also need to have prepared other outlets and to know where they should carry the grain, in the event that they have speculated wrongly, so that they are not forced to sell it on at a loss.

Because one cannot see to everything oneself, and will be all the less able to as one undertakes more extensive and far-flung trade, it will be necessary to have intelligent and attentive correspondents, whose competence is known: otherwise false advice would drag one into ruinous enterprises. It is no less necessary to make sure of the accuracy and good faith of all those to whom one entrusts the protection or the sale of one's corn. And one must have men used to transporting it, on whom one can count equally; it is through the co-operation of a host of agents always moving about that the circulation of corn takes place. People in the towns are far from conceiving of it.

It is relevant to distinguish two kinds of corn merchant. The one type are wholesale merchants who, undertaking this trade in a big way, undertake to supply distant provinces whether inside or outside the kingdom. The others are small merchants who, in retailing in a restricted area, seem to limit themselves to stocking a canton. It is by the latter in particular that trade is carried on from place to place. They are called *corn chandlers* [*blatiers*].

The merchants require large warehouses in more than one place, many servants to watch over their cereals, correspondents or associates everywhere, and carriers of some kind on all the ways. It is clear that while they can make great profits, they also run great risks. The more extensive their trade, the more speculative the investments they have to make, and the more uncertain is the success of the enterprise.

As they have made great outlays, they wish to make large profits. So they are not in a hurry to sell. They seek out the moment. But because corn is a foodstuff which one cannot keep for a long time without great expense, and in keeping it there is ever-growing wastage, and always more risks to run; if the opportunity for a huge profit is delayed too long, they are forced to be satisfied with a smaller profit. So their hand is forced, and they serve the public in spite of themselves. It will not take them much experience to learn that it is in their interest to sell every time that they find in the sale all their expenses and a profit.

The corn chandlers buy from the farmers to sell on. They hardly need a warehouse. If they have one, the protection of it is not costly; and they have little wastage to fear because they empty it almost as soon as they have filled it. One servant is enough for them. They only need a donkey or a mule to transport their grain; and they have no need of agents, as they carry on their trade in a small canton where they live.

They have less outlay than the great merchants, fewer expenses, fewer risks, and they are satisfied with a smaller profit; they are always in a hurry to take their profit, because they are not rich enough to risk waiting for a larger one. Their interest is to sell promptly, so as to buy again in order to sell again. In order to subsist they need repeated purchases and sales to make their first outlays pass continually through their hands with a profit.

The circulation of corn is thus handled by a great number of merchants and by a larger number of corn chandlers.

If we need corn, all these merchants have no less a need to sell it. We shall not lack for it therefore, if the greatest liberty gives rise to the greatest competition.

Let us assume that a rich merchant buys, or makes a down payment, on all the corn of a province, intending to put a high price on it, he will probably cause an increase in price, but a temporary one. Because corn will flow in from all the nearby provinces; and the merchant, disappointed in his attempt, will be forced by a great number of competitors to lower the price of his corn. So he will not be tempted to repeat this operation. In this monopoly there would only be risks and losses. A clever merchant will not try it.

Instead of planning to cause dearness in a region that has a plentiful supply of grain, where in consequence the price will not be able to be kept up, a merchant has a surer and easier way to carry out profitable trade in his corn: that is to send it wherever a high price is the natural consequence of dearth. Let him cast his eyes over all Europe, and always be ready to send shipments: if he is well informed of the state of the crops, or only of the view held of them in each nation, he will be able to anticipate in which places prices will rise, and to take measures to send shipments there in time.

So it is that a host of merchants watch over the needs of all the peoples, when trade is completely free. Let us therefore rely on the interest they have in not letting us lack for corn; leave them alone, and we shall not want for it. Since there is always somewhere a natural rise in price which offers them a certain profit, why should they busy themselves with ways of causing artificial price rises, which will not guarantee them the same profit? The more self-interested we consider them to be, the more we should believe that they will be enlightened about their own interests.

Driven by this self-interest, merchants, great and small, multiplied by reason of our needs, will cause the corn to circulate, will put it everywhere at a level, everywhere at the true price; and each one will be drawn by the general movement, which he will not be able either to slow down, or to precipitate.

You will say that monopoly would then be impossible. Certainly it would be, in the situation where the corn trade enjoyed full, entire and permanent freedom. Now it is with this assumption that I have just examined the circulation of corn. We shall see elsewhere how monopoly becomes only too easy.*

---

*I often see that many objections can be raised against my arguments. They arise in great number in the complicated subject I am treating, and which I seek above all to simplify. I should like to reply to them all at once. But that is impossible. To be understood I must take myself from proposition to proposition: as, in the last resort, if no one understood me I should be wrong to write. Happily my reader cannot interrupt me, however much he wants to. He must necessarily put down my book, or wait for my response to his problems. However, I do not delude myself that I can reply to all; as people might make some very strange objections.

## 23 Corn Considered as a Measure of Value

OF ALL GOODS metals are the best suited to serve as a common measure of value; we have seen why. But because, from one century to another, they are scarcer or more plentiful, and, in consequence, have more or less value, they cannot be taken as a fit measure to determine the relationship a good has held in one age with the value of the same merchandise in a different age. For instance, I assume that in the twelfth century when silver was scarce, an ounce was the price of an ell of cloth; nowadays, when silver is much more plentiful, to pay for that same cloth one would need two or three ounces, or perhaps four.

The value of silver is thus itself too variable to serve as a measure of all values in every time. We have also noted that in a century when at one time it is scarcer, one is as rich with an income of fifty ounces as one would be with an income of a hundred ounces in a century when at one time it is more plentiful.

Not only is silver not a precise measure for all ages, it is not even an exact measure for all places. That is, it does not have the same value everywhere.

As we are drawn by habit to judge prices according to the amount of silver that things cost us, we rush to assume that when we pay two ounces of silver for something in a large market town, it is a price double that for which we pay one ounce in a province, where commerce has few outlets. But, in such a case, the difference between the prices cannot be exactly like the difference between more or less silver. This metal is then a false measure. It has greater value in a province without trade where it is scarcer; it has lower value in a market town where it is more plentiful. How then could it measure the relationship between the prices which are current in the one with those which are current in the other?

The circulation of money slows down from country area to country area, because of their distance from the main towns; and, if we assume the distance to be the same, it again slows down because of obstacles which make the transport of goods more expensive. Once money circulates less, it is scarcer; once it is scarcer, it is worth more; once it is worth more, one gives less of it for the things one buys; and, consequently, these things seem cheaper than they are.

So to judge incomes by the amount of money one receives each year, one seems richer in a town than one is, and one is richer in a country area than one appears to be. The position is that since metals have been taken as the common measure of values, one is drawn to see wealth only where one sees a lot of gold and silver; and this misconception began in the towns, where silver constitutes all the wealth. But our way of seeing does not change the nature of things. Indeed, what does the greater or smaller quantity of silver matter, when the smaller amount is worth the greater? If I can make the same consumption in a rural area with a hundred ounces of silver as you make in a town with three or four hundred, am I not as rich as you?

A good would always have a stable value if, always equally essential, it was in all ages and in every place in the same quantity in relation to need. Then it would be a measure with which one could assess the value of silver in every century and in every place. Corn is this good.

It would be superfluous to prove that corn is always equally necessary: it is enough to prove that there is always a similar quantity of it in relation to demand. That is easy because this question, like all those one makes on political economy, resolves itself.

In a time when the population is larger, more corn is eaten, and it is reproduced in a larger amount.

In a time when the population is smaller, one eats less corn, and it is reproduced in a smaller quantity. That has been proved.

Thus in normal years, production is always in proportion with consumption; and, in consequence, the quantity in relation to the demand is always the same, in normal years. Now it is according to the quantity in relation to the demand that corn is valued. So it always has the same value, a fixed and permanent value.

It would not be the same for a foodstuff for which one could substitute others; and which, consequently, would be a lesser necessity. For example, wine cannot have a fixed and invariable value.

However, we must note that corn itself cannot have a fixed and invariable value unless we assume that trade in this article is carried on with complete and lasting freedom. If it is hampered by duties, prohibitions, monopolies, it cannot place itself at its true price; and if it cannot be at its true price, it will have a constantly shifting value. When, at intervals, the people are forced to chew grass, it is not possible to determine the amount of corn in relation to need, and consequently, it is no longer possible to fix its value. I leave you to judge if Europe has a measure to reckon values in every age and in every place.

In the normal practice of leasing lands for money, there is damage for the farmer if corn falls to a low price; and if it rises to a high price, there is damage for the landowners. This custom is all the more harmful, in that the farmers, all being obliged to pay in the same quarters, and in consequence to put everything on sale at the same time, cause the price of corn to fall every year in the same months to their great loss and to the benefit of monopolists. It would thus be beneficial for the landowners, for the farmers, and for the state, if the price of leases were paid in foodstuffs. There would be benefit not only when the grain trade is shackled, there would also be benefit when it is unrestricted, because it would be made freer; because farmers would no longer be forced to sell at one time rather than another.

## 24 How Production Regulates Itself According to Consumption

NOW THAT I have explained all that relates to the true price of goods, I intend to look at the reason for the progress of agriculture and the arts, the use of land, the employment of men, luxury, public revenues, and the respective wealth of nations. There you have the purpose of the chapters by which I end this first part.

The need that citizens have of each other places them all in mutual dependency.

As masters of lands the proprietors are masters of all the riches the lands bear. In this respect, it seems that they are independent, and that the other citizens depend on them. Indeed, all are in their pay: it is on the wages that they pay that the farmers, the artisans, and the merchants subsist; and there you have the reason why the *économiste* writers judge them independent.

But if the lands were not cultivated, the artisans would be without raw materials, the traders would be without merchandise, the landowners would lack all kinds of products, and the land would not be adequate for the subsistence of its inhabitants. There would no longer properly be artisans, merchants or owners.

Farmers as the prime movers of production seem then in their turn to hold all the citizens in their dependency. It is their work which enables the citizens to subsist.

However, if raw materials were not worked up, agriculture and all the arts would be without all the most necessary instruments. There would be no arts in consequence; and society would be destroyed, or reduced to a wretched state. Therefore all the citizens still depend on the artisans.

Our tribe had no need of merchants when the settlers, sole owners of the land, lived on the lands they cultivated. Then each person could get himself the things he needed by exchanges with his neighbours. Sometimes someone bought a foodstuff which he did not have with the surplus from another; sometimes with the same surplus he paid the artisan for the raw material he had worked up. These exchanges were made without money and no one as yet thought of estimating the value of things exactly.

But as the landowners establish themselves in the towns it becomes all the more difficult for them to obtain all the goods they require, now that they consume much more. So shops need to be set up where they can supply themselves.

These shops are no less essential to the artisans, who need raw materials from one day to the next, and who cannot go each time to buy them in the countryside, which is often distant. Finally, they are essential to the farmers, to whom it is important, each time that they come to town, to sell their produce rapidly, and at the same time to buy all the tools they need. There you have the era when all the citizens fall into dependence on the merchants, and where goods begin to have a value estimated by a common measure.

Such is in general the nature of men: the person on whom one depends wants to draw advantage from his position; and all would be despots if they could. But when, in different respects, dependence is mutual, all are forced to give way to each other, and no one can abuse the need one has of him. So interests come together: they merge: and although all men seem dependent, they are all in fact independent. There you have order: it is born from the respective and combined interests of all the citizens.

Among these respective and combined interests is one which seems the moving power of all the others: it is that of the landowners. As the greatest consumption is made in the towns, and they have the largest share of it, their taste will be the yardstick of farmers, of artisans and of merchants. People will grow, by choice, the foodstuffs with which the landowners like to nourish themselves, people will work at the objects in which they are interested, and people will set out for sale the merchandise they seek.

It is natural for this to happen. Since the proprietors, as owners of lands, are masters of all the products, they alone can pay the wage that gives subsistence to the farmer, the artisan and the merchant. All the money, which must circulate and which in consequence must be the price of all tradable effects, originally belonged to them. They receive it from their farmers and they spend it as they please.

This money must return to the farmers, either immediately when they themselves sell to the landowners, or through an intermediary when they sell to the artisan or the merchant, to whom the landowner will have given some of this money as a wage.

Now this circulation will be rapid if the farmers, the artisans and the merchants study the tastes of the landowners and adapt to them. They will do it, because it is their interest.

Let us assume that, from generation to generation, the landowners have accustomed themselves to the same consumption; we shall assume from it that, in so far as there has been no variation in their tastes, people have grown the same products, worked at the same crafts and carried out the same kind of trade.

There we have the state through which our tribe must have passed. As it is accustomed to a simple life, for a long time it will be satisfied with the first products it has had occasion to know, and there will have been no others in commerce.

As later the tribe becomes more refined, it will vary in its tastes, preferring in one period what it has rejected, and rejecting in another what it has preferred.

But then the goods which it most seeks after would not be in proportion to the need it has formed for them, if the farmers, the artisans and the merchants did not vie with each other in busying themselves to supply the increase of this type of consumption.

Now they have an interest in seeing to it; because initially, as these goods were not plentiful enough, they were at a higher price; they can thus count on a higher wage.

They will not even be satisfied with observing the variations which bring them new profits. Once they have noticed they are possible, they will put all their effort into creating them, and there will be a revolution in commerce, in the arts and in agriculture. Previously consumption adjusted to the products; now production will adjust to consumption.

A more extensive commerce will embrace a greater number of objects. It will awaken the efforts of artisans and cultivators, and all will take on a new life. But that is only true with the assumption that commerce will be perfectly free. If it were not, it would soon degenerate into a state of convulsion which, in causing the price of goods to rise and fall without rules, would create a thousand disastrous enterprises for a few which would succeed, and would spread disorder in fortunes.

Our tribe has not yet reached this point. Its commerce, which I assume is confined within its lands, must naturally produce abundance. It opens up all the sources of commerce, it spreads them, and the previously sterile fields are cultivated and become fertile. It is certain that, so long as its commerce is supported by the produce of its soil alone, the mass of consumption, whether in foodstuffs, or in raw materials, can only encourage the farmers to draw from this soil all the wealth it encloses.

There you have the effects of free, internal commerce. A people is then really rich, because its wealth belongs to it, and only to it. It is in its possessions alone that it finds all the sources of its wealth, and it is its work alone that directs them.

Consumption, multiplied simultaneously by new tastes and revived tastes, must therefore multiply products, so long as there remain lands to cultivate, or lands which can be made more productive. Up to that point wealth will keep on growing and will only have a limit in the final advances of agriculture. Happy is the free people which, rich from its own soil, will not be drawn into commercial dealings with others!

# 25  Of the Use of Land

ONE CAN ONLY multiply products in proportion to the amount of land, its extent and the care one takes over its cultivation.

If we assume that all the lands are developed and that they each produce as much as they are able to produce, the products will be at the ultimate point of abundance and it will no longer be possible to increase them.

Then, if we want to have a greater quantity of one kind of foodstuff, we shall necessarily have to accept that we shall have less of another kind. For instance, to have more forage we should have to put down to meadowland fields which used to be sown; and so one would have a smaller crop of corn.

The same products are not equally fitted to the subsistence of animals of every kind. Consequently, if the lands are used to nourish a large number of horses they will not be able to feed the same number of men.

According to the use of the lands, the population will thus be larger or smaller.

But men consume more or less in proportion as they have more or fewer needs. The population must thus diminish in proportion as needs multiply all the more; or, if the population does not diminish, people must have found the means of increasing products in proportion to consumption.

In a word, a country never has just the number of inhabitants that it can feed. There will be fewer, all other things being equal, if each of them consumes more; there will be even fewer if a part of the land is given over to produce on which they do not feed themselves.

Let us observe our tribe now. Let us assume that in the country where it lives it has ten million arpents equally fitted for cultivation; and so that they cannot extend their possessions, let us place them on an island, in the bosom of the ocean; or, to take away from them even the resources which the sea could provide, let us transport these lands to the middle of a vast desert, sandy and arid in every direction.

At first, as we have noted, the tribe has few needs. Dressed in bark or in coarsely sewn skins, without comforts, not even aware of what it lacks, it sleeps on straw; it does not know the use of wine; it only has berries, vegetables, the milk and flesh of its herds for food. Yet it is not exposed to suffering from hunger nor from the abuses of the atmosphere, and that is enough for it.

In the early years, as it is small in number in relation to the country it lives in, it is easy for it to proportion its production to its consumption. Because, through the foodstuffs which are exchanged at the market, it will judge the type and amount of what is consumed and will use its lands accordingly.

Once it has grasped this proportion, the tribe will live in abundance, because it will have everything to meet its needs; and as long as this abundance can be reconciled with a greater number of inhabitants, the population will grow. It is a matter of fact that men multiply every time that fathers are assured of subsistence for their children.

I assume that in the country which our tribe inhabits each working man can live on the produce of an arpent and cannot subsist on less. Now the tribe has ten million arpents fit for cultivation. The population will therefore be able to grow to ten million inhabitants; and having reached that number it will no longer grow.

It has only increased to this point because men have carried on living in their original coarse fashion, and have not created new needs for themselves.

But when, by the means we have indicated, some landowners have increased their possessions, and, gathered in a town, seek more commodities, in food, clothing, lodging; then they will consume more, and the product of an arpent will no longer be enough for the subsistence of each of them.

If they make a greater consumption of meat, more herds will have to be fed; and in consequence corn fields will have to be turned to pastureland.

If they drink wine, some of the fields which used to be sown will have to be used as vineyards; and some of the fields will have to be used for plantations, if they burn more wood.

So it is that consumption, which multiplies like needs, changes land use; and one can see that products necessary for man's subsistence diminish in proportion as other needs increase.

The more that new forms of consumption multiply, the more movement there will be in trade, which will every day embrace new goods. This will produce the need to maintain a large number of horses to transport the merchandise from the country to the towns, and from province to province: a fresh reason for multiplying pastureland at the expense of cornland. What will happen if the owners who live in the towns want to have horses for their convenience, and pride themselves on having a large number? What will happen if they convert once cultivated fields into gardens or parks? One can imagine that in this state of affairs a single man could consume for his subsistence the product of ten, twelve, fifteen, twenty arpents, or more. So then the population will have to fall.

But it is natural for the merchants and artisans who have become rich to imitate the proprietors, and raise their consumption too. Each of them, according to his faculties, would wish to enjoy the commodities which custom brings in.

The men who change their way of living least markedly are those who, subsisting from day to day, earn too little to improve their condition. Such are the small traders, the small artisans and the ploughmen. However, each of them will endeavour to enjoy, in his station, the same commodities that others enjoy; and they will succeed bit by bit, because they will obtain higher wages by degrees. So in emulation all will consume more. The ploughmen, for instance, will take as models the large farmers, who consume more because they see the landowners, their masters, consuming more, and they have the ability to do so.

So, step by step, following each other's example, all will consume more and more. It is true that in general each person will order his expenses by what he sees men of his own estate doing: but in all conditions, expenditure is bound to be greater. The humblest ploughman will thus no longer be able to subsist on one arpent alone, he will swallow up two, three or four.

If we only consider the needs of the ploughman, the population might then be reduced to a half, a third, a quarter; and it could be reduced to a twentieth part, if we only consider the landowners who consume the product of twenty arpents. So, out of twenty ploughmen, new consumption will cut back fifteen; and, out of twenty landowners, it will cut back nineteen. There is no need to try to make the calculation more precise. I just want to make you understand how the population, which we have assumed to be ten million, might be no more than five or six million, or even less.

Since changes in the mode of existence are not sudden, the population will decrease so imperceptibly that our tribe will not notice. It will believe in the later stages that its country is as populous as it has ever been; and it will be amazed if one asserts the opposite. It will not conceive that population can decrease in a century, or that each citizen enjoys greater plenty and more comforts; and that it is none the less for that reason that the population is decreasing.

This revolution happens between generations and imperceptibly. Since with each generation consumption increases as do needs, there can no longer be so many families, and they will not be able to be so large.

Indeed, each man wants to be able to keep his family in that comfort which custom has made a requirement for all those of his estate. If a ploughman estimates that for that upkeep he needs the product of two or three arpents, he will only think of marrying when he can command that product. So he will be forced to wait. If the moment does not come, he will give up the plan to marry, and will have no children. If that moment comes late, he will only marry when he is advanced in age, and he will no longer be able to have a large family. There will doubtless be some people who will marry without thinking of the future. But the wretched state into which they will fall will be a lesson for the others; and their children will die for lack of subsistence, or will leave no posterity. One can make the same calculation with regard to merchants, artisans and proprietors.

We may conclude that the use of land is different, when needs, being multiplied, increase consumption and that then population necessarily shrinks.

It is true that if we had put our tribe in a totally different position, it would find resources in the lands with which it was surrounded. It could put out colonies; and, in that case, it is possible that the population would not decrease; it could even grow further. But if these lands were occupied by other peoples, it would need to arm; and war would kill the inhabitants whom the land could not feed.

I agree too that, when herds consume the produce of a large number of arpents, the lands reserved for human subsistence become more fertile, because manure is more plentifully spread there. But you will also agree with me that this fertility will not be enough to compensate. Even if, as is not possible, these lands taken on their own were to produce as much as all lands put together, how could they be enough for the same population, at a time when men are always consuming more at will?

People often say that one can judge the prosperity of a state from its population. But that is not quite right. Because one would certainly not call the time when I depicted our tribe, when I carried its population to ten million souls, one of prosperity. However, the increase of men can never be so great as when they are content to live, like that tribe, on the product of an arpent each.

So it is not the largest population taken by itself which makes one judge a state prosperous: it is the largest population which, examined with regard to the needs of every class of citizen, is reconciled with the abundance they all have the right to claim. Two kingdoms could be unequally populated although the government was equally good or bad in each.

China, for instance, embraces a huge population. That is because the sole food of the masses is rice, which produces three abundant harvests each year in several provinces: because the land does not rest at all, and often yields a hundred for one. This multitude, which has few needs, is almost naked, or is dressed in cotton, that is to say, in a crop that is so plentiful that an arpent can provide enough to dress three or four hundred people. This great population proves nothing therefore in favour of the government: it simply proves that the lands are very fertile, and that they are cultivated by hard-working men who have few needs.

Lands will have value wherever agriculture enjoys complete freedom; and then the population, in proportion with consumption, will be as large as it can be. There lies the prosperity of the state.

One might ask whether it is better for a kingdom to have a million inhabitants who subsist, one supporting the other, on the product of ten arpents a head: or ten million who subsist each on the product of a single arpent. It is clear that that question comes down to this, *Is it better for a kingdom that its inhabitants have the fewest possible needs, or that they have many?*, or again, *Is it better for a kingdom that its inhabitants remain in the first condition, in which we have conceived our tribe; or is it desirable that they leave it?* I reply that they must leave it. But at what stage should we be able to check them? That is what we shall examine in the next chapter.

## 26  Of the Employment of Men in a Society Which Has Simple Tastes

IN AMERICA, on the lands abandoned to their natural fertility and covered with forests, each savage needs the product of eighty or a hundred arpents for his subsistence; since the animals off which he chiefly feeds cannot increase their number much in the woods where they find little pasturage; and because, besides, the savages destroy more than they can consume.

With these huge, almost desert lands we can contrast those of our tribe, when the number of men was equal to the number of arpents. There you have the two extremes of population.

This tribe has the advantage over a horde of savages of finding abundance in the places where it is settled: but it needs many arts to leave the coarse condition in which it finds itself initially.

I shall not undertake to explain how it makes this discovery: that research is not my subject. I move to the time when it will know those arts which go back to remotest antiquity: the art of grinding wheat and making bread from it; the art of raising herds; the art of making cloth with the wool of animals, with their hair, with cotton, linen, etc., and finally, a beginning of architecture.

Then it finds in bread a more refined food than the corn which it previously ate in its harvested state. It has, in the milk of its herds and in their flesh, an additional food which lets it subsist with greater ease. The stuffs or materials with which it clothes itself protect it better from the elements than skins coarsely sewn together, and they are all the more suitable as they have a suppleness which gives the body freedom in all its movements. Finally, buildings, which are more solid and larger, are a better shelter for things the tribe wants to keep and it finds more commodities there.

When materials are suitable and long-lasting, it is of little importance that they should be worked with more refinement: if food is plentiful and healthy, it would perhaps be dangerous for it to become more delicate: and when solid buildings are large enough to lodge a family and enclose all the things it needs, is it really essential to find in them all the commodities to which a less hardy people has become accustomed?

Between a coarse and an indulgent existence, I should like to mark out a simple life, and if possible, to fix the notion of it with some precision.

I picture to myself a coarse life in the original state our tribe was in: I picture to myself a soft life in those times when every kind of excess had corrupted behaviour. These extremes are easy to grasp. It is between the one and the other that we should find the simple life. But where does it begin and where does it end? There you have what one can only show roughly.

We pass from the coarse life to the simple life, and from the simple life to the soft life, by a succession of those things which custom makes essential to us and which for this reason I have called *of secondary need*. So the arts must make some progress to draw us from a coarse life; and they must halt after some progress, to prevent our falling into a soft existence. The movement from one to the other is imperceptible, and it is only ever more or less that the simple life distances itself from one of the extremes, as it is only ever more or less that it approaches the other. It is therefore not possible to speak of it with exact precision.

It is easy to picture to oneself what the simple life was, when men, before gathering together in towns, lived in the fields they cultivated. Then, whatever progress the arts had made, all concerned agriculture which was the prime art, the art prized above all.

Now, so long as agriculture was regarded as the first art, as that to which all others must refer back, far from being able to become soft, men were necessarily sober and hard-working. The government, which was simple then, required few laws, and did not involve itself in long discussions. Cases between individuals that were put to arbitration had as judges neighbours whose fairness was known. Matters of general import were dealt with in the assembly of heads of household or of the chiefs who represented them; and order, in some sense, maintained itself among a people who had few needs.

There you have the simple life: it is marked out in the work men do in an agricultural society which supports itself with few laws. This simplicity will last, so long as the citizens are only cultivators; and it will retain some vestiges in every period when agriculture is of some esteem among them.

After the founding of towns, government could no longer be as simple, and disturbances began. The landowners, being the richest, found themselves possessed of the chief authority: they seemed to have more right to it, as, being masters of the land, they had a greater interest in the general welfare.

Everyone wanted to have the same share of power, and yet all could not. Wealth gave the advantage to some; greater shrewdness or more ability gave it to others; and, in this conflict, authority was bound to shift until the head of a party became possessed of it, or the assembled nation had given a form to government. So it was then that a senate was formed to look after the interests of all; and it was given a head with the name of *king,** a name which became what we call a title, when the kingship had drawn to itself the supreme power. But in the early days the kings only had a very restricted authority.

Under this new form of government there were still only a small number of laws, and this small number is a proof of the simplicity of manners. It is in corrupt times that laws multiply. People keep making more because the need for them is constantly felt, and it seems that they are always made to no purpose, as they soon fall into disuse, and people are forever forced to enact them again.

It is with reason that one judges that when a nation is not refined, in its food, or its dress, or its lodging, it is enough for it to live in plenty and comfort, if a quarter of its citizens are employed in the daily tasks of cultivation and the unrefined arts.

Another quarter, or thereabouts, are too young or too old to contribute by their work to the advantage of society. So that would leave half without a job. It is this half which withdraws to the towns. It includes the landowners who find themselves naturally entrusted with the main cares of government; the merchants who enable the greatest possible sale of all the necessities of life; and the artisans who work with greater skill on raw materials.

If the arts remain in this state, where the work of a quarter of the citizens is enough for everyone's subsistence, most of those who have no land in their ownership will be unable to subsist, since they will be without jobs, and that will be the majority.

One cannot fail to recognise that therein lay a source of disturbances. Now if it is important on the one hand that each citizen can live off his work,

*In the early days *king* only signified what we now understand by chief: *1798 footnote.*

it is certain on the other that one will not be able to give everyone work, except when the arts have made fresh progress. It is therefore in society's interest that this progress should be made.

The artisans who succeed in these perfected arts make finer linen, finer cloth, vessels of a handier shape, tools which are more solid or more useful, utensils of every kind adapted to new uses, or better-suited for old uses than those which one used to employ. All these arts, so long as too much refinement is not put into them, will be consistent with simplicity.

What I call *refinement* can be found in the raw material and in the work. In the raw material, when people prefer those which are drawn from abroad, simply because they are rarer and without finding any other advantage from them; in the work, when people prefer a more finished article even though it is neither more solid nor more useful.

Now, as soon as there is less refinement in prime materials and work the artefacts will be less costly. Once the artefacts are less costly they will be better adjusted to the citizens' means. Their use will therefore not be forbidden to any of them: all will enjoy them, or at least will believe they can enjoy them. It is above all exclusive pleasures which cause simplicity to disappear. Once a person starts to believe that he is of more consequence, because he enjoys things which others do not, he will only ever seek to be appreciated by these types of things: people believe they are marking themselves out by pretending to enjoy them, even when they no longer feel the enjoyment; and people cease to be simple, not only because they are not like others, but also because they want to seem to be what they are not.

Such then is the employment of men in our tribe. It has magistrates whom it has charged with the cares of government, ploughmen who till the land, artisans for the coarser arts, other artisans for the perfected arts, and merchants who place all the citizens within reach of goods for their own use.

Everyone works in competition in this society; and because each one has the choice of his occupation, and enjoys complete freedom, one person's work does not harm another's work. Competition, which distributes the jobs, puts each person in his place: all subsist, and the state is rich from the labours of all. There you have the point to which the arts should lead, and at which they should remain.

Indeed, if, to make further progress, they put too much refinement into customary goods; if they create in us the need for a multitude of things which are only for ostentation; if they give us another need for a mass of frivolities: it is then that the citizens, far from helping to raise and consolidate the structure of society by their work, seem on the contrary to sap its foundations. Luxury, which we shall discuss, will take artisans away from the most useful arts; it will take the ploughman from the plough; it will raise the price of the most basic necessities; and, for the small number of citizens who will live in affluence, the mass will fall into wretchedness.

A people will not leave simplicity at all when, instead of walking barefoot, it has comfortable footwear; when it prefers sturdier vessels, made with common metals, to vessels of wood, stone, earthenware; when it uses linen; when its clothes are of a shape better-fitted to the uses to which it intends them; when it has tools of every sort, but at a price related to everyone's means: in a word, it will never leave it when it only seeks goods of common use in the arts it creates or perfects.

Let us conclude that, since all citizens should be occupied in a society, it is beneficial or even necessary for the arts to make enough progress to provide work for all. It is the goods of which custom makes the need felt which should be the rule of men's employment, and procure for some the means of subsistence by working, without exposing others to a descent into softness.

The subject of this chapter will become clearer in the next, where we shall deal with luxury, that is to say with a type of life which is most removed from simplicity.

AS SOON AS one writes on luxury, some excuse it, others satirise it, and one proves nothing. The fact is that people do not try to agree.

We speak of luxury as of something of which we have a perfect notion, and yet we only have a comparative notion of it. What is luxury for one people is not for another; and for the same people what used to be luxury can cease to be so.

Luxury, in the original meaning of the word, is the same thing as excess; and when one uses it in that sense one begins to agree on it. But when we forget this first meaning, and so to speak rush to a host of associated ideas, without stopping at any one, we no longer know what we want to say. For the moment let us substitute the word *excess* for *luxury*.

The rough and ready life of our tribe, from the point of its settlement, would be an excess of refinement in the eyes of a savage, who, being accustomed to live from hunting and fishing, could not understand the purpose of the needs it had created for itself. Because the land, without being worked, provides for his subsistence, it seems to him that those who cultivate it are too fastidious about the means of subsistence.

There you have, in his judgement, an excess, which is not so in our judgement, or in that of our tribe.

But even among our tribe, each new comfort which custom will introduce can be seen as an excess of refinement by all those who do not yet feel the need for it. Is the tribe thus condemned to fall from excess to excess, according to its progress in the arts?

Men only differ in their judgement as to what all are agreed to call excess, because, as they do not all have the same needs, it is natural that what seems excess to one, does not seem so to another. There you probably have the reason why one has so much difficulty in knowing what one means when one speaks of luxury.

I distinguish two sorts of excess: those which are only so because they seem such in the eyes of a certain number; others which are so because they seem so in everyone's eyes. I make luxury consist of the latter. So then let us see what are the things which must appear a luxury in everyone's eyes.

However refined goods might have appeared at the beginning, they are in no way an excess when it is in their nature to become of common use. Then they are a consequence of the progress it is so important to make in the arts; and there will come a time when everyone will be agreed in considering them necessary. One can even see that they can be reconciled with simplicity.

When, on the other hand, goods of a kind that can never become plentiful are kept back for the smallest number to the exclusion of the majority, they must always be regarded as an excess: even those who have the greatest pleasure in their enjoyment could not disagree. Therefore luxury consists in the articles which appear an excess in the eyes of all, since by their nature they are reserved for the minority to the exclusion of the majority.

Linen, which was a luxury in its early days, is not so today. Gold and silver which, in movable goods and clothes, have always been a luxury, will always be so.

Silk was a luxury for the Romans, because they drew it from the Indies, and consequently it could not be a common good among them. It began to be less of a luxury for us when it started to be a product of our climate; and it will become less so, to the degree that it becomes less scarce.

Finally, potatoes would be a luxury on our tables, if our fields produced none; and if we had to make them come at great expense from North America, whence they came originally. Rich folk, whose taste is proportional to the rarity of the dish, would judge them excellent; and a plate of this root, last resource of peasants without bread, would be the talking-point of a meal.

To judge whether there is luxury in the use of some goods, it is therefore often enough to consider the distance of the places from which one draws them. Indeed, when commerce is carried on between two neighbouring nations, luxury cannot creep in to either of them; because through exchanges the same goods can become common in both.

The same is not the case when trade is carried out between two much-separated peoples. What is common among us becomes luxury in the Indies, where it is necessarily scarce; and what is common in the Indies becomes luxury among us, where it is necessarily also scarce.

So luxury can exist in the use of goods which one summons from afar: but that is not the only kind. There may be luxury in the use of goods which one draws from a neighbouring nation, and even in the use of goods which one finds in one's own country.

It is asserted that if France paid in champagne for Brussels lace, it would give the product of more than sixteen thousand arpents of vines for the product of just one arpent of flax.* Lace, though it does not reach us from far away, is thus an article whose use cannot be common, in other words a luxury good.

But, if lace were made in France, it would be no less a luxury: it would be at an even higher price and, in consequence, of less common use.

The cost of labour thus converts into luxury goods the raw materials which our soil produces in the greatest abundance. There is plenty of this luxury in our furniture, in our carriages, in our jewellery, etc.

Although all these luxuries tend to corrupt behaviour, they are not all equally harmful. Let us consider them first of all with regard to the state; we shall consider them next with reference to individuals.

Two nations will trade with the same advantage, every time that each of them receives in products a quantity equal to what it hands over. But if one gives the product of sixteen thousand arpents for the product of a single one, it is clear that it will be hurt sensationally. The luxury of lace is thus harmful to France. It takes away a large amount of subsistence, and so it tends to reduce the population.

It could be beneficial to Europe to send the surplus of its products to the Indies. But if it only had a surplus because it was depopulating itself, it would do better to use its lands for the subsistence of its own inhabitants, and to increase its products in order to increase its population.

It was especially useful for it, in this commerce, to get rid of part of the gold and silver which America provided it in excess. But the luxury goods which it draws from the Indies cost it in exchange millions of men. How many perish on the journey! How many in unhealthy climates where it is obliged to have depots! How many in wars with the Indians! I will believe this luxury beneficial for Europe when it has been proved that she has a surplus population.

---

*Cantillon, *Essai sur la nature du Commerce*, Part 1, Chapter 15.

As for the luxury goods which come from our soil and our hard work, they may have some utility, but they are not without abuse.

When a rich man buys a litron of small peas from the first crop it is a luxury, everyone agrees. But one could wish that all the excesses of moneyed men were of this type: because their wealth would discharge itself straight away on the fields, like manure fit to make them fertile.

It is not to be doubted that the sums which we spend on furniture, on carriages, on jewels, are likewise poured on our fields, when we employ our own workmen for these artefacts; since these workmen return them individually to the cultivator who gives them their subsistence. But they are not poured out there immediately. They begin by making the artisan wealthy; they get him used to pleasures which are a luxury for him; and these possessions excite the envy or the emulation of all those who hope to succeed in the same trade.

Indeed, as this artisan is a peasant whose relatives are ploughmen, his improved condition will demonstrate to all in his village how industry in towns has advantages over the labours of the countryside. So people will leave the villages. Out of ten peasants who have taken up crafts, one will succeed, and nine will not earn enough to live off. So there will be ten men lost to agriculture, and nine more paupers in the town. There you have the undesirable consequences of luxury for the state, when it consists in pieces of work for which we use our own workers.

To judge the undesirable consequences of luxury with regard to individuals, I distinguish three kinds of it: luxury of splendour, luxury of useful goods, luxury of frivolities.

The first seems to me the least ruinous, since some of the things which have served for splendour can be used for it again; and besides, when they are of a sort that is not used up, they keep a great value, even after they have been used for our purposes. Of this kind are gold or silver dishes, diamonds, vessels of rare stones, statues, paintings, etc.

The luxury of commodities, more contagious because it is proportionable to the means of a much greater number of citizens, can be very expensive because it becomes greater along with increasing softening of manners, and most of the things one uses for it lose all their value.

Finally, the luxury of frivolities, subject to fashion's whims, which renews itself continuously in fresh forms, throws people into expenses to which no limits are seen; and yet, for the most part, frivolities only have value at the point when people buy them.

What is the fortune that can prove adequate for all these kinds of luxury? So resources are needed, and sadly people find them to bring about their ruin. You will doubtless say that luxury helps a vast number of workmen to live, and that when the wealth remains in the state, it is of little importance that it passes from one family to another.

But when there is disorder in all fortunes, can it avoid being in the state? What becomes of manners when the chief citizens, whom one takes as an example, are forced to be at one and the same time greedy and spendthrift, knowing only the need for money, so that any means of making it is accepted among them, and none dishonours? Luxury gives subsistence to a host of workers, I agree. But are we to shut our eyes to the wretchedness which spreads in the countryside? Who then has the greater right to subsistence, is it the craftsman who makes luxury goods, or the ploughman?

It is a statement of fact that only the simple life can make a people rich, powerful and happy. See Greece at her zenith: she owes the power which astounds decadent nations to her residuum of simplicity. Even see the peoples of Asia before Cyrus. They had vices, they knew gorgeous display; but luxury had not yet spread its mortal poison over every part of society. If splendour was evident in the treasures amassed for future need, in great enterprises, in works as gargantuan as they were useful; if it was evident in movable goods, in clothes; at least they did not know all our comforts and they were even less familiar with all the frivolities which we are not ashamed to have made necessities for ourselves. Even the luxury of the table, such as it was, only occurred at state feasts. It consisted in plentifulness rather than in refinement. There was not twice daily a profusion of dishes, even in individuals' houses, prepared with elegance and spread out with luxury.

I would happily excuse the luxury of the ancient peoples of Asia. I see it reconciled with a residuum of simplicity, even in the palaces of kings. If it is great, I see it supported by even greater wealth, and I understand that it may have been of some use. But we who, in our wretchedness, have only resources which ruin us, and who to obtain these resources do not fear to dishonour ourselves, we want to live in luxury, and we expect our luxury to be useful!

IN CONSIDERING how wealth is produced, distributed and preserved we have seen that commerce needs a power to protect it. I call *public* or *state income* the revenues one allows this power. It is a matter of knowing why and by whom this must be paid.

A civil society is based on a contract, clear or implied, by which all the citizens undertake, each for his own part, to contribute to the common benefit.

In general, to contribute to this benefit, it is enough to be useful; and one will be, every time one has a position and one fulfils its duties.

This way of contributing is an obligation which all the citizens, without exception, have contracted in coming together in the body of society.

Thus a useless man is not a citizen. Living at society's expense he does nothing for it: it owes him nothing.

But it is not always enough to have a position and to fulfil its duties. In the government of every civil society there are necessary and indispensable public expenses to which in consequence the citizens must contribute.

They can only do that in two ways: one is by themselves working on public projects, the other is by providing subsistence to those who work. Now since this subsistence and this work can be valued in money, for greater simplicity we shall bring down to a money contribution these two ways of contributing. Such a contribution, if regulated by the nation itself, is called *a subsidy* or *free gift;* and if it is imposed by the government, one calls it *a tax.* You ask who should pay subsidies or taxes?

There are in general only two classes of citizen: that of the landowners to whom all the land and all the products belong; and that of the paid workers who, having neither land nor produce of their own, subsist on the wages that are due for their work.

The first class can easily contribute; since, with all the products belonging to it, if it does not have all the money, it has more than the equivalent* and besides it passes entirely through its hands.

---

*One must remember that, whatever amount of money there is in a nation, it cannot ever have a value equal to all of its production.

The second class would not be able to do so. It cannot provide subsistence to those who work, because it has absolutely no products of its own. It cannot give them the money they need to buy their subsistence, because the only money it has is its wages; and these wages, reduced to the lowest level by competition, are no more than the exact amount it needs to subsist itself.

Let us stand in the shoes of people who have none of our prejudices, will the first idea that occurs to people such as I have conjured up be to say: "Those who have nothing must contribute to public expenditure like those who possess something"; or else, "Those who have their arms and their hard work as their sole possessions must contribute to public expenditure the money they do not possess?" Now the class of wage earners only earns the money needed for its subsistence, so putting a tax on it is wanting it to pay with money it does not have.

Taxes on industry seem reasonable and fair to us, because, without having thought of the matter, we judge them reasonable and fair whenever they are in the established order. However, this order is often only an abuse. Our behaviour proves it, even when we do not wish to agree.

Indeed, if we go to the merchants on whom a new tax has been imposed, we are not surprised if they want to sell for a higher price. We even reckon that they have good reason, and we pay the price they demand. So we are contradicting ourselves; we want the merchants to contribute to public expenditure, and when they have contributed, we want to reimburse them. Would it not be easier for us to undertake all this expenditure ourselves?

But there are merchants and artisans who are making themselves wealthy. There, no doubt, you have what sustains our prejudice. Well, let us make them contribute, they will ensure that they are reimbursed. It is therefore impossible for them to contribute.

You will probably say that, with the need they have to sell, they will not always succeed in being reimbursed in proportion to the taxes; and that consequently they will bear a part of them.

That may be: but it should be noted that the portion on which they remain taxed will be taken from their wage, and that as a result they will be reduced to consuming less than they would have done. So there you have, in a state such as France, several millions of citizens who are forced to cut back on their consumption. Now I ask whether the land will return the same income, when people sell a smaller amount of their produce to several million citizens. So whether the wage-earners are totally reimbursed, or whether they are only partially reimbursed, it is clear that, in the one case as in the other, the tax that one places on them falls equally on the owners.

Indeed, the landowners must certainly pay for the wage-earning class, since it is the landowners who pay the wages. In a word, no matter how one approaches it, they must pay everything.

Either the country which a nation inhabits supplies in plenty all that is necessary for its citizens' requirements; or it provides only a part of that, no matter what care one takes over cultivating the land.

In the first case, the nation which is rich through its soil is self-sufficient. But the products which are its entire wealth belong totally and solely to the owners of the lands. So this class alone can bear all public expenditure.

In the second case, I make the assumption that this nation is on not very fertile coasts, whose product is only enough for the subsistence of a tenth of its citizens. Condemned by its soil to poverty, it can only be rich in so far as it takes for itself the products which grow on an alien soil. Now it will obtain them by its industry; or rather it has developed by stages only because it has obtained them gradually. It carries out trade. It is through this that the peoples, who did not trade straight away, or on their own behalf, exchange their surplus; and it finds, in the profits which it makes on the one and the other, the products it needs.

As it is rich simply through its industriousness, it only has a precarious wealth, which will be taken away from it, just as soon as the other peoples should want to carry out their exchanges themselves. It will lose population, to the extent that it loses its trade; and when it has totally lost it, it will find itself reduced to a tenth of its citizens; since we assume that in the product of its own soil it only has the wherewithal to make that tenth subsist.

But so long as this trade is flourishing, the nine-tenths of the wealth of this nation or of the products it consumes belong to the merchant class which has obtained them from foreign peoples by its own work and industry. If this class were to pay no subsidies, those paid by the landowners would be inadequate to meet public expenditure. So the merchant class must contribute nine-tenths when the landowners contribute one-tenth.

However, when that class pays nine-tenths, the position is that it arranges for them to be paid by the people whose agent it is; and consequently the public expenditure of a merchant state is, for the most part, paid by the owners of lands in foreign countries.

This nation does well to demand subsidies from its traders, since it has no other way to provide for public expenditure. It does all the better, as it is not its landowners who pay for the traders; it is the landowners in other nations. It is precisely on them that it makes the taxes fall back; it is with their products that it subsists, and it makes all the peoples with whom it deals pay taxes.

Such is near enough the position of Holland. So because in this Republic industry pays taxes, one should not conclude from this that industry ought to pay taxes in France.

But you will say, do there not exist in France, as in Holland, traders who cause landowners in foreign countries to pay taxes? There would therefore be the same advantage for France as for Holland to make the traders pay taxes.

My response is that in France the traders will begin by passing the taxes on to native landowners: it is these owners whom they will cause to pay the lion's share of the tax placed on industry and in consequence they will not pay it themselves. I admit that some will cause foreign landowners to pay a part of it; but this benefit would not be a reason to place taxation on French traders.

If Holland places taxes on traders, it is not because it finds an advantage in taxing foreign nations, it is because it cannot do otherwise.

Indeed, you will agree that this Republic would have a much more flourishing trade if it could exempt those who undertake it from every tax. It cannot: it is forced to demand subsidies on the part of its traders. It is forced to by its very constitution, which is a necessary consequence of its position: in a word it is forced because its subsidies would be inadequate for public expenditure if they were only imposed on the lands. The tax on industry is therefore in its country a vice inherent in the state's constitution and it must live with this vice. Such is the fate of a nation that has but a precarious wealth.

But France is not forced to place taxes on industry: France, I say, where the land-owning class has all the wealth, and wealth which would certainly be in surplus, if the land were better cultivated.

France is rich in products and the surplus of these products is the stock with which its merchants trade. They export this surplus which would be useless to us, they exchange it, and in bringing us back useful products they increase the sum of our wealth.

Let us tax our traders, they will sell the surplus they export at a higher price, and so buy less; and they will bring back to us in exchange a smaller quantity of foreign merchandise, whose price will rise for us.

So we shall be less rich, since the surplus which ceases to be consumed is no longer reproduced; and we shall be deprived of wealth which it would have procured for us through exchanges. Taxation on industry is always deceptive, because, on all assumptions, it always falls back on the landowners; so it is a vice which must not be suffered, except when it belongs to the very constitution, and cannot be eradicated. It necessarily diminishes consumption; and in reducing consumption it hinders reproduction. Therefore it tends to damage agriculture.

WE HAVE distinguished landed wealth and movable wealth.

Within landed wealth I place not only all products, but also all the animals: indeed they must be considered as a product of the lands which feed them.

Within movable wealth I place everything to which labour has given a new form. There you have the categories to which all wealth is reducible, it would be impossible to imagine a third kind.

If you were to say that gold and silver are of another type, I should ask whether these metals are not formed in the ground, and if it is not true that they only really show themselves for us when we draw them from the mine and refine them.

Gold and silver are thus landed wealth, which, like corn, are the product of the land and of our work; and these metals are mobile wealth, when we have caused them to take the forms which make them suited to various uses; when we have made from them coins, vessels, etc.

We have seen that all this wealth only increases by reason of our work. We owe all the products to the cultivator's work; and we owe to the artisan or the artist all the forms given to raw materials.

We have further seen that all these riches are only at their true value in so far as circulation makes them pass from the places where they are surplus to the places where there is a shortage of them. This circulation is the result of trade. The value of wealth is thus in part due to the work of the merchants.

Finally, we have seen how much wealth depends for its production and preservation on a power which protects the cultivator, the artisan, the artist and the merchant; that is to say, which keeps order without having preferences.

The works of this power therefore combine for the increase of wealth, as for its preservation.

Following this résumé it is easy to judge which is the nation that must be the richest.

It is the one where there is simultaneously the most work of every type.

Are all the lands as well cultivated as they can be? Are all the workshops of artisans and artists full of workers constantly occupied? Do an adequate number of merchants cause the whole surplus to circulate promptly and constantly? Finally, the vigilance of the sovereign power, this toil watching over all labour, does it maintain order and freedom without partiality? Then a nation is as rich as it can be.

Therefore I beg people not to ask if one should prefer agriculture to manufactures, or manufactures to agriculture. One must not prefer anything; one must see to all.

It is for the individual to have preferences; he has by law the right to choose the type of work that suits him. Now he would lose this right if the government protected one type of work exclusively or if it favoured it.

Will a nation, destined by its soil to be agricultural, neglect the products which nature wants to heap on it, this wealth which belongs to the nation and only to it, and which one cannot take away from it?

Will it neglect them, I say, to spend its days in workshops? In truth it will acquire real wealth but this is wealth of the second order; it is precarious and other nations will take it to themselves.

Because these people are agriculturalists, shall they scorn all works which do not have direct relevance to agriculture? Will they wish to have no artisans or artists? They will then draw all movable goods from outside and be compelled to pay a higher price for them, because they will have transport costs to pay. They could have had among them a large number of workmen who would have consumed their produce, and they will send their products at great expense to enable these workmen to subsist in foreign lands.

So whether a people gives preference to agriculture, or whether it gives it to manufactures, it is certain that, in the one case as in the other, it is never as rich as it might have been.

Shall it neglect agriculture and manufacturing to concern itself principally with commission trade [trading: *1798*]? It will then bring itself down to being no more than the salesman for other peoples. It will have nothing for itself, and it will only subsist so long as the nations do not envy the profit it makes at their expense. Commission trade can only be preferred when a people that lacks from its own resources enough foodstuffs or primary materials in relation to its population has no other resources for subsistence.

So in order for an agricultural country to be as rich as it can be, it needs to concern itself at the same time with every type of work: the different occupations must be spread among the citizens, and in each profession the number of workers must be proportionate to the need for them. Now we have seen how this allotment comes about naturally when commerce enjoys full, complete and permanent freedom.

Allow me to assume for a moment that all the nations of Europe work according to these principles, which perhaps they will never understand.

With this assumption, each will acquire real, tangible wealth, and their respective wealth will reflect the fertility of the soil and the industry of its inhabitants.

They will trade among themselves with complete freedom; and they will each find their own advantage in this trade which will cause the surplus to circulate.

With all equally involved, they will feel the need they have of each other. They will not consider at all taking away from each other manufactures or trade: it will be enough for each to work and to have work to exchange. For example, what does it matter to us that a certain type of cloth is made in France or in England, if the English are obliged to exchange their cloth for other products of our manufactures? Just let us work, and we shall have nothing to envy other nations. As much as we need to work for them, so they need to work for us. If we were to wish to do without their manufactures, they would want to do without ours: we would hurt them, they us.

Every type of work, and freedom of choice given to all citizens, there you have the real source of wealth; and you can see that this spring will spread plenty to a greater or lesser degree; according to whether it is more or less free in its course.

This chapter would be finished did I not have prejudices to fight.

Does a nation attempt a new trade? All want to carry it out. Does a new manufacturing process establish itself in one nation? Each nation wants to establish it. It seems that we only think of doing what is done elsewhere, and that we do not give a moment's thought to what we can do at home. It is that, lacking the freedom to do what we want, we think to find that freedom in a new type of trade or of manufacture which seems to assure us government protection.

If we were to start by concerning ourselves with the things for which our land and our industry intend us, we should not work in vain, since foreigners would seek out our work. Our goods will stay on our hands in contrast, if we work on the types of goods where they must succeed better than us.

But when we have succeeded as well as them, have we done all we can in our wish to make everything that others make? If our old manufactures languish, why should we establish new ones? And why should we multiply our manufactures if we have fields fallow, or if those we cultivate are not fully exploited? We have work to do, we do not do it, and we envy other nations the works they do! Still, if we only had articles similar to theirs to exchange with them, there would no longer be trade between them and us. These reflections are trivial indeed: but why should I fear to say trivial things when people are not ashamed to ignore them? Do we recognise these trivial matters when we prohibit foreign merchandise to give preference, as they say, to our manufactures, or when we subject it to exorbitant duties?

Busy as they are in hurting each other, the nations would each like to enjoy the advantages of trade exclusively. Each one, in the exchanges it makes, would wish all the profit to be for itself. They do not see that in the nature of exchanges there is necessarily profit to both sides, since on each side one gives less for more.

An individual who does not know the market price may be deceived in the purchases he makes. Nations are merchants: it is on their own soil that markets are held; the price of goods is known to them. So by what art shall we force them always to give us more for less where they are concerned, when we only ever give them less for more where we are concerned? This art is however the great object of politics: it is the philosopher's stone that it seeks and that it certainly will not find.

But you will say, we must draw to ourselves as far as possible the gold and silver of foreign nations. Therefore we must prevent them selling us goods produced or manufactured in their lands, and force them to buy goods produced or manufactured in our country.

So you think that a million in gold and silver is greater wealth than a million in products or a million in worked-up materials! Are you still at the point of being unaware that products form first-order wealth? What will you do then, if other nations which reason as badly as you also wish to attract your gold and silver to themselves? That is what they will attempt. All the peoples will therefore be busy preventing foreign goods entering their lands; and if they succeed it is a necessary consequence that native merchandise will not leave any of them. So, as a result of each having wanted to find exclusively a great profit in trade, they will cease trading among themselves, and in rivalry they will deprive themselves of all profit.

There you have the effect of prohibitions. Nevertheless who would dare to assert that Europe will open its eyes? I desire it: but I know the force of prejudice, and I have no hope of it.

Indeed, for Europe trade is not an exchange of works in which all the nations will each find their advantage; it is a state of war in which they only think how to plunder each other. They still think as in those barbarous times when peoples only knew to enrich themselves from plundering their neighbours. In perpetual rivalry they only worked at hurting each other. There is not one of them that would not wish to destroy all the others; and not one of them considers ways to make its real strength grow.

You ask what would be the benefit or the disadvantage for a nation, France for example, if it were the first to give full and complete freedom to export and import.

I reply that if it was the first, and consequently alone in giving this freedom, it would have no advantage or disadvantage for it; since then it would export nothing and nothing would be imported on her soil. Since for export to be possible in France we must be able to import on foreign soil; and the foreigner must export for import into France to take place.

This question is thus badly presented. I ought rather to ask what would be the benefit or the disadvantage for France if she were to give export and import permanent and never-interrupted freedom, while elsewhere export or import were now allowed, now forbidden.

Cereals form one of the branches of commission trade that Holland engages in; and that Republic always allows their export and import. It appreciates that if it hindered that trade it would be all the more exposed to a shortage of cereals as its lands do not produce enough for its consumption.

In Poland, the export of cereals is always allowed, because in normal years the harvests there are always in surplus. Since it draws all manufactured goods from outside, it needs this surplus for its purchases, and it guarantees itself the surplus by its work. If it had at home all the manufactures it lacks, its crops would be less overflowing, because it would be more populous, and perhaps it would forbid export.

In England export is seldom forbidden: but freedom to import is restrained to a greater or lesser extent by the duties which rise or fall according to circumstances.

Finally, elsewhere export is allowed when cereals are cheap, and import is allowed when they are dear. However, the freedom, whether to export or to import, is never full and complete: it is always to a greater or lesser degree limited by tariffs. There you have, more or less, what happens in Europe. I say, *more or less* since it is enough for me to reason on assumptions. It will always be easy to apply my reasoning to the changing conduct of government among the different peoples.

France, we assume, is alone in giving export full, complete, permanent freedom without restriction, limitation or interruption. All her ports are always open and no one ever demands any duty on entry or exit there.

I say that, on this assumption, the trade in grain must be more profitable for France than for any other nation.

It is certain that the seller sells to greater advantage when a larger number of buyers make him a greater number of offers in competition with each other. So France will find advantage in the sale of her cereals if, not limiting herself to selling to domestic consumers, she sells as well to consumers in those states where import is allowed.

It is clear that if she could import equally throughout Europe she would sell with even more benefit still, since a larger number of buyers would make her a larger number of requests. If her benefit is not all that it might be, it is therefore because she cannot import everywhere equally.

You will doubtless say that cereals will become dearer in France if we sell them to all the foreigners who request them.

But we have assumed that import into France is as unrestrained as export, and we have noted that there are nations which export their grain: now these nations will import into our country when they find in the high price a profit in selling to us. On that point it must be seen that that high price is not dearness; it is the true price fixed by competition, a true price which has its high, its low and its middle limit.

So long as this price has not reached its highest point, people will not bring us grain, and we shall not need them to bring it to us. When it has reached its ceiling all the grain-exporting nations will bring us grain; and we shall buy to all the more advantage, as a larger number of sellers will make us a larger number of offers. We shall buy with all the more advantage still if grain is brought to us from every part of Europe, since the offers will multiply with the sellers. Kindly reflect on the position of France: as she is placed to be the depot of the north and of the Midi, can she fear doing without or having to buy dear? One sees on the contrary that she will be the common market of all Europe.

Whether she sells or whether she buys grain, France will, on our assumption, thus have a great advantage over the nations which forbid export and import, over those which allow only the one or the other, and finally over those which only allow both temporarily and with restrictions. Because by forbidding export, they reduce the number of purchasers, and consequently they sell at a lower price; and by forbidding import they buy at a higher price, because they reduce the number of those selling to them.

We may conclude that if the states of Europe persist in denying complete freedom to trade, they will never be as rich or as populous as they might be; that if one of them gave complete and permanent liberty, while the others only allowed a temporary and restrained freedom, it would be, other things being equal, the richest of all; and that finally, if all ceased to place obstacles in the way of commerce, they would all be as rich as they could be; and then their respective wealth would depend, as we have already noted, on the fertility of the soil and the hard work of its inhabitants.

# 30 A Concise Recapitulation of the First Part

THE VALUE OF things, or the estimation we make of it, based on utility, is in proportion to our needs. From this it follows that the surplus, considered as surplus, has no value whatever, and that it can only acquire value in so far as one judges that it will become necessary.

Our needs are natural or artificial.

Natural needs in the isolated man follow from his makeup. In man as a citizen they follow from the constitution, without which society could not continue to exist.

These needs are small in number and only give value to things of primary need. Artificial needs, in contrast, multiply with our customs, and give value to a host of products and worked materials which we have placed among the goods of secondary need.

The value of these things, in proportion to their scarcity and their abundance, varies again following the true or false notion we have of that scarcity and that abundance.

These values, estimated by comparison, are what one calls the price of goods. From this it follows that, in exchanges, the goods are reciprocally the price of each other, and that we are all at the same time, in different respects, buyers and sellers.

Prices are settled through competition between sellers and buyers. Prices can only adjust themselves at markets, and they will vary little if every one is allowed to bring to the market what he wishes in the quantity he chooses.

Now these exchanges, which are made in markets, are what one calls trade.

They suppose on the one hand surplus produce, and on the other, consumption to be made.

It is thus the surplus which is traded, whether the farmers make their own exchanges, in which case trade is made directly between producers and consumers; or whether exchanges are made through the intervention of merchants, traders or dealers; and then the merchants are like channels of communication between producers and consumers.

The surplus, which had absolutely no value in the hands of producers, acquires a value when it is placed in the hands of consumers. Trade therefore gives value to things which had none. It therefore increases the stock of wealth.

This stock also grows with the arts, which, in giving form to raw materials, give them value as they make them suitable for varied uses.

Society owes all its wealth to the work of the farmer, the artisan and the merchant. This work should merit a wage. This wage, regulated by competition, adjusts the consumption which each has the right to claim, and the citizens find themselves arranged by classes.

We have two kinds of wealth: landed wealth, which we owe to the farmer, and which is self-replacing; movable wealth, which we owe to the artisan or the artist, and which accumulates.

All these kinds of wealth are produced, distributed and preserved by virtue of the labour of the farmer, of the craftsman, of the artist, of the trader and of the sovereign power which maintains order and liberty.

Wealth abounds especially after the foundation of towns, since then greater consumption gives a new impetus to industry. The lands are better cultivated and the arts increase and perfect themselves.

All those who share this wealth acquire a right of property over it that is sacred and inviolable. We acquire this right ourselves through our work, or we acquire it because it has been ceded by those who have acquired it. In the one case as in the other, a person alone disposes of the goods he owns; no power can, without injustice, place a lower price on them than that which we place ourselves; and it is for competition alone to regulate the price of each good.

Just as the field belongs to the settler who cultivates it [landowner: *1798*], and all those whom he employs in the cultivation acquire a right of co-ownership of its product: so in every enterprise there is a capital which belongs to those who have provided it, and a product which they must share with the workers whom they set to work. This co-ownership is represented by the wage which custom fixes and of which no one may be deprived.

Once wealth has increased, a more extensive commerce makes the need felt to judge the value of each good with more precision. So one looks for a common measure.

Since in exchange values measure themselves reciprocally, any kind of merchandise could be used to this end. We give the preference to metals, as being the commodity with which one can most conveniently measure all the others, and we create money.

It is thus because they had a value as merchandise that metals had one as money; and in becoming money, they do not cease to be merchandise.

The use of money, in facilitating exchanges, gives more movement to commerce, and increases the stock of wealth. But it causes what we call value to be misunderstood. When one thinks one sees the price of things in a measure, such as an ounce of silver, which is always the same, one does not doubt but that they have an absolute value; and because one judges that they have an equal value each time that they are estimated equal in value to the same amount of silver, one falsely supposes that in exchanges one always gives equal value for equal value.

Silver only facilitates commerce because one gives it constantly in exchange. It is collected up to be distributed, it is distributed to be gathered up; and never ceasing to pass and pass again from one hand to another, it circulates constantly.

So long as this circulation is made freely, it matters little whether there is more or less silver in trade. Its quantity can be smaller as it can be greater. One could not determine it with precision. One can simply surmise that, whatever the quantity is, it is at most equal in value to the value of the products which are consumed in the towns.

The circulation of silver is called exchange when, by the exchange of two sums which are at a distance, one makes them both in some manner bridge a gap to replace the one with the other.

Exchange has become a branch of commerce, in which money is the sole good which is bought and sold. The workings of exchange, which are simple, are regulated according to the reciprocal debts which exist between towns; and they assure the greatest profit to the dealers who have won confidence.

Just as silver has a price in exchange, so it has one when loaned, and that price is what one calls interest. Now as money in trade has a yield, the person who lends must have an interest in this yield, just as a landowner must have an interest in the yield of land he gives or leases to be farmed. This rate of interest, which rises and falls following circumstances, can only be regulated in commercial centres. The rate of interest is fair when it only puts silver at the price which dealers have placed on it freely and publicly; it is usurious when this price is arbitrary and clandestine.

The metals from which one makes coinage are scarcer or more plentiful, depending on whether they are used for more or fewer purposes: they tend to find a common level among the nations which have free and never-interrupted trade between themselves. That is why their relative value settles itself in all the markets of these nations, just as it would in a single market. Gold and silver each have the same price in all nations, because in all nations these metals are in the same relationship to each other.

As a free, never-interrupted trade tends to make gold and silver equally common among many nations, and for this reason gives each of these metals the same price in all: so a free and never-interrupted trade would tend to make corn equally common among many nations, and would give it the same price among them all.

This price, based on the quantity in relation to the consumption, would be the true price for all: because it would be the most beneficial for each. Then wages would always proportion themselves to the permanent price of corn: they would never fall too low, and each article would be constantly at its true price.

But when trade is not free, if corn is lacking in one nation, it stays deficient, and it rises to an excessive price which is to the detriment of the consumer: and if it is in surplus in another nation, it carries on being so, and it falls to a paltry price which is to the detriment of the producer. There is thus no longer a true price: there is only an excessive or a bargain price, that is to say harm for the buyer or for the seller.

So it is that when the number of merchants is not as great as it might be, monopoly, which raises itself on the ruins of liberty, places corn for sale in excessive or inadequate quantity, according to whether it is in its interest to lower or raise the price. However, if it matters that some corn is always on sale, because one constantly consumes it, it is no less important that it is only put on sale in the quantity one needs to consume. Now this proportion will never be grasped, except when the largest possible number of merchants make corn circulate everywhere with prompt and never-interrupted movement.

It is because this circulation has always been more or less halted that Europe cannot have in corn a measure fit to determine value in different ages and in different places. Once cereals can never be at their true price, once they can never have a permanent price, how can they be a common measure for all ages and all places?

Freedom alone can give each good its true price and cause commerce to flourish. It is then that order establishes itself naturally, that products of every kind multiply as does consumption; that all the land is brought to value; that every citizen finds his subsistence in his work, and plenty spreads. It spreads, I say, because habits are simple: but wretchedness spreads with luxury.

To sustain this plenty a power is required that will protect the arts and trade, that is to say, which will maintain order and freedom. This power has outlays to make, and it is for the landowners alone to pay the subsidies or taxes that it needs.

If this power maintains order and freedom, a nation which busies itself with everything without an exclusive preference, will be as rich as it can be. In every government see that all kinds of work are equally protected, and let the export and import of all goods, even necessities, be without restriction or interruption; then all nations will be rich, and their respective wealth will be by virtue of the fertility of the soil and the hard work of the inhabitants.

*END OF THE FIRST PART*

# SECOND PART

*Commerce and Government Considered
in Relation to Each Other Following
Some Assumptions*

ALTHOUGH WE are almost completely alike through the needs which follow from our physical constitution, we differ in particular through the needs
which follow from our customs, and which, multiplying in proportion to
the progress of the arts, develop our sensitivity and intelligence by degrees.
The peoples are as brutes when they are limited to the needs which I have
called natural. It appears as though nothing summons their attention: they
are scarcely able to make some observations. But in step as they acquire new
needs, their gaze rests on new objects. They notice what they never noticed
before. One might say that objects only begin to exist for them when they
have an interest in knowing that they exist.

However beneficial this progress may be, it would be dangerous for a
people to pride itself on excessive sensibility, and to have a profusion of
intelligence only to apply it to frivolous objects. However, there you have
what happens wherever needs multiply to excess. More than ever a play-
thing of constantly changing circumstances, a people then changes itself
continuously and applauds every change. Its customs vie with each other,
destroy themselves, reproduce themselves, change: ever different in itself,
the people never knows its identity. It behaves randomly according to its
customs, its views, its prejudices. It has no thought of reforming itself: it
does not think it needs to. As it is preoccupied with what it believes to exist,
laws or abuses, order or disorder, all seem indifferent to it; and its delusion
is such that it thinks it sees its prosperity in the very things that prove its
decadence.

Is it by fighting the customs of such a people head on that one might flatter oneself to be enlightening it? It is too blinded and its eyes would shun the
light as soon as one showed it truths that it does not wish to see.

For it to judge its errors it must be unaware that they are its own. Now
one might, through assumptions, attempt to point them out to it in other
peoples, where it would have some trouble in recognising itself. One might
at least make it see perceptibly the advantages of which it deprives itself, if
one has caused it to notice those enjoyed by a people which does not share

its prejudices. That is what I intend in this second part. Besides, this method is the unique way to simplify overcomplicated questions which are raised about commerce, considered in relation to government; and one must simplify them if one wishes to treat them with precision.

# 1  The Distribution of Wealth, When Trade Enjoys Complete and Permanent Freedom

I ASSUME that the country that our tribe occupies is as large as England, France, Spain, or as these three kingdoms put together. It has to have a certain extensiveness, and commerce must find a considerable stock-in-trade in the variety of products that the provinces will need to exchange.

This country is filled with hamlets, villages, boroughs, towns. It is a multitude of free cities which govern themselves near enough by the same laws; and which, remembering their origins, regard themselves as one and the same family, although they already form several peoples.

All these peoples, busy with agriculture and the arts which relate to it, or which tend to make it flourish, live a simple life, and live in peace. The magistracies are the ceiling of ambition for the citizens and none of them has yet thought of aspiring to tyranny.

These peoples know neither tolls, nor customs dues, nor arbitrary taxes, nor privileges, nor the police forces which hamper liberty. Among them, everyone does what he wishes and freely enjoys the fruits of his labour.

Finally, they have no enemies, since we have placed them in a country inaccessible to any foreign nation.

There you have the assumptions following which you can form an idea for yourself of what I understand by commerce which enjoys complete freedom. It simply mattered to make that notion perfectly clear; and it hardly matters that some of the assumptions do not appear realistic.

To make trade flourish in all the provinces where I spread out cities, it is essential that the surplus pours out without hindrance, reciprocally from the one to the other, and that it supplies what is missing in the places where it spreads. It is a kind of ebb and flow where things balance out by alternating movement and tend to place themselves on a level.

Among the peoples we are observing, nature alone can place obstacles in trade's way, and we lift them, or at least we lessen them. Navigation on the rivers is made easier, canals are dug, roads are constructed. These works which amaze us, as we, who do nothing except by dint of money, are rarely rich enough to undertake them, cost little to a sober nation which has willing arms. It sees its interest there; it feels that it is working for itself; and it carries out the greatest undertakings. It is not forced to impose taxes since all contribute voluntarily, one of his labour, another of his foodstuffs, to provide the workers' subsistence.

The transport of merchandise is thus carried out with the minimum expenditure. Everywhere we have outlets to make surplus goods leave: everywhere these outlets are so many doors to allow essential goods to arrive; and, in consequence, exchanges between all the provinces are always made with equal facility, at least to the extent that the nature of the ground allows. If there is some difference, it only comes from the obstacles which nature has placed, and which it has not been possible to flatten out equally everywhere. But where there are more obstacles there is also more industry; and skill seems to make good the wrongs of nature. Let us see how wealth spreads naturally everywhere in a land such as the one I have just invented.

The country districts, each abounding in varied types of products, are rightly the first source of wealth.

In the boroughs, in the villages, in the hamlets, even on the farms, people work up the raw materials to make them ready for the needs of the settler who cultivates his field, or of the farmer who cultivates another's field. There they make ploughs, yokes, carts, tumbrils, pickaxes, spades, coarse linen, heavy cloths and other works which require little skill, and are used in the neighbourhood of the places where they are made.

These manufactures, however coarse they are, give a new value to raw materials. They are thus so many channels through which the spring of wealth is distributed to spread from one side to the other at a certain distance.

I say *at a certain distance,* because the works which come out of these manufactures are only a stock-in-trade for the canton where they are established. Being of little value in themselves, and made expensive by the costs of transport, they would not be marketable in distant places where people make similar goods.

The wealth of the towns consists in the revenues of the landowners and the industry of the inhabitants, an industry whose income is in money. So it is money that forms the principal wealth of the towns, just as produce forms the principal wealth of the countryside.

It is in the towns that the greatest consumption is made. It is the place where the most skilled artisans in every kind of work set up valuable manufactures. There are permanent markets where people come from the countryside to buy works which are not made in the villages, or which are not made so skilfully there. There you have the channels through which wealth in money circulates in greater abundance. [more appreciably: *1798*]

If a town's industry were only paid for by the landowners who lived there, it would not increase the quantity of money which circulated in that place. However, it would make it circulate faster and that speed would make the same amount of money equal to a greater one.

But if, as we have noted, the articles which are made in the countryside are not of a type to be sold far away, it is not the same with those which come from the manufactures established in the towns. As they are at a greater price, the increase occasioned by transport costs is very little in comparison with this price. The artisans are thus not reduced to being paid only by the landowners of the towns they live in. Money reaches them from all the places where their works are sought after. It is really they who dig the channels through which wealth comes together in the towns; channels which form more branches and more extensive branches in line with industry's progress.

Such in general is the distribution of wealth between the countryside and the towns; it is that the country districts are rich in products through the ploughman's work and that the cities are rich in money through the incomes of the landowners and the work of the artisans.

[*1798 addition:* But you must not think I mean that money is wealth exclusively for the towns. Doubtless it moves continually through the countryside where it is exchanged for products: but it always returns to the towns as to reservoirs from which it flows back again into the countryside.]

But from one country area to another, and from town to town, this distribution is not and cannot be made in an equal fashion.

The ploughman sees the foodstuffs that are for sale. The more he is asked for, the more he demands from the fields he cultivates, and he applies all his effort to bring each piece of land to value. The countryside neighbouring the main towns, where people consume more, is thus the richest in produce.

In the remote countryside this wealth will be in proportion to the greater or lesser ease in transporting foodstuffs into the principal towns. Whatever trouble people have taken to make roads, to dig canals, to make rivers navigable, it has not always been possible to open up equally convenient outlets everywhere. Nature often placed obstacles in the way, which, even after being smoothed out, caused further great expenses for the transport of goods.

It is not in the ploughman's interest to have foodstuffs beyond what can be consumed. So the provinces where export is less easy will be less rich in products. Less rich, I say, in comparison with the others; but rich enough for themselves because they will have as much as they need for their consumption.

In the provinces whose soil is the most unyielding the inhabitants will be harder working and they will have more ingenuity. They will develop the land right up to the rocks which they will cover with crops. In the seasons when they do not have enough work at home they will go in search of it in neighbouring provinces. They will return to their villages with profits which will place them in a position to form some small enterprises. They will increase the number of their animals, they will clear some scraps of land; and they will set up some common manufactures to work up their soil's raw materials themselves. It is in that way that, in proportion to their extent, the least fertile provinces will be able to be almost as populous as the others.

Towns are not all in an equally favourable position for trade because they do not all have the same means to communicate afar. There cannot everywhere be large rivers, channels of communication and usable roads. There will therefore be towns which are more accessible, more engaged in marketing as a result, and more populous. These are the principal ones.

If a city conquered all the others, its town, now the seat of sovereign power, would be the capital, and could fill itself with people to the point where it would confine a twentieth of the citizens. We shall see elsewhere what such a capital must produce in a state. But there are not yet any among the peoples who have developed from our tribe. Up till now they have only been busy each governing itself separately, and none of them has had occasion to discover what it might do with conquests. It takes many circumstances to prepare the means of conquest for a people; and when all these circumstances come together, it does not nourish the ambition of dominating afar, except when, after making unintended conquests, it judges that it is capable of making them: this ambition is not therefore the first idea that proposes itself to a people.

All the cities are consequently free and independent, and if we consider them at a time when dissension has not armed them against each other, we shall judge that their towns communicate among themselves without hindrance.

On this assumption wealth divides itself among the towns by reason of the consumption made in them.

In the chief towns, which enclose a great population and which count many wealthy landowners among the citizens, there will be a great assembly of artisans and merchants of every kind, and money will circulate there more rapidly and in greater quantity.

In the smaller towns there will be less wealth, or less money in circulation; because being less populous they will consume less, and as they consume less they will not have as many artisans or merchants.

But although richer or poorer in money, all the towns have plenty of the things on which they have become dependent; because in all of them, the population is proportioned to the subsistence they can obtain for themselves. The less rich have only been formed because they have found subsistence in the places where they are settled. Now they find every day all the more to subsist on, as their citizens possess more industry as the days pass, and this industry is not held up by any impediment.

Let us conclude that the spread of wealth among the towns condemns none of them to lack necessities. Comparing some with others they are richer or less rich in money as they are more or less populated, but there is abundance in all.

Having seen what is the wealth of the provinces, the countryside and the towns, it remains for us to observe the division of it which must be made among the citizens. They have only one means to enrich themselves, trade.

Now we have distinguished the trade of products which is that of the settler and the farmer, the commerce in manufactures which is that of the artisan, and the commission trade [or long-distance trade: *1798*] which is that of the merchant.

In all these kinds of commerce one only earns in relation to the high price one can set on the goods one sells. It will therefore be according to these prices that the division of wealth will be made among the merchants.

If, under the pretext of provisioning the towns, privileged companies had exclusive permission to carry corn there, you can conceive that they would rapidly enrich themselves on a fantastic scale. They would buy corn at the lowest price in the country districts where the harvests had been plentiful, because corn could only be handed over to them; and soon after they would sell it at the highest price, because, by keeping it back in their warehouses and putting on sale only an amount that was below consumption, they would cause a scarcity, even in places where there was abundance. This monopoly is not known in our cities.

Since everyone is free to sell to whom he wishes and when he wishes, it is the sellers and buyers who decide, alone and freely, on the price of each commodity.

This price, as we have seen, will rise or fall from one market to another. However, if we except the cases of glut or of great scarcity, prices will in general vary imperceptibly because competition will always be nearly the same.

It is rare too, when commerce is free, that the move from abundance to scarcity causes considerable variation in the price.

That would happen if in the same year all provinces experienced the same plenty at the same time, and the same dearth at another time. This cannot happen in a country of a certain extent whose parts are in a different situation. Normally when one province is in dearth another is in abundance.

Now abundance in one province causes the price of foodstuffs to fall very little there, when trade is free to export the surplus.

Likewise dearth raises the price little in another where trade is not slow to bring in the surplus.

So it is not in proportion to a localised abundance or scarcity that prices vary most perceptibly: it is rather in proportion as trade has less freedom. So we have demonstrated that, when freedom is complete and permanent, goods tend to make themselves equally common everywhere at the same price, or near enough.

Whatever this variation may be, wealth cannot be spread very unequally between those who carry out trade in products amongst peoples where this trade enjoys complete freedom, and where, in consequence, competition between sellers and buyers is the sole regulator of prices.

So it will not be in the power of some settlers or farmers to sell their food-stuffs for as much as they would like. The market price will necessarily be the price of everything: and they will be mutually forced to content themselves with the same profits.

In this state of affairs, the commerce in products will not enrich some at the expense of others, because no one will gain too much, and all will gain. All will share in the pleasures to which custom gives them claims; and if some, harder-working, live in greater comfort, the others will not fall into wretchedness; because to subsist it will be enough to work as one generally works. It is not to be feared that market prices will deprive anyone of the profits he ought to make. For that to happen all the cultivators would have to agree to sell at a loss, which cannot be.

Commerce in manufactures will spread wealth in the same manner. Competition will regulate the artisans' wage according to the type of work. Some will earn more, some less. But all will subsist, and each, in his branch of work, will be happy to enjoy those things which in general those who make them in competition with him enjoy.

It will be the same for the commission trade, as for the two other trades, since competition will regulate the wage of the merchants.

If goods came from a distant, foreign country we should not know in our cities what they had cost in those places; and by capitalising on that ignorance, merchants would be able to make huge profits, especially as they would have few competitors. But, following our assumptions, this disadvantage is not to be feared. Since our cities only trade among themselves, the goods offered for sale are the products of their soil, or the works of their manufactures; that is to say, goods whose prices, known by everyone, are always regulated by competition.

In proving in the first part of this work that the true price is the same in the common market where all nations come freely to sell and buy, I have noted that this price is higher or lower for them depending on whether they are far away or adjacent to the common market.

Prices will therefore not be the same wherever our cities have been established. First of all, they will be higher in the towns than in the country districts. That is because, besides the wages due to the merchants, we also owe them the carriage costs and an indemnity for the risks they have run.

Secondly, prices will be higher in the chief towns since that is where people make the largest consumption. There one is better fed, better clothed, better housed, better furnished. Now the more one consumes, the more one demands; and the more one demands, the more one buys at a high price, other things being equal.

Besides, in proportion as consumption becomes greater, people will have to go to look for products in a greater extent of territory. There will thus be more risks and more transport costs to pay.

But lastly, although prices are not the same everywhere, they will be regulated everywhere by competition: everywhere they will be what they should be, and wealth will be spread with little inequality among those who compete in the same branch of trade. Everyone will have what he needs to subsist according to his condition, and no one will be able to make himself much wealthier than his rivals.

Someone who has not enough money income to live in a town will have enough in products to live in a country district: the worker who has no kind of income will find his subsistence in a wage proportioned to the price of foodstuffs; and because no one will be able to make himself surpassingly rich, so no one will be able to fall into wretchedness.

I estimate that a present-day merchant who gains 40 or 50 per cent will accumulate great wealth if, continuing to live with the sobriety to which he has become accustomed, he reinvests each year the lion's share of his profits in trade. So it is not because he spends little that he becomes rich: it is because he earns a lot; and if he earned little he would not become wealthy whatever his savings were otherwise. But among the peoples whom we are observing the gains will be limited to procuring for the merchants the use of things necessary to their status.

There is only one class of citizen whom savings could enrich, that is the landlords. By making savings on their incomes, they would be able to increase the value of their lands, and it is to be wished that they should do so. This method of getting richer would help the day-labourers, for whom they provide work, to live more comfortably; and it would be beneficial to the state, for which it would provide products in greater quantity. But it can only be very slowly that one acquires wealth by this route, and the wealth is necessarily limited.

So everything comes together among the peoples whom we have conjured up to place limits to the fortunes of individuals; it seems that they cannot know the passion for money. Among them each person has his essentials: a large number live in ease; few are rich; no one is opulent. That is what freedom of trade must naturally bring about when it puts every good at its true price and it proportions wages to the price of subsistence.

## ～ 2  The Circulation of Wealth When Trade
Enjoys Complete Freedom

THE ARTS multiply the goods of secondary need, they perfect them; and in proportion to their progress, they place in trade a greater quantity of goods, and goods of greater value.

We have seen manufactures right down to the villages; but these are manufactures which are not sold far away, and which, in consequence, only cause wealth to circulate in their localities.

So it is for the manufactures set up in the towns to produce a general circulation between all our cities. The works which come out of them, being made to be sought after everywhere, are on sale everywhere, and the trade made in them causes a sequence of exchanges on every hand which brings everything to value.

I call *mercantile* the provinces where there are manufactures of this kind and *agrarian* those where there are none. Let us look at the trade between the one and the other kind.

If an agrarian province buys cloth and linen with the surplus of its products, or with a sum of money equal to that surplus, it makes a profitable trade. Because in handing over the surplus of its products for sale, it gives up something which is useless to it; and in handing over an equivalent sum of money, it gives up money with which this surplus will be bought, and, as a result, the money will come back to it.

This trade is equally profitable to the mercantile provinces whether they are paid in products or whether they are paid in coin. Because they need these products and this money for their subsistence and for the upkeep of their manufactures. It will often happen that they subsist in part on the product of the agrarian provinces; but the latter will not suffer from that if they only ever give up their surplus.

This respective position of the provinces would secure the same plenty for all, if it could always stay unchanged.

It is not to be denied that in mercantile provinces manufactures to a greater or lesser extent harm the cultivation of products necessary for man's subsistence. By preference, people there will grow the raw materials for which manufacturers are accustomed to pay a higher price, and the lure of gain will draw the inhabitants to become artisans rather than ploughmen. These provinces will thus be forced to carry their money into the agrarian provinces to provide themselves with those foodstuffs lacking for their subsistence; and they will carry all the more there as they become more populous. Now the manufactures, which are a magnet for industry, will make new inhabitants come every day from all over.

Subsistence in a mercantile province is thus not in proportion to its population. But it is easy for it to put this disadvantage right, since with the product of its manufactures it can buy everything it lacks.

The more need the mercantile provinces have of subsistence, the more they demand from the agrarian provinces; and in consequence, they make agriculture flourish there. For the same reason, the fewer manufactures the agrarian provinces have, the more they cause them to flourish in the mercantile provinces. So it is that as the ones lack what is surplus in the others, they all come together for their common advantage.

However, there is a disadvantage for an agrarian province, which is that it is never possible for it to buy except by reason of its surplus. Indeed, as each individual is free to dispose of his property as he pleases, by what means could the province come to regulate its expenditure in this proportion? To increase its expenditure beyond its surplus, would it not be enough, for instance, for the use of fine cloths and fine linen to become more common? It would then have to give up part of the foodstuffs needed for its consumption, or to give a sum with which people could come to buy them.

In the one case as in the other, it would not have enough foodstuffs left: that would make them rise to a higher price, and would force some of the inhabitants to go and live elsewhere.

The more it consumed in cloth and expensive fabrics the more everything would become expensive for it; because the subsistence it would be forced to give in exchange would become scarcer every day.

However, the cloths and fabrics of which it was consuming more would become still more costly, and cause a greater amount of money to pass into the mercantile provinces.

As the latter become richer they form new undertakings. They extend their trade more and more, and they summon new citizens from every part because they offer industry copious wages. That is how these provinces seem bound to enrich themselves and populate themselves at the expense of the agrarian provinces, and seem to be preparing their ruin. But they will not cause it.

You may perhaps judge that it does not matter to the state that wealth and men pass from one province to another, provided that the total of wealth and of men always finds itself the same. However, it is not right, in order to make some provinces more populous and to enrich them, to make of the others so many deserts, or only to leave a wretched people there. If agriculture decayed in the agrarian provinces, because they were no longer populous or rich enough, the mercantile provinces which had caused their ruin would destroy themselves in reaction, because they would not be able to extract anything from them, nor carry anything to them.

Everything would seem to draw towards this general ruin, if the trade in manufactures belonged exclusively to the mercantile provinces.

This is not how they possess it; it can be shared with them, and it will be. In step as the mercantile provinces make everything more expensive, industry will revive in the agrarian provinces, where people would like to go on wearing fine linen and fine cloth, and where they find that it is progressively more difficult to buy them at the price set by the mercantile provinces. It is easy for the agrarian provinces to judge how profitable it would be for them to have their own manufactures, where labour is at a lower cost.

Now if there are flourishing manufactures in the mercantile provinces, there are also others which are hardly so. The attraction of profit has multiplied them excessively and they harm each other by rivalry. There are therefore manufacturers interested in setting up elsewhere. They move into the agrarian provinces where they are called for.

At first, they only make poor-quality cloths, because they do not have the choice of workers; the most skilled having remained in the mercantile provinces where rich manufacturers give them higher wages.

But they offer their cloths at the lowest possible price, and they find a sale in a region where people in general are not rich enough to buy finer ones.

Bit by bit they train up better workers. Then they make cloths which rival in beauty those of the mercantile provinces; and they sell them for a lower price, because labour costs them little and they live very economically.

So the mercantile provinces see some of their trade escaping them. To keep it, as far as they are able, they lower the price of their cloth, of their fabrics, etc. They are forced to do so by the competition of the manufactures set up in the agrarian provinces.

In this way there will be a continuous balancing of wealth and population between all the provinces: a balancing which will be maintained by industry and competition, and which, without reaching a permanent equilibrium, will always seem to lead towards it, and will always be close to it. In a word, all provinces will be rich and populous by reason of the fertility of their soil and their industry.

If a province believed it could become wealthier by concerning itself with the ways of attracting and retaining gold and silver from all the others, that would be an error on its part as fatal as it was gross. Soon everything would become costlier for it: it would lose population: sooner or later it would be forced to spread abroad its gold and silver; and it would have no more idea how to bring them back because, as everything became more expensive, it would have lost its manufactures, and it would need a long time to set them up again.

So gold and silver must be able to enter and leave freely. That is the way that wealth balances itself between all the provinces: all will be in plenty through the exchange of their work.

It is true that, when one province is richer in metal, it seems to have an advantage over others. Since the price of the land's products and of work are evaluated in money, they are higher in it. They will double, for instance, if it has twice as much money in circulation. With the product of one of its arpents, valued at four ounces of silver, it can buy the product of two arpents, which would only bring in two ounces each in silver in another province. In the same way the product of the work of one of its inhabitants will be the equivalent of the product of the work of two inhabitants of another province. In consequence, it will sell for twice as much money what people buy from it, and it will pay half as much money for what people sell to it.

This advantage would be huge and real for it, if it had the exclusive privilege of the trade in manufactures. It does not. If it believes it is richer because it has more money it is thus harbouring an illusion.

In reality the provinces which have been harmed will concern themselves with ways to draw money to them, and they will succeed through the cheapness of their manufactures. They will sell a lot, while the province that is rich in metal will sell little, or nothing, and nevertheless it will buy all the more, as its consumption will be far greater. So money will leave it, not to return, and it will enter the others, not to leave them, or at least only to leave when they have made the same mistake.

To develop my ideas I have had to show how it appears that provinces must get rich at each other's expense. All the same this cannot happen when one assumes that they give trade complete and permanent freedom. Because if the circulation of wealth can be carried on with some inequality, it is not to be feared that this inequality can ever go as far as to place wretchedness in sharp contrast to opulence. All the peoples will work in emulation of each other, because they will all want to join in the same benefits. In this competition manufactures will gradually decay in the provinces that they have enriched, and where the price of labour has risen; while they will recover in the other provinces which they must make wealthier, and where the price of labour is lower. They will pass from province to province. Everywhere they will set down a part of the wealth of a nation; and trade will be like a river that divides itself in a host of channels, to water all the lands in succession.

This revolving motion will finish only to begin again. When, in one province, the high price of labour starts to make manufactures decay, the low price will raise them up again in another. They will thus be more or less rich in turn. But because none will be too rich, so none will be poor. That is, wealth will flow back continuously from one to the other; following the different gradients that trade will make them take, they will pour out in succession everywhere. This revolving motion will be without drawbacks, because it will happen naturally and without violence. It is imperceptibly that some provinces will lose a part of their commerce; it is imperceptibly that others will recover what they have lost. Freedom has thus the benefit of guaranteeing them all against poverty, and at the same time checking the advance of wealth in each, when excess of this kind could be harmful.

At the start of this chapter I was obliged to distinguish two kinds of provinces, the one mercantile and the other agrarian: but you can see that, through freedom of trade, they are all at the same time both agrarian and mercantile. That is to say that, in each, people are concerned with everything, and no one knows exclusive preferences.

# 3 The Simple Ways of an Isolated Nation Within Which Trade Enjoys Complete Freedom

PLACED CLOSELY enough under the same heavens, the people whom we observe generally enjoy the same products, only in more or less abundance, depending on the nature of the soil and the hard work of the cultivators. A foodstuff, which is rare in one province, will be common in another, where a foodstuff which is common elsewhere will be scarce.

For trade between them, these peoples possess a stock in the products of which each of them has more than enough; and, as skills develop, they have another stock in their industry.

This double stock gives them the wherewithal to make exchanges of every kind; and through these exchanges, all enjoy the same products and the same goods.

They enjoy the same products, because, with the surplus of those which grow in their lands, they buy those which do not grow there.

They enjoy the same comforts, because they either develop the same skills or they trade with those who develop them.

Now it is the needs we have created for ourselves, and the means we use to satisfy them, which make our customs, our practices, our habits, in a word our behaviour.

Needs are the same for all the peoples we have imagined: the means of satisfying them are also the same. Therefore their ways are yet again the same.

So in order to give them a new way of life one would have to carry to them products foreign to their soil, or comforts unfamiliar to their skills.

But not only do they have the same mode of existence: I also state that their ways are simple and can only be simple. That is to say that it is impossible for them to know luxury.

We have seen that luxury consists in those pleasures which are the portion of a small number to the exclusion of the majority; that these pleasures only occur as people scorn common goods in order to seek out rare and expensive goods; and finally, that these goods are only rare and expensive because they come from a remote region, or because they have been worked up with great skill.

Now, following our assumptions, no foreign rarity can arrive among the peoples whom we are observing. It will not be any more in their power to obtain these works for themselves, works to which considerable labour will give a high price. As no one would be rich enough to pay for them, no artisan would dream of making them.

We have just proved that among such peoples there cannot be those over-whelming fortunes, which form from the despoilment of a host of families reduced to ruin. How could this disorder occur in a land where commerce, the sole means of obtaining ease for oneself, sinks and recovers in turn from one province to another, and everywhere keeps wealth at more or less the same level, or constantly tends to bring it back to it?

Now once this wealth cannot get lost in a small number of families, there will not be those exclusive pleasures which mock public misery, and which seem to efface the majority of the citizens from the ranks of humanity.

I do not mean that all will enjoy the same pleasures on an equal footing; doubtless not all, for instance, will wear cloth of equal fineness: but they will all wear cloth. Each, according to his position, will enjoy the comforts that the arts bring. Each one will be in plenty and ease, since all will have the use of the articles which their station in life allows them to make necessities; and if fortunes are not equal, it will only be because talents are not equal. Yet, once more, no one will be able to make excessive expenditure, because no one will be able to enrich himself exclusively.

I can see only one way to introduce luxury among these peoples: that would be to substitute exclusive privileges for freedom of trade. Then there would soon be a great disparity of fortunes, and articles which had previously been common would become scarce through the high price to which they would be raised. In such a case glass and earthenware, for instance, would become a luxury; and it is just so that china and mirrors are a luxury in our country.

WE HAVE SEEN what freedom can achieve. It is time to sow dissension among our peoples, and to place constraints on trade: our assumptions will be the more plausible for that.

Divided by wars they form several nations which have opposing interests.

Now if we may assume that each of these nations trades freely within its boundaries we may no longer assume that they all trade freely with each other.

External trade, always hampered and sometimes suspended, will be all the less flourishing as it will be more expensive, whether from the losses to which it is exposed, or through the efforts made to sustain it.

These nations therefore do themselves mutual harm: firstly, because they each deprive themselves of the advantages which they would obtain for each other through exchanges.

Secondly, they harm themselves more, because they lay waste each others' lands. Each time they take up arms, they destroy a stock of wealth which they could have put into circulation, and which cannot be there any more. There will be fields which warfare will not allow to be sown: there will be others, where it will not allow any harvesting. Consequently, products will diminish, and the population with them.

I want some of these nations to cover themselves with glory, with that glory which the peoples, in their stupidity, attach to conquest, and which historians, stupider still, love to celebrate to the point of boring the reader: what will be their advantage? They will rule far away in countries once populous and fertile, and now in part deserted and uncultivated. Because it is not by exterminating that they will assure their sway over previously free peoples. Let us assume that our cities are reduced to four enemy nations, more or less equally powerful, or which attempt to maintain themselves in a kind of equilibrium.

Are they equally powerful? They will hurt each other equally.

Do they try to keep themselves in a kind of balance? Two or three will join against a power whose dominance threatens to subject them, and they will hurt themselves again. The war will cost even the conquering nation provinces; because I regard as lost, provinces where the population and cultivation have been ruined or markedly damaged. Indeed, an empire which lost population and let lands fall fallow would not be the greater for having pushed back its boundaries.

But this balance, will one succeed in establishing it? Never: only false steps will be made, and anxiety will seem the sole moving force of the powers: they will confidently abandon themselves to the most ruinous projects, to carry them out in a more ruinous manner still.

Now, in this disorder, will the lands be as rich in products as when they were divided between a host of peaceful cities? They will be all the less so, as, with war taking away all freedom to trade, the surplus will cease to pass reciprocally from one nation to another. So it will not be consumed any more: now once it ceases to be consumed it ceases to reproduce itself.

While agriculture is damaged, many manufactures will collapse; and those which still exist will not have the same market any more. Normally they will only be able to sell to the nation in which they are established; and they will sell less to it, because that nation will itself be less rich.

No doubt you will say that these peoples will not always be at war. Indeed, there will be intervals of peace: but in those intervals you will not make good all the evils war has caused; and yet people will place new obstacles in the way of trade.

## 5 Blows Directed Against Commerce: Customs Dues, Tolls

THE FOUR NATIONS which we postulated in the previous chapter are now four monarchies, whose monarchs rival each other in the ambition to be rich and powerful: but sadly they do just what is needed to be neither the one nor the other. They are in a deluded state from which they cannot escape. Because each of them believes he has nothing to fear from his neighbours, and even sees that he has sometimes made himself feared, they believe that they are all equally powerful, or near enough. The same faults that they repeat, copying each other, hold them in a balance of weakness, which they take for a balance of power: their great maxim is that one must weaken one's enemies. There you have the essence of policy which must give them turn by turn the upper hand; furthermore they have no maxim for obtaining real strength.

One of them, to increase his income, conceived of putting taxes on all foreign merchandise that enters his states; and to that end he established customs and tolls. The others also set up customs and tolls.

Some time later he persuaded himself that the income would increase further if he placed taxes on the goods leaving his kingdom; so he placed them and the others set them following his example.

When it was no longer permissible to export or to import anything, unless one had paid in advance a certain tax, everything became more expensive in these four monarchies by virtue of the taxes imposed; and this increase in price which first of all reduced consumption, and then production, suddenly slowed down trade. There were manufacturers who, not being able to be certain of selling, no longer worked. Those who continued in their business worked less, and the ploughmen neglected every surplus which was becoming useless to them. So it is that customs duties and tolls injured agriculture, the arts and trade, and reduced to beggary a large number of citizens who had previously lived by their work.

Free trade between these four kingdoms would have caused the surplus of all to flow back from one to the other; and each sovereign would have based his power on a numerous people made wealthy by the arts and by agriculture.

That is not how our four monarchs saw things. On the contrary they doubled taxes because they thought they were doubling income, which they did not double. They tripled and quadrupled taxes; and they did not understand how, far from having more income, they had less. They did not see that they had caused consumption to fall.

Trade languished, and they thought they had found the reason. How, people said in the four monarchies, could our manufactures not fall since we are in the habit of preferring articles made abroad to those which are made at home? So one of the monarchs conceived of subjecting imports to new taxes and of suppressing some of those which he had placed on exports. But the three others, who were no less crafty, did the same, and trade did not pick up anywhere.

There was a great profit in defrauding the duties at tolls and customs, and people defrauded them. So it was forbidden in the four kingdoms, under severe penalties, to sell foreign goods for which one had not paid the tax imposed. But people carried on selling fraudulently: they simply sold at a higher price, compensating for the risks to which they were exposed. The traders who committed this fraud were called *smugglers*.

It was necessary to spread troops on all frontiers to stop the smuggling, which was not prevented. So there you have the four monarchies armed in time of peace in order to stop all trade between themselves.

Under the pretence of levying the sovereign's rights, employees in the customs and tolls committed a great deal of harassment; and the government, which protected them, seemed to be in league with them, to compel all the traders to become smugglers.

These employees were large in number; men armed with the intent to prevent fraud were in even greater number. All these men consumed a large part of the customs duties and tolls dues at the expense of the state, and yet they were so many citizens taken away from crafts and agriculture.

## 6 Blows Directed Against Commerce: Taxes on Industry

OUR CITIES FROM their foundation, and consequently a long time before the monarchy, had recognised the obligation citizens have to contribute to public expenditure.

Composed solely of settlers, it was only from the settlers that they could ask for subsidies. Consequently they levied them on each field and everyone paid by reason of the products he harvested.

This subsidy was raised at little expense. Its assessment was made in each canton by the settlers themselves. Each person paid without being forced, and as no one could complain of being overcharged, so no one thought of paying less than he owed. When, afterwards, some citizens found themselves without belongings, people did not think of demanding subsidies from them. It could not even occur to anyone to make men who had nothing pay. Custom, which determines the rules when it is reasonable, did not allow it.

These citizens who only had their strength thus lived on their work, or on the wage they received from the settlers, and they paid nothing.

This custom continued with the progress of the arts because every custom lasts. Therefore the artisans and the merchants, as well as the farmers and the day-labourers, lived on their wages and no one thought at all of asking them for subsidies.

So long as this custom lasted, everything flourished. Industry, assured of a wage regulated by competition alone and from which nothing had to be deducted, busied itself with ways of increasing this wage, whether by creating new crafts or by perfecting already known skills.

Then everything became useful. The surplus found a use in step with the progress of the arts and commerce. People consumed more: products grew by reason of consumption; and the lands were better cultivated every day.

Matters continued in this state right up to the time of the monarchy. They remained there still even under the first kings. But at length there had to be a transformation.

Because the artisans and merchants lived in ease, people asked: but why should these men who are rich not make a contribution to the subsidies? How have they been able to be exempt? Must the settlers alone [landowners alone: *1798*] pay all the expenses, and does not every citizen have the duty to contribute to public expenditure? This reasoning seemed a gleam of enlightenment.

So taxes were placed on industry, and it was no longer permissible to undertake any kind of work, unless one had paid a certain sum of money to the state. *It was no longer permitted to work!* There is a very strange law. However, when one wishes someone who has nothing to pay for a licence to earn his subsistence, it is very necessary to forbid work to those who do not pay; and in consequence to take from them every means of subsistence.

One does not make the same profit in every occupation any more than in every kind of trade. It therefore seemed fair to create different classes, whether of artisans or of merchants, in order to tax each of them in proportion to the profits they could make.

This operation was not easy. How is one to estimate the amount a man can earn from his hard work? It is bound to happen that in the same occupation and in the same trade the person who earns less will pay as much as the person who earns more. That is a disadvantage which was not seen or which people did not want to see.

The name *Guild* was given to the different classes of artisans; and because one could only be admitted to them if one had passed as master, they were further given the name of *Masteries*. As for the classes of merchants, they were called *Corporations*.

As many guilds were created as the trades that could be distinguished in the mechanical arts; and as many corporations were created as branches of trade were distinguished.

When these distinctions had been made, the tax that each guild or corporation had to pay was set; and, in consequence, those who formed themselves into these bodies not only had the right to work, they also had the right to forbid all work to those who had been excluded; that is to say, to reduce them to begging for their bread.

To work without being a member of one of these bodies was a misdemeanour; and because an individual would not have wanted to stay idle, or rather, because he had been forced to work for his own and his family's subsistence, he was apprehended and condemned to a fine he could not pay, or that he could only pay to fall into wretchedness.

As the chief branches of trade meet at the trunk from which they arise, still more are joined to these principal branches, and so forth; you may imagine that it will be all the more difficult to disentangle all these branches, as one divides the corporations of merchants and subdivides them again. However, they will divide and subdivide, because the sovereign, seeing that he is paid a new tax as each new corporation emerges, will believe himself richer when he has caused them to multiply.

Then the corporations will entangle like branches at the trunk they join. They will no longer be able to distinguish their privileges: they will blame each other for encroachment, and law suits will be born. It will be the same with the guilds.

All these bodies will be forced to incur great expense, whether to pay taxes, or to pursue their law suits, or to hunt out those who are working without having been incorporated into a guild or a corporation.

Forced to this expense, each of them will levy common funds from its members; and these funds will be wasted in assemblies, meals, buildings, and often in embezzlement.

These expenses will be recouped on the merchandise they sell. They will lay down the law to the consumers because, having the sole right to work, they fix the price of their work as they please. However many artisans and merchants there are, everything must become more expensive; because the guilds and corporations must always find the wherewithal to renew the common funds that they waste.

Besides, there exists in these guilds and corporations an *esprit de corps*, a kind of point of honour, which forces people to sell at the same price as the others. A person would pass for a traitor if he sold at a lower price; and he would expose himself to unpleasantness if he gave the slightest suspicion there.

Accustomed to laying down the law, these bodies sell dear the advantage of sharing in their privileges. It is not enough to pay for apprenticeship. So long as it lasts one only works for the master's account; and one must expend many years to learn a trade which one could sometimes know at the end of a few months. The person who has the greatest aptitude is sentenced to an apprenticeship as long as the person who has the least aptitude. From that it results that all those who have no means are excluded for ever from every guild. Have you been received? If you do not succeed there is no more time to serve another apprenticeship: you would no longer have the means to pay for it, and you are condemned to beg.

When the professions were free in our cities, the artisans somehow found themselves scattered widely. The ploughmen, in the moments when they did not apply themselves to cultivation, could work at some mechanical art. They could give work to some children who were not yet strong enough to work in the fields, and they used the profits they had made for cultivation. This expedient was taken from them when all the trades had been formed into guilds.

Thus the guilds and the corporations take all comfort away from the country inhabitants: they reduce to beggary the hard-working citizens who have not the means to pay for an apprenticeship: they force them to pay a high price to a master to learn from him what one could often learn much better on one's own: finally, they deliver a blow to commerce because, by making everything more expensive, they reduce consumption and consequently production, cultivation and the population. Can one reflect on these abuses and not recognise how contrary they are to public welfare?

## 7  Blows Directed Against Commerce: Privileged and Exclusive Companies

THE PRIVILEGES accorded to guilds and corporations are iniquitous rights which only seem in order because we find them established. It is true that the competition of a large number of artisans and merchants places limits on the profit that guilds and corporations might draw from their monopoly. But it is no less true, according to what we have just shown, that these bodies take away comfort from many citizens, reduce others to beggary, make everything more expensive, and bring damage to agriculture as to trade.

However, once people became used to regarding monopoly as in the order of things in a large body, it was natural to see it again as in order when it was found in smaller bodies. An abuse which has passed into custom becomes a rule; and because one has judged badly at first, one carries on judging badly.

It was easy to foresee that the profits stemming from a privilege, which were great for each member in a large body, would be greater still as one reduced the number of members. It was no more than a matter of establishing this new monopoly and few obstacles were found in the way.

Salt, which is very common in our four monarchies, was, through free trade, at a price proportionate to the means of the less well-off citizens; and it was consumed on a large scale since it is necessary to men, to animals, and even to the land for which it is an excellent fertilizer.

There was thus bound to be great profit in exercising a salt monopoly. The project for it was made and to that end a privileged and exclusive company was created. The company gave the sovereign a considerable sum, and it gave the great men who protected it a share in its profit. Those who made up this company called themselves *contractors* because they had contracted with the king. They alone carried out, in his own name, the salt trade in the length and breadth of the kingdom. The first king who found this source of wealth caused the others' eyes to open, and he was copied.

The price of salt rose suddenly from one to six, seven or eight; and yet the contractors, who alone had the right to buy it at source, paid so poorly for it that people ceased to work several salt pits.

Such was the abuse of this monopoly that the consumption of salt fell to the point where, to make this branch of trade pay, it was necessary to force each of the citizens to take a certain amount per head. Salt was thus a fertilizer taken away from the land: people stopped giving it to animals; and very many subjects only continued to consume it because people forced them not to do without a necessary substance.

The company of contractors cost the state a vast amount. How many employees spread throughout the provinces for the sale of salt! How many armed men to prevent contraband! How many searches to make sure that all the subjects had bought the required amount! How much vexation! How much expense in arrests, seizures, fines, confiscation! In a word, how many families reduced to beggary!

There you have the troubles that this privileged and exclusive company produced. However, it did not yield the king half what it took from the citizens. The greater part of the other half was consumed in expenses. The rest was divided among the contractors: and if they did not have enough profit, as indeed they never found they had enough, they were given ordinance upon ordinance to give them every day greater scope for their privileges; that is to say, to permit them to harry the people more and more.

Once the profit of this monopoly was known, it spread a spirit of greed and plundering. One would have said that it was essential for every branch of trade to be carried out exclusively by companies. They were formed every day: patrons begged for them, often with success. They sold their credit, and they did not hide it. Everyone thought he could permit himself what he saw happening. It was the monopoly of the great.

These companies always had as an excuse the good of the state; and they did not fail to demonstrate in the privileges they were given great advantages for the very trade. They were particularly successful when they proposed to set up new manufactures.

It is clear that new manufactures deserve to be given advantages, that is to say to be multiplied; and the more useful they can be, the more one should reward those to whom the manufactures are owed. But exclusive privileges were granted, and straight away luxury came out of these manufactures. The works which were sold there became costly and scarce, whereas they could have been cheap and plentiful. I return to the consequences I have already repeated: *reduction in consumption, in production, in cultivation, in the population;* and I add, *birth of luxury, growth of misery.*

## ~ 8  Blows Directed Against Commerce: Taxes on Consumption

THE TRUE WAY to make everyone contribute was to place taxes on consumption and our four monarchs placed them on every kind. They persuaded themselves that this imposition would be very productive for them and at the same time an indifferent burden on their subjects. Because in matters of administration one often reconciles the contradictory.

But they deceived themselves, both on the yield which is not as great as it appears, and on the burden which is greater than they thought.

First of all, the yield is not as large as it appears.

It is true that since everyone is forced to consume, everyone is forced to pay; and if one pauses at that consideration alone, one can see that the yield grows by reason of the number of consumers.

But one must first deduct the expenses of collection; expenses which themselves grow by virtue of the number of companies to which one farms out or gives the administration of each of these taxes, and by virtue of the number of employees they have on their payroll.

Besides, these companies alone know the potential yield of each of these taxes, and they put all their skill into concealing it from the government, which itself often closes its eyes to the abuses it sees. The collection would enlighten the public if it was simple, and would be less expensive: but they deliberately make it more complex, as it is not on them that the expenses fall; and it is all the easier for them to make the collection complicated, as the mass of taxes ends by making a totally incomprehensible science from this part of the administration.*

There you have a large part of the yield which is bound to be wasted; and the best that one can imagine for the monarch is that about half the yield

---

*One knows how Sully, who was naturally clear-sighted, had difficulty in unravelling this chaos.

comes to him.* But he deceives himself further if he believes that his income is increased by this half.

Taxes, multiplied like consumption, have made everything more expensive for the monarch as for his subjects; and this price rise bears on all expenditure since it raises the cost of labour in every type of work. Should one estimate his revenue to be increased by a third, he would not be richer if for what he used to pay an ounce of silver he in future paid an ounce and a half.

He thinks he is only placing the tax on his subjects and he is placing it on himself. He pays his share and this share is all the larger as he is compelled to greater expenditure. For industry which consumes, this tax is only an advance which it is forced to make. It makes the law in its turn and it forces even the sovereign to reimburse it.

The raw materials on which one works in manufacturing pass through the hands of many artisans and many merchants before they reach the consumers; and with each artisan and each merchant they take on an increase in price, because one must replace turn by turn the taxes that have been paid. So one thinks one is only paying the final tax, placed on the merchandise one is buying, and yet one is reimbursing many more still.

I do not intend to seek the result of these increases through calculations; an Englishman has done it.† It is enough for me to make it understood how much taxes placed on consumption necessarily increase the price of everything; and that consequently the king's revenues do not grow by virtue of the yield that they pour into his coffers. Let us see if they are burdensome for the peoples.

The government did not suspect they were. It assumed that everyone can at his discretion place such limits to his consumption as he judges right; and it drew the conclusion that no one would pay more than he was willing to pay.

---

*There are writers who claim that for a million to come into the king's coffers the subjects must pay three. I am not in a position to make exact calculations on this matter.

†See Remarques sur les avantages et les désavantages de la France et de la Grande-Bretagne par rapport au Commerce [Louis-Joseph Plumart de Dangeul (Paris, 1754)], 394, where the English work [Matthew Decker, *An Essay on the Causes of the Decline of the Foreign Trade* (Edinburgh, 1743)] is cited.

According to it, this levy did no harm to anyone. Could one imagine a less onerous one? It left complete freedom.

The government, which reasoned thus, probably only considered as subjects the rich men who consume lavishly at the court or in the capital; and I agree with them that those people had the power to reduce their own consumption, and that it would have been desirable that they should have used the freedom given them. I agree besides that all those who lived in ease could also use this freedom, which is only so in name, since in reality one is compelled to do without what has become necessary.

But the subjects, who only earn from one day to the next just enough for themselves and their families to subsist, are they free to cut back their consumption? However, there you have the majority, and perhaps the government is unaware that there are many among them who scarcely have bread: because I am not talking about those who are begging, many of whom have only been reduced to it by the errors of government itself.

But I want everyone to be free to cut back his consumption; what will be the effects of this supposed freedom?

The monarch, I assume, will be the first to set an example. Economies will be suggested to him, and sooner or later he will have to make them, as, at the high price to which everything has risen, his income is no longer adequate for his expenditure.

I might note at this point that these economies are an evil; because they are at the expense of the cultivator, the artisan and the merchant, who no longer sell the same amount of goods. Consequently, agriculture and trade suffer. But let us go on.

I assume similar economies at the court and in the capital; I also assume like ones in other towns: and step by step I reach the cultivator, who having no surplus on which he can economise does so on the number of his animals, his horses, his ploughs. The final outcome of these economies is thus harmful to agriculture.

Do you wish to see them all from another standpoint? I shall say: comfortably-off men will make fewer clothes. As a result less cloth will be sold from the merchants and less will be made at the drapers, and fewer sheep will be raised in the countryside. So when we follow all these economies in every type of consumption, we see, as a result, the ruin of several manufactures in the towns, and the ruin of agriculture in the countryside. Then a host of citizens who previously found work will seek it in vain. Those unable to find it will beg or steal: and those who do find it will be forced to offer their labour on the cheap and will subsist wretchedly.

In this state of affairs the sovereign, who does not understand why his income is falling, doubles taxes and his income falls again. So it is that, through the economies, which he does not weary of forcing blow by blow on his subjects, he finally succeeds in ruining the arts and agriculture.

I pass over a demonstration of the constraints that the inspections at the gates of towns place on commerce; the processes needed to value the goods, the disputes and law-suits to which these processes often give rise; the harassment by employees who often only look for excuses to make charges; the losses that merchants sustain when, forced to leave their goods at the customs, they lose the right moment for sale. I could yet point out that the duties that are placed on entry and departure are necessarily arbitrary and unfairly distributed. Wine in the cask, for instance, which is only worth ten ounces of silver, will pay as much as a cask worth fifty; and, for the one as for the other, this tax will be the same in a year of scarcity and in a year of plenty, that is to say when they will each of them have changed in price. But, without repeating platitudes already repeated so often and always uselessly, it is enough to have shown that the duties on consumption are the deadliest of all.

# 9 Blows Directed Against Commerce: Variation in Coinage

WE HAVE SEEN that pieces of money are portions of metal, on to which public authority has placed a stamp to make known the amount of gold and silver they contain.

If, among pieces of coin, one only used pure gold and silver, it would be enough to weigh them to know their worth. But because these metals are amalgamated with a certain amount of copper, whether to work them more easily or to pay the costs of minting, one needs to know further in what relation the amount of gold or silver is to the amount of copper.

A gold piece considered as a whole is made up of twenty-four parts called *carats*. If these twenty-four parts were so many parts of gold one would say that the standard of the piece was twenty-four carats. But because there is always some alloy, the standard is always below twenty-four. If there is one part of copper, the standard is at twenty-three, if there are two it is at twenty-two; if there are three it is at twenty-one, etc.

In the same way, one considers a silver piece as a whole to be composed of twelve deniers; and one says that the silver standard is at eleven deniers if the piece contains one part of alloy; that it is at ten if it contains two parts, etc. It is understood that these divisions into twenty-four carats and twelve deniers are arbitrary, and that any other would have been equally suitable to fix the standard of the coinage.

The right to coin money can only belong to the sovereign. That is to say, he alone is worthy of public confidence, he alone can state the standard and the weight of the gold and silver pieces in circulation.

[*1798 addition:* The sovereign, that is to say, the king in a monarchy, and in a republic the nation or the body which represents it; the sovereign, I say, alone worthy of trust, can alone fix the denomination and the weight of pieces of gold and silver in circulation. The right to coin money can only belong to the sovereign.]

He is not only owed the expenses of minting, he is also owed a duty or a profit for his stamp, which has a value, since it is useful.

[*1798 addition:* But from whom should he demand his due? The money which is mine today will be yours tomorrow: if it is not fair that you should be made to pay since you do not yet have it, it is no more just that I should be made to pay since it is going to slip away from me. Indeed, it is neither for you nor for me that one coins money, it is for the citizen body: so it is up to this body to pay; in consequence it is for the landowners to pay if the old taxes do not cover this expense.]

But it is in his interest to limit this duty, because too great a profit on his part would invite counterfeiting. He alone sells coins. This monopoly, based on public utility, would become wicked if he abused it. He would have himself to blame for the crimes he had caused, and the need he would be under to punish them.

It is easy to judge that our four monarchs have abused this right and multiplied counterfeiters. They have done more.

In the early days, a livre in coins weighed twelve ounces of silver; and with these twelve ounces, twenty pieces called sous were made, and they were each a twentieth part. So twenty sous made a livre in weight.

Now our four monarchs changed the coinage by degrees. They sold, as the twentieth part of twelve ounces of silver, sous which were only the twenty-fifth part, the thirtieth, the fiftieth; and they finished by making sous which were only the hundredth part of an ounce. However, the public, which had at first judged that twenty sous make a livre, continued through habit to judge that twenty sous make a livre, without much understanding what it meant by sous and by livres. One might have said that their language concealed from them the deceit perpetrated on them, and conspired with the sovereign to deceive them. It is one of the most striking examples of the abuse of words.

When it was recognised that one no longer attached any precise idea to the denominations *livre* and *sou,* the monarchs noticed that they had a simpler way of raising or lowering the value of the coinage without changing it. That was to declare that what was worth, for instance, six livres, would in future be worth eight, or would be worth no more than five. So the pieces of money in commerce were, with the same quantity of silver, worth more or less according to what they judged fitting.

This operation is so absurd that if it were an assumption on my part you would say that it was unreal. People would object to me: How do you expect it to enter the sovereign's mind to persuade the public that six is eight, or only five? What gain would he draw from this clumsy fraud? Would it not rebound on him? And would people not pay him with the same money with which he pays? Monarchs however have regarded these frauds as the great art of finance. Indeed, the least realistic assumptions that I have made are more realistic than many of the facts.

I shall not dwell on all the drawbacks that arise from variation in the coinage. It is enough for me to show how they damage commerce.

Confidence is absolutely necessary in commerce, and to establish it one must have, in the exchanges of value for value, a common measure which is exact and recognised as such. Gold and silver had that advantage when the stamp of the sovereign authority truly attested the standard, and never deceived.

But once the monarch had changed the coins, one could no longer accept them with confidence, because one no longer knew what they were worth. One had either to be deceived or oneself to deceive. So the sovereign's deception placed deception in lieu of confidence in trade, and people could neither buy nor sell unless forced to by need.

When it pleased the monarch to raise and lower the value of the coins by turn without having changed their standard or their weight, the abuse was greater still; people did not know how to use a measure which, as it varied continually, was no longer a measure.

It is true that they could have disregarded the pretended value which was only in the name given to the piece of money: they could have calculated the amount of silver it contained and used it according to that valuation. That is what the prince did not permit. He wanted an écu, which contained an ounce of silver, to be taken for a hundred sous, six francs or eight livres, at his discretion; and he wanted this, because otherwise he would not have drawn from the fraud the profit that he found in having himself paid when money was low, and in himself paying when money was high. But we must look at the government procedures, to judge better the chaos these changes must produce.

Usually he did not make the coinage fall suddenly to the lowest limit at which he intended to halt it. He brought it down by steps. He issued an ordinance through which he declared that in the space of twenty months écus, for instance, which were worth a hundred sous, would lose 1 per cent a month; and that way he brought it down by degrees to be worth no more than four livres.

One could surmise that the coinage would rise after having fallen; because that was the government's method of proceeding in this operation, as it thought it would find a profit in these alternate rises and falls. So people no longer knew on what they could count. Cautious people who did not want to lay out their money at the risk of losing it locked it up again. They waited for the moment to use it again with less risk, and trade suffered from this.

Others, less wise, seeing that at the beginning of the reductions one made twenty livres with four écus and that at the end it took five to make the same sum, hastened to put their money in the market place. For the same reason those who were indebted hurried to pay their debts.

So people found it very easy to borrow. This ease deceived incautious merchants who thought they must seize this opportunity to form some new enterprises. They took this money that was offered them, and they bought, but dearly, either because their competing demands raised prices, or because they paid with money which, from one day to the next, was to fall in value.

However, after several reductions, the king himself began to lock up the silver in his strongboxes. Payment at his treasury ceased. So mistrust was general and one saw no more silver in circulation. Merchants who had borrowed it did not have enough for everyday essential expenditure. Then, forced to empty their warehouses and to sell at a 50 or 60 per cent loss, they saw how they had been deceived in their speculations. The majority became bankrupt.

At the height of this crisis, the government suddenly raised the écu of four livres to a hundred sous, and it thought it had gained 25 per cent. But this gain is imaginary, and the harm it brought to the people real.

When I say it raised the écu, I am not speaking with enough precision. It banned the écu whose value it had lowered. It laid down that it should be carried to the mint where it was only received on the basis of four francs; and it made a new écu at the same standard, which it made worth a hundred sous.

Because it raised the duties of its mint to 20 per cent it thought it was finding 20 per cent profit in this operation. But counterfeiters bought the old écus for four livres five, four livres ten; and they made new ones which they sold, like the king, for a hundred sous. The government had thus grossly deceived itself.

For the rest, it matters little what is the standard and the weight of the coinage. It is enough that the stamp guarantees the amount of silver that each piece contains and that the prince, by abusing words, does not embark on placing a value that is imaginary, and hence always variable, in place of a real value which is permanent.

## 10  Blows Directed Against Commerce: The Exploitation of Mines

IN ONE OF our monarchies mines were found which, being very plentiful in gold and silver, suddenly made the owners, the entrepreneurs, the smelters, the refiners and all those who worked these metals wealthy.

When one becomes rich only slowly and by dint of work, one can be economical: but one is wasteful when money easily reproduces itself and seems bound always to reproduce itself in greater quantity. Now the mines that were plentiful in themselves were even richer still in the public estimation.

So those whom they made wealthy hurried to increase their expenditure; and consequently they shared their wealth with the artisans to whom they gave work, with the merchants from whom they bought, and with the farmers whose products they consumed.

The artisans, the merchants, the farmers, become wealthier also in their turn, spent more than they had before, and, in step with the growing consumption among citizens of every estate, prices rose in all the markets.

This rise in prices did harm to those who had lands whose leases they could not yet renew. But that was only for a while. It was more disastrous for people living as rentiers or on wages. It took from them permanently part of their subsistence and forced many to leave the kingdom. Thus the population fell.

Consumption increased further still when the leases of all the lands had been renewed. Then the kingdom appeared to be flourishing. Everyone was rich. The owner of an estate saw his income doubled. The merchants rapidly emptied their shops: there were scarcely sufficient artisans for the works sought from them: the farmers raised more animals, cleared more lands and cultivated them all more intensively.

In this moment of prosperity, people said: Mines are the power of a state. It is a plentiful spring which so to speak causes the other springs to overflow with wealth. You can see how they make the arts, trade and agriculture flourish. This truth was only momentary and one had to hurry to voice it.

Indeed, when a larger quantity of silver had again raised prices, people bought from abroad, where everything cost less, what they had previously bought in the kingdom. Bit by bit the artisans ceased work, the merchants gradually stopped selling and the farmers gradually stopped growing the products that were no longer wanted from them. Manufactures, agriculture, trade, all fell; and among those who previously lived from their work some left the kingdom, others remained there to beg.

So in the last analysis the product of the mines was depopulation and misery. The silver drawn from them crossed the provinces and passed abroad without leaving traces.

However, no one tired of exploiting the mines, and silver was no easier to come by for all that. People lacked it all the more as everything became more expensive in the neighbouring monarchies, where merchandise doubled and tripled in price, because silver had doubled and tripled there.

At last the increase in prices reached the point where people were obliged to abandon the mines. The costs of extracting the gold and the silver became so great that there was no longer profit in exploiting them. Richer ones were sought: none were found.

So a time comes when the exploitation of mines can no longer be carried out profitably. It is not the same for the cultivation of products which are consumed to reproduce themselves. By the abundance with which they renew themselves they increase each time, by reason both of the amount needed for our consumption and of the advances made and to be made; so that, whatever the costs, the product always ensures a profit. It is a spring which does not dry up. The more one takes from it, the more it increases. That is the advantage of the exploitation of the land over the exploitation of mines.

What would have happened if gold and silver had become as common as iron? These metals would have ceased to be the common measure of value, and it would no longer have been possible for the landowners to receive their incomes in the towns where they lived. When they had been forced to retire to their lands, because they would not have been able to cultivate them all by themselves, they would have left the larger part to the settlers whom the lands had enabled to subsist. So, no more towns, no more large fortunes. But also no more begging; and in place of our four monarchies where wretchedness and depopulation grow constantly, we should see a host of agricultural cities which would become more populous every day. How happy we should be if we could find mines rich enough to make all our gold and all our silver useless!

## 11 Blows Directed Against Commerce: Every Type of Government Borrowing

IN THE TIME of our cities, justice was administered in the simplest fashion, that is to say, with few laws and few magistrates. Under the monarchy, laws proliferated with tribunals, magistrates and henchmen of every kind.

Of all the causes which contributed to this abuse, there is only one which enters into my scheme: it is the creation of a host of offices; a creation from which the sovereigns obtained money.

In a monarchy the offices of the magistracy must be venal; since if they were not, intrigue would sell them, and the administration of justice would be plunder.

But, to sell them himself, the sovereign must not multiply efficient offices beyond the need for them, even less create useless ones. If it is a source of income for him, it is only temporary, and it remains charged with debt for eternity. Because an office he sells is rightly a loan, whose interest he pays under the name of wages.

However, when our four monarchs had found this income, they abused it to the point that the magistrates were often obliged to pay out to avoid the tribunals being overburdened with an excessive number of useless members. But this expedient, instead of producing the expected result, was yet another way for the sovereign to make money. So they paid up, and some time later new offices were created.

The nobility was exempt from a large part of the taxes. This ridiculous exemption, which is inexplicable among peoples who were agricultural in their origins, such as those I assume, is easily explained among peoples who were barbarous in origin.

Since the ancient nobles were exempt from taxation, people wanted to become noble to share this prerogative with them; and offices were created simply to sell nobility.

Then the people found itself more and more overburdened. Not only did it bear as an additional burden all the load that the ennobled commoner no longer bore; it also had new taxes placed on it to pay the wages of the new offices.

One would tire of seeing the four monarchs using the same means to make money. But then they had many which they gave up by turn and to which they returned at long intervals.

They especially found great resources in the privileged companies. These had credit. The monarchs borrowed from them, sometimes at 10, 15, 20 per cent, sums which the companies normally borrowed at 5.

At first the people did not deem these loans to be a new expense for it. It did not see that it was itself contracting debt when the sovereign borrowed. However, a part of the taxes was transferred to pay interest to the companies; and soon after, new taxes were imposed to equate tax receipts to total expenditure.

These loans were an endless expense for the state; an expense that was all the greater, as a part of the interest each year went abroad to foreigners who had also lent. The government did not abandon this income but it created another in the borrowings on life annuities; and to tempt greed it thought up tontines. It congratulated itself on contracting debts that snuffed themselves out, and on having found the secret of taking money from the citizens without doing violence to anyone.

This expedient, like all the others, placed it in the need to multiply taxes so as to balance income and expenditure; and it had to lay heavy taxes, as its debts were great. It is true that the debts died out; but the taxes remained; and they were piled up, because life annuities or tontines kept on being created. This operation which had no end filled the towns with idle, useless people who nevertheless lived at the state's expense.

The companies, in borrowing to lend to the king, had spread among the public an amazing number of bills payable to the bearer and carrying interest at 5 per cent. There were ones of fifty ounces of silver, of a hundred, of a thousand, so as to make it easy for everyone to have the means of lending.

This paper currency seemed to put great impetus into the circulation, and people thought themselves wealthier. With lands, it was said, one always has repairs to carry out: a poor crop takes away some of one's income, and one often has a lot of trouble getting paid by one's farmers. Besides, if the circumstance occurs of an exceptional expense, one cannot take it from one's capital, and there is difficulty in borrowing. But, with a portfolio, one has stock which pays well at maturity; and since, if needed, one can sell some bills, one can always face up to misfortunes.

You can imagine what a blow this new way of thinking delivered to agriculture. Land fell in price. Losses in livestock were not made good: farms were allowed to fall into ruin: farmers were harried for payment; and people bought bills. One needed to have a huge money surplus to contemplate buying an estate: and when a person had done so, he thought of ways of getting a lot out of it without putting anything back.

However, the state's debts were growing, and the companies, which the government repaid poorly, could no longer keep their undertakings. Then the government put itself in their place and declared that it would pay for them, that is to say, it reduced the rate of interest on public paper from 5 to 4 per cent, to 3, to 2, finally to nothing. Then the ruin of a great many individuals, who had previously been rich, brought down with it a crowd of traders. One saw no more than bankruptcy on bankruptcy; and people learnt that it is not the same with papers, which only have a pretended value, as it is with gold and silver, which have a real value.

People ought at least to have learnt the lesson. But wealth in paper was so convenient that they only sought to deceive themselves; and after a while they again received it with confidence. It seemed that people did not know what to do with their silver.

We have seen how a banker put to work for his own account the funds that several traders entrusted to him. Now let us assume that bankers, rich in silver and especially in credit, associate and form a joint fund to exploit for their mutual profit. This association is a company which will give each of its members a written recognizance of the sum that each of them has provided. This promissory note or bill will be called a *share* [*action*] since it gives a title on the bank's funds called an *action* in legal terms.

I assume that the capital of this bank amounts to a hundred thousand ounces of silver, and that to make its circulation easier, this capital has been split into a thousand shares, each of a hundred ounces.

These shares will yield 5, 6 per cent, sometimes more, sometimes less, according to the bank's profit. The more they yield the more they will gain favour; and there will soon be several thousands of them among the public.

Every owner of a share has a credit on the bank and finds several advantages in it. The first is security for his money that he is afraid to keep on his premises. The second is the interest he will draw on it, interest which may grow from one day to the next. The third is to be able to place in small portions, and over the length of time he chooses, all the money he will not use for the moment. The fourth is the convenience of being able to pay large sums by the simple conveyance of these claims. The last is to hide one's property in a wallet, and only to show it when one wants people to see it. These advantages, which everyone weighed up according to his whim, could cause shares originally valued at a hundred ounces to rise to a hundred and ten, a hundred and twenty, a hundred and thirty, etc.

The bank, which wanted to respond to the public's eagerness, sold these shares, I assume, for a million ounces of silver. Now it does not need to have this million in hand, because, so long as it is trusted, it is confident that the shareholders will not all come at the same time to ask for their money. It will be enough for the bank to keep sufficient to pay those who will be in the position of needing ready money; and this will be, for example, a hundred thousand ounces, more or less, according to the circumstances.

These shares, like all other negotiable bills, gained or lost value depending on the eagerness with which they were sought after. If many people wanted to buy them, and few wanted to sell them, they rose in price: they fell, on the other hand, if many people wanted to sell, and few wanted to buy them. Sometimes a rumour, true or false, which will cause a loss to the bank will spread alarm and everyone will want to sell: at other times a rumour, just as true or false, will restore confidence, and everyone will want to buy. With these possibilities stock-jobbing will become the profession of many of those persons who will only be busy spreading confidence and alarm by turns. The bank itself, when it is confident of being able to re-establish its credit, will let it fall at intervals so that it can practise jobbing its own shares. It will buy them when it has caused them to fall: it will re-sell them when it has caused them to rise again.

The government could borrow from this bank, and it borrowed at high interest rates. But it turned it to its account in another way. The government had paper which was losing heavily; in particular the revenue farmers' bills had fallen massively on all markets. It obliged the bank's directors to create shares, whose value they had not received, and with these shares it caused the revenue farmers' bills to be bought. Immediately these bills rose in price. People rushed for them: they rose still more. The rumours that were sown maintained the public delirium; and people rushed all the more to buy them as they believed they must always rise. When, by this manipulation, the bills had been made to rise above par again, the bank's directors sold them to withdraw the exceptional shares that they had created, and they withdrew them with profit. So it was that in turn the bank's bills and the tax farmers' bills were promoted: sometimes the latter were good, sometimes the former; and the public did not perceive that all were bad.

It was only left now for the government to bank on its own account, and it did so. When it had borrrowed from the bank to the point where it could no longer pay, it took the place of the bankers. Then it created more shares, and it did so all the more, as it believed that in future the paper would serve it in place of silver.

These shares, multiplied to excess, fell in price from one day to the next. Soon no one bought any more, and the shareholders demanded their capital. Much skill was now required. A great display of gold and silver was made. However, payment was made slowly, with the excuse that everyone could not be paid at once; and trusted persons came to receive huge sums in public which they secretly took back to the bank. But though such deceits could be repeated, they could not always succeed. The collapse of the bank in the end produced a general upheaval.

## 12  Blows Directed Against Commerce: The Policing of Grain Import and Export

W HAT   O NE understands by *grain policing* is the regulations that the government makes when it wants to direct the grain trade itself. To judge the effects of this policing, I assume that this trade had enjoyed complete and entire freedom at all times in our four monarchies; and that in consequence, as merchants have multiplied in response to need, the circulation of grain was unimpeded and put cereals everywhere at their true price.

This was the state of affairs when, in one of our four monarchies, it was asked which could be more profitable, to allow the import and export of grain, or to forbid them both; and soon the decision was taken for prohibition. It is not the case that disadvantages had been noticed in the freedom. But if, in the normal way, those who govern let matters carry on as they did before them, it also sometimes happens that they innovate for the joy of innovating. They want their ministry to be epoch-making. Then they make changes under the pretence of correcting, and disorder begins.

Our lands, they maintain, produce in normal years as much as we consume. It follows that our corn will fall to too low a price if more than we need is brought to us; and we will be short of it if we export some of the cereals we need. This problem has not yet arisen; but it is possible, and it is wise to anticipate it. Such was the cause of the prohibitions.

It is not true that this disadvantage was possible. You will be persuaded of that if you recall how free circulation necessarily puts corn at a level everywhere. People do not import more than is needed, because this excess would not sell, or would be sold at a loss; and one does not export cereals that are needed, since there would not be a profit in selling them elsewhere. These prohibitions thus rest on false assumptions: let us see what were their results.

In a first year of surplus the price of corn fell: in a second it fell further: it became dirt cheap in a third. The people cheered a government which procured it bread so cheaply. But this surplus was a calamity for the growers; and it would have been a source of wealth for them if it could have been sold abroad. So it is that the favours of Heaven turned into scourges through man's supposed wisdom.

The people did little work. They could subsist without needing to work much. Often they did not think of asking for work and, for the most part, the cultivators did not think of giving them any. The labourers, previously hard-working, acquired a habit of idleness; and they demanded higher wages when the growers could scarcely pay meagre ones.

Cultivation fell: fewer lands were sown; and years of dearth occurred. The price of corn was excessive.

The people then asked for work. Forced by competition, every kind of worker offered to work on the cheap. They only earned low wages, and yet bread was dear.

There you have the result of the regulations which forbade export and import. It was no longer possible either for corn or for wages to find their true price; and there was only wretchedness, now among the cultivators, now among the common people.

You will say that all that was needed was to allow import. And that is what they said too in the other monarchies which perceived all the benefit they could draw from it. They offered corn and it was taken. But if the need of the moment had greater force than the regulations, it did not get them revoked. The government persisted in its maxims.

It is very well done, the government in another monarchy was saying, to forbid export because one must not expose oneself to scarcity. But one must never forbid import, which can make good the deficiency in a year of dearth. So export was forbidden and import allowed.

But as soon as export was no longer allowed, the grower sold in lesser quantity and at a lower price. As he was less rich, he was in less of a position to cultivate, and he grew less. Therefore, from year to year, the harvest was always less abundant; and export which had been banned to avoid exposure to scarcity produced an opposite effect: people went short. To add to the misery, import provided for nothing.

It must be noted that when I say that export was forbidden, it is the case that heavy duties had been placed on the exit of grain; and when I say that import had been allowed, it is that no duty had been placed on its entry.

In this state of affairs the merchants had several risks to run.

If a large number of competitors simultaneously brought a large quantity of grain, they caused the price to fall; and it could happen that most of them did not find an adequate profit in the sale. They made a loss, if they sold at the low price to which the grain had fallen; and if they wanted to take it back, they made another loss as they had to pay exit duties. Often they were even forced by the people or the government to give up their corn at a fixed price. So you can imagine that, since the country, which was open to them on entry, was closed to them on exit, they were not going to bring corn at the risk of being forced to sell it at a loss; and that, consequently, permission to import provided for nothing. We may conclude that, however free import may appear, it is ineffective whenever export is not allowed.

It is not export that one should forbid, they said in another monarchy. The more one exports, the higher the price of our corn: the higher its price, the more profit there will be for the grower, and the more profit there is for the grower: the more he will grow; and the more he grows, the more flourishing agriculture will be. So one must encourage export: one must even allow a bounty to the exporters. But one must not allow import, as it would make our corn fall to a miserable price.

One cannot deny that, in this monarchy, people reasoned better than in the other two. Export produced abundance, as had been expected.

But the bounty was too much: because export carries the bounty with it, since one exports whenever one finds more advantage in selling abroad than at home. Besides, this bounty had the disadvantage of preventing corn from reaching its true price; because the native merchants, who had received the bounty, could sell at a lower price than the foreign merchants.

There were still more disadvantages in forbidding import. This prohibition was not complete: it consisted in entry dues that were stiffer or weaker.

They were stiffer when corn was at a low price; because it was judged that import, if allowed, would have made it fall all the more. That was an error because merchants do not carry their corn into markets where they sell it less favourably.

These duties were weaker when corn was at too high a price in the monarchy. It was then that there was a need to have prices lowered; and since import would produce this result, people were right in judging that it should be approved.

There were several years during which this monarchy enjoyed the plenty it owed to export, when, a bad harvest having brought dearth, the entry duties were reduced: they were even cut back completely.

But the foreign merchants, who, for a long time, had not been at all accustomed to congregate in this monarchy's markets, could not immediately take every necessary measure to bring it enough corn. Most of them lacked carters, agents or representatives for this purpose. So too few of them came and the dearth continued.

Then the government forbade export. A useless precaution. Could it imagine that native merchants would take abroad cereals they could sell more profitably in their own country?

As it had forbidden import, this monarchy deprived itself of any expedient in a dearth, and placed itself at the mercy of monopolists.

Now when monopolists have a stranglehold on trade, the price of corn can no longer be permanent. It rises and falls suddenly in turn, and as though by shocks; it is costly or cheap depending on the rumours that it is or is not arriving.

During these variations the government does not know what course to take. From one day to the next it increases the entry duties on corn: from one day to the next it reduces them.

Therefore foreign merchants themselves have no idea on what they may count. If, when the import duties were slight, they got ready to make consignments in the hope of the profit that the high price seemed to promise them, often, when their corn arrived, the import duties had risen, because cereals had fallen in price; and they found that they had incurred large costs to bring their corn and to take it away at a downright loss. You can imagine that they tired of trading with this monarchy and that consequently when it was in dearth they left it there.

So there were only abuses in these three monarchies. In the fourth it was reckoned that one should have no permanent prohibition or interdiction, either of export or of import; but that one should, turn by turn, allow and forbid export and import, following the circumstances. This course seemed the wisest, and yet it was the least wise. It had all the drawbacks we have mentioned and even greater ones still.

It had, I say, all the drawbacks when it forbade export or import: and it had even greater ones, because it injected an uncertainty into trade which constantly held up the circulation of grain.

Since, in this monarchy, the policing varied following the ever-varying circumstances, prohibitions and permissions could only be transitory. Export was permitted with the proviso: *until it is otherwise ordained,* when the corn fell in price; and when it rose import was allowed, always with the proviso: *until it is otherwise ordained.* This proviso was necessary, because circumstances could change from one day to the next; and they were bound to change, without the government being able to predict the variations, since it rested with the monopolists to make the price of cereals fall when they wanted to import, and to make them rise when they wanted to export.

But when import was allowed for an uncertain time, people in the heart of the monarchy did not know if one could export before the permission was revoked; as a result there were risks in taking steps to export; and those who did not want to incur them, only saw in the permission the equivalent of a prohibition. So the internal provinces did not benefit from these outlets, which seemed to be closed to them almost as soon as they had been opened.

Merchants on the frontiers who foresaw a new prohibition rushed to send their corn abroad. They set up their storehouses outside the country to remove them from the police. Then the corn rapidly rose in price, because export was happening in rapid succession and in a large amount.

Permission to export, favourable to the merchants alone, came too late for the ploughman. As he was obliged to pay his lease, his taxation, wages of the day-labourers, he had sold the corn when it was at a low price; or if he had not sold it, permission still came too late, since the season that was right for the work of tillage had already passed. In the one case he had lost on the sale of his grain, in the other he could not use his profit to ensure for himself an abundant crop for the next year.

Finally, these short-lived permissions were all the more harmful as the cultivator, fearing a prohibition, hurried to sell; and consequently sold badly, or at too low a price.

However, all the surplus corn had been exported, when a harvest was reaped that was inadequate for consumption. Then the government banned export and allowed import, still with the clause which left its duration uncertain. Immediately the native merchants, who congratulated themselves on having sent their corn abroad, hurried to bring it back at various times, but each time in a small quantity; and people bought back from them at a very high price what had been sold to them cheaply.

The dearness lasted. They sustained it because they were the only sellers. The foreigner did not come at all, either because, lacking the time to take measures for sending consignments, he feared he would only arrive when import had been forbidden, or because he feared being forced by some blow from authority to leave his corn at a low price.

There you have the results of temporary permissions. There are no rules, either for giving them or for revoking them. All the duties on the entry or exit of cereals are necessarily arbitrary, and one could not say why one placed them at one rate rather than another. So export and import are only carried out at risk every time they occur following uncertain and changeable regulations. Then trust is lost, and trade, given up to monopolists, is continually stopped in its tracks. Let us move on to the regulations which it has been thought necessary to make on the internal circulation of grain.

## 13 Blows Directed Against Commerce: The Policing of the Internal Circulation of Grain

IF IMPORT AND export had always enjoyed complete and full freedom, the government would never have been in the position of interfering in the internal circulation of cereals. It would not have felt the need, because within each state cereals would have circulated themselves just as from one state to another.

But when it had once been disturbed in a part of its course, circulation could no longer carry on anywhere regularly; and we have just seen the disturbance wrought in our four monarchies by regulations that people felt obliged to make on export and import.

If governments had seen that these regulations were the prime cause of these disturbances they would have spared themselves a lot of trouble: they did not see it. So, to cure the ills they had produced, they placed themselves in need to make fresh ones, by making regulations on the internal circulation of grain.

In our four monarchies, the various regulations on export and import have had the same effect as exclusive privileges given to native merchants: hence the excessive price.

With this excessive price, dearth might merely appear to be there. But often it must have been real, because, when export was allowed, people hurried to send out the corn; and, when import was allowed, people were not in such haste to bring it back.

But since foreigners did not bring it, whether the dearth was real or merely in appearance made little difference; all the government could do was to busy itself with ways of getting it to arrive. So there you have it forced to become a corn merchant.

It caused corn to come in at great cost, and it sold none. However, the price fell: the fact is there merely appeared to be a dearth. Up to that point the merchants had held back from putting it on sale because they hoped for a greater increase in price. But when they saw that corn was coming, they hurried to carry theirs to market, to profit from the time when the price was still high.

Since the government had not sold its corn, on another occasion it caused less to arrive, and it sold that. It had assumed that the dearth was never more than in appearance. But this one was found to be genuine. So there was not enough corn, and the dearth continued.

As it was still persuaded that the dearth was only in appearance, the government had the granaries opened, and compelled several merchants to sell their corn at the price it set. But authority could not strike everywhere at the same time. People concealed corn to keep it away from coercion. So while corn was cheap, or below the true price in one place, it was dear or above in another. Soon the dearth was dreadful and widespread.

Then, as it had been convinced that dearths are sometimes genuine, the government feared they were always so. It had not caused enough corn to arrive, and not to fall into the same trap on another occasion it had corn brought, and sold it in such a huge amount that everywhere it fell to a dirt-cheap price.

So it made nothing but mistakes. It had been wrong to place itself in the position of itself having to provide for the people's subsistence; and it made a second, even greater mistake, a consequence of the first, that of forcing open the granaries and claiming to fix the price of grain.

It did not know either the population, the production or the consumption. So it did not have the slightest idea in what ratio the quantity of corn stood with regard to the need. The disproportion could be stronger or weaker. There was such a province where on occasion it could be huge: sometimes too it could be almost negligible everywhere. What rule should one follow to assess the exact amount of corn one needed?

But should the government have known the relationship between the quantity and need, had it calculated all the costs of cultivation, of storage, of transport to require the cultivators and the merchants to give up the corn at the price fixed?

Forced to commit unjust actions to put right its mistakes, the government thought by these acts of authority to set right the disturbance it had caused, and it caused even greater ones.

It ordered all those who had corn to declare its amount. Therefore it felt that it needed to know this. But it should have begun by winning trust; and that order alone would have caused trust to be lost, if it was not already. For why should it want to know the amount of corn that each person was keeping in his barns unless it was intending to dispose of it by fiat? People made unreliable declarations.

False declarations are not always made with impunity. Often people were betrayed, and often the accusations themselves were false. The government ordered searches; but the force with which they were made caused such great disturbances that it reckoned it had better at least suspend them. So it remained in its ignorance, and each individual hid his corn.

When trade is perfectly free, the quantity and the need are apparent in all the markets. Then goods put themselves at their true price, and plenty spreads equally everywhere. That is what we have proved sufficiently.

But when one has once taken all freedom from trade, it is no longer possible to judge, either if there is really an imbalance between the quantity and the need, or what it is. If it were slight, it grows from day to day, through the people's fear and the monopolists' greed. Then circulation is constantly suspended by the obstacles it finds in its path; and it can happen that all the provinces have shortages at the same time, or at least that they experience scarcity one after the other.

It is true that the government redoubled its efforts in these circumstances. But its operations, always slow, could not bring help equally everywhere, as a crowd of merchants spread out on every side would have been able to do. Yet it found itself compelled to all the greater expenditure as the purchases on its behalf were made lavishly and sometimes dishonestly.

It was making useless attempts to settle the disorders. Its first regulations had produced them: its last regulations were bound to perpetuate them, or even to make them grow more.

It persuaded itself that the high price or dearth resulted from a residue of freedom. Consequently, *It was forbidden to all persons to undertake trade in grain without having obtained permission for it from officials appointed for that purpose.*

*It was forbidden to all others, farmers or landowners to interfere directly or indirectly in carrying out this trade.*

*Any association between grain merchants was forbidden unless it had been authorised.*

*It was forbidden to pay a deposit on corn or to buy corn unripe, standing, before the harvest.*

*It was forbidden to sell corn other than in the markets.*

*It was forbidden to make hoards of grain.*

*It was forbidden to let it move from one province into another without having obtained permission.*

There you have what in an abuse of language was called *police regulations*, as if order could have emerged from these regulations.

Yet the farmer could only sell to licensed merchants, who alone had permission to undertake the grain trade.

He was forced to sell his corn within the year; because the prohibition on amassing it did not allow him to place one crop upon another.

On the other hand, however much he needed money, he could not sell before he had harvested. So he only had a limited time for selling; and he saw himself placed in the power of a small number of merchants.

The prohibition on selling anywhere except in the markets caused him to have to leave the cultivation of his fields at intervals. He could have sold his corn to his neighbour; but his neighbour was obliged to go to the market to buy it. So they were both forced to expenses they could have been spared.

If he wanted to pay a debt or the wages of his day-labourers with his grain, he was accused of having sold elsewhere than in the market. He was treated with the same injustice if he advanced grain to a ploughman who did not have enough for sowing. This generous action was a fictitious sale, a fraud, in the jargon of the officers of the grain police.

Even the freedom given to merchants was limited. They needed leave to form an association, that is to say, to get together on the ways to provision the state. Without this leave it was left to each of them to carry on this trade individually, and as best they could.

Finally, a province suffering from dearth could not draw grain from a neighbouring province where there was a surplus. If permission was never refused, even if it was given the moment it was possible, it always came too late because it had to be awaited. The disorder was all the greater when, in order to cause a fresh price rise, permission was deliberately delayed. That is what happened on occasion.

On the one hand, the prohibitions removed all freedom from trade: on the other, the prohibitions authorised monopoly. Normally the officials from whom permission had to be sought did not give it for nothing, and you can judge why people bought it from them.

In this disorder the townspeople could not be assured of subsistence. So it was down to the government to provide it, and it created privileged companies to provision the towns, especially the capital. They alone might buy in the countryside what was set aside for this provisioning: or at least, you could only sell to others after they had made their purchases; and because you could only sell to them, you had to hand over the corn at the price they wished to pay. This final regulation, which was always fatal for the countryside, was sometimes so for the towns themselves, in whose favour it had been made. However much care was taken that bread should not become dearer in the capital, it could not always be prevented because the privileged companies introduced high prices in succession everywhere.

# 14 Blows Directed Against Commerce: The Manoeuvres of Monopolists

WE HAVE SEEN monopoly born from the regulations made for the policing of grain. In my design to make known the monopolists' manoeuvres I should need them to give me some notes themselves. I shall limit myself to a few observations.

You could not carry on the corn trade at all without having obtained their permission. But it was not enough to ask for it in order to get it; you also needed to have protection; and protection was hardly ever granted except to those who would pay for it, or who would give up a share in their profit.

So the right to make a monopoly of corn was sold in some way to the highest and last bidder; and often when a person had bought it he also had to give money to prevent its being sold to others. Few people could therefore enjoy this privilege. Also the monopolists were too small in number to carry out a sufficiently extensive trade to deal with the needs of all the provinces. But they were not concerned with trading on a large scale: they simply cared about making a huge profit.

This profit was guaranteed to them, if they bought cheaply and sold dear.

Small farmers are forced to sell early from the month of September, October or November in order to pay the landowners, taxation, and the expenses of cultivation. So then the price of grain falls through the surge of sellers. That is the time that the monopolists seize on to fill their stores; and they dictate to the farmers, who can only sell to them.

However, they used deception, as it would be dangerous for them to take advantage too openly of the exclusive right to carry on the grain trade. They provisioned themselves in the provinces where the harvest had been most plentiful, and they spread the rumour that it had been even more plentiful elsewhere. To confirm these reports, they made fictitious sales between themselves in public view in the markets, and delivered corn at the lowest price to each other. Then, as they had been given the privilege of buying everywhere, they went to the farms and they bought, or paid a deposit, on corn at the low price they had themselves set in the markets.

So now their only rivals are the large farmers who, not having been so pressed to make money, have waited for the moment to sell more advantageously. But these farmers have only a limited time in which to sell, as they are forbidden to hoard grain. The privileged merchants, on the other hand, sell when they wish. In the end it will happen that they are the sole sellers.

Then they put on sale a little at a time. They spread rumours about the latest harvests. They persuade that these have not been as plentiful as had been thought. Once again they do not fail to confirm this by fictitious sales, and they deliver corn to each other in public at the highest price.

So there is dearth; it is not that corn is lacking, but that it has been withheld from consumption.

However, the dearth is not general, because it matters to the monopolists themselves that it should not be. They must be able to pride themselves on the low price they maintain in some provinces in order to acquit themselves of the high price they set in others; and it is enough for them that dearth passes over all the provinces in turn. They caused such great disorders that sometimes in a province one saw the people compelled to feed themselves on all sorts of nasty roots; while in a nearby province the best wheat was thrown to the animals.

As they alone were responsible for making cereals flow back everywhere they were lacking, they did so slowly, with various excuses; and they found great profit in their slowness because they made the high price last.

Thus these monopolists made themselves wealthy, because they bought at a low price and they sold dear. There were others who made themselves no less wealthy, and yet bought at a high price and sold at a low one. I mean to speak of the commissioners who made purchases and sales of grain on the government's account.

They were given 2 per cent profit on each purchase and 2 per cent on the sale.

The more grain they bought and the dearer they bought it, the more profit they had as a result. So they bought whatever the price was.

To make their operations easier, the merchants had been ordered to notify their associations, to make a declaration of their storehouses, and only to deal in the regulated markets on such and such a day and hour.

As all the merchants were known and all their storehouses revealed, it was easy to abort all their schemes. Wherever they might turn up to buy, the commissioners outbid them; and wherever they might present themselves to sell, the commissioners sold at a discount. So as the merchants could not keep up the competition without ruining themselves, one after the other they gave up the grain trade, and then the commissioners alone bought and sold.

The commissioners had an interest in buying much and dearly, since the 2 per cent profit was greater because of the high price of the purchases; and although the 2 per cent profit on the sale was smaller because of the low price, they had no less interest in selling cheaply, because they became the sole grain merchants.

It was the government that made all the advances for the purchases, as it made all the losses on the sales. It cost it several millions a year; and if it is true that to find one million, it was obliged to set three million in taxes, you may judge how this monopoly was in every way at the state's expense.

The advances were paid to the commissioners in ready money. For the most part they turned their money to account in the capital, and they paid in the provinces or abroad with exchange operations. So this monopoly became a banking capital for them, or rather a veritable speculation.

## 15 Blows Directed Against Commerce: Obstacles to the Circulation of Grain, When the Government Wishes to Restore to Trade the Freedom It Took from It

MONOPOLISTS WERE always placing dearth, or at least high prices, somewhere, when in one of our monarchies this branch of administration was given to a minister who returned freedom to trade.

But when disorder has reached a certain point, a revolution, however good it may be, is never accomplished without causing violent shocks; and it is often necessary to take countless precautionary measures to restore order.

The new minister who wanted the public good, and whom even his enemies recognised as enlightened, took all the measures that prudence had suggested to him. But there was one thing which did not depend on him: that is the weather, and it was wanting.

In dealing with the circulation of cereals we have seen that it can only be carried out by a host of merchants spread everywhere. These merchants are so many canals through which the grain circulates. Now these canals had been broken and it was time to mend them.

Indeed, to succeed in any type of trade it is not enough to have the freedom to carry it on; one must, as we have already noted, have obtained contacts, and these contacts can only be the fruits of experience, which is often slow. One must also have capital, stores, carters, agents, correspondents: in a word one must have taken many precautions and many measures.

So the freedom returned to the grain trade was a benefit that could not be enjoyed the moment it was granted. A word from the monarch had been enough to wipe out this freedom; a word did not restore it, and there was high price a few months later.

"Look at what freedom produces." That is how the common people reasoned, and they were almost the entire nation. They thought that the dearness was a result of freedom. People did not want to see that monopoly could not have fallen under the first blows directed at it, and that there could not be enough merchants yet to set cereals at their true price.

But, people were saying, we need bread every day. Now, because people are free to bring it to us, is it certain that they will bring it to us and will not put us in danger of doing without?

So they forgot the high prices and dearth that had occurred in turn in all the provinces, when the ministers took away all freedom on the pretext of not leaving the people's subsistence to chance.

So they were counting on a small number of monopolists who could make a large profit by selling little, rather than on a large number of merchants who could only make a large profit by selling a great deal.

The merchants must have a wage: it is their due. But it is not for the sovereign or the people to set this wage: it is for competition, for competition alone. Now this wage will be smaller in proportion as competition is greater. Thus corn will be at a lower price when merchants multiply with freedom, than when their number is reduced by the police regulations. I add that one will be more assured of having it. For it will only be at a lower price because all the merchants, vying with each other, will offer it cheaply, and will be happy with a smaller profit.

They have as much need to sell as we to buy. Busy in anticipating where corn must go up in price, they will hurry all the more to come to our help, as those who arrive first are those who sell at the highest price. There is more cause to judge that they will bring us too much corn than to fear that they will not bring us enough.

These reasonings counted for nothing in the people's mind. They thought that the one task of government was to procure them cheap bread. The police regulations seemed to have been issued for this purpose. In truth, they produced an opposite effect: but this was not known; and people wanted the police regulations, because they wanted cheap bread. So every time that it became dearer the people asked the government to have the price lowered.

There were only two ways to satisfy them. The government had to buy grain itself to sell again at a loss, or it had to force merchants to deliver their corn at the price it had fixed.

Of these two ways the first tended to ruin the state; the second was unjust and odious; and both accustomed the people to think that it was for the government to obtain cheap bread for them, whatever it cost either in money or in injustice.

From this another prejudice arose, even more opposed to the grain trade, if that is possible. That is, the people, who believed these violations just, since they were enacted for them, regarded the grain merchants as grasping men who took advantage of their needs. Once that opinion was rooted, a person could not engage in this trade if he cared for his reputation: it had to be left to those vile creatures who counted money for everything and honour for nothing.

It was the behaviour of the government that had produced these prejudices. They had so triumphed that often even those possessed of integrity, and what is called wit, were not shielded from them. No doubt we must respect the rights of property, said people whom one could not suspect of evil purpose; but we claim the rights of humanity for the people. From that they concluded that the government can, must even, regulate the price of corn and compel merchants to deliver it at the prices it has set.

The rights of humanity opposed to those of property! What gibberish! It was so decreed that one should say the most absurd things to oppose the operations of the new minister. But you, who believe you care for the people, would you like the strong-boxes of wealthy men to be broken open under the pretence of giving alms? Doubtless not: and you want the barns to be forced open! Are you also ignorant of the fact that cheapness is always, of necessity, followed by dearness; and that in consequence it is a calamity for the people, as much as for the merchant and the landowner? If you are unaware of this, I refer you back to what I have said.

It seemed that everyone was condemned to reason badly on this matter: poets, geometricians, philosophers, metaphysicians, in a word almost all literary men, and especially those whose trenchant tone hardly allows one to take their doubts for doubts, and who do not permit one to think differently from them. These men always saw excellent matter in the works which were written in favour of the grain police. These were, however, works in which, in place of clarity, exactitude and principles, one found only contradictions; and one could have proved that the author had written in favour of the freedom he wished to contest. The fact is that it is impossible to establish anything exact when people want to put limits on freedom to trade. Where indeed should one place these limits?

Deaf to all the suggestions, the new minister showed courage. He let them speak and write, and carried on with his initial moves. However, people were still very far from feeling the effects of freedom. Corn was dear in one province while it was cheap in another. The fact is that it did not circulate; there were not yet enough merchants. Besides, the people, who believed that export was necessarily the precursor of dearth, became alarmed at the sight of grain on the move. "There will be none left for us," they said; and at that seditious cry [seditious is omitted in *1798*], they rose in revolt. Then evil-minded men went round the markets, spread new alarms and caused riots. Such are the chief obstacles in the way of the re-establishment of freedom. Time will remove them if the government perseveres.

# 16 Blows Directed Against Commerce: The Luxury of a Great Capital City

OF THE FOUR monarchies I have postulated, I no longer make more than one, and I build a great capital city in that place where people come from all the provinces. Those who are rich enough to enjoy all the comforts found there gradually settle there. Others come there for business, others out of curiosity, many because they do not have the means of living elsewhere. Because, with nothing, one can often make great outlays in that place, as it offers resources of every kind. It even offers some which ought to be inadmissible, and yet which people do not hide.

Wealth brings forth the arts. There will thus be a large number of craftsmen. They will occasion great consumption. They will make foodstuffs rise in price, and they will attract money from the provinces, where people will be rich enough to seek out the goods in demand in the capital. Their handiwork will be at a higher price than it would have been had they chosen another place for their establishment: because their subsistence and their raw materials will have to be brought there at great expense.

If they had been spread throughout the provinces they would make the capital's money flow back. They would bring plenty because, wherever they established themselves, they would increase the number of consumers, and they would help to spread wealth with less inequality. These considerations brought about the wish that manufactures should be established in the provinces; but this project remained a pipe dream.

Craftsmen do not mind that their products are costly, provided they are assured a sale. Now, where could they sell better than in a town of luxury, where without ever appreciating goods, people only value them in so far as they are highly priced? Where will they be in closer reach of realising their talents, whether they deal with the individuals to whom they sell their work themselves, or whether they deal with traders who vie to offer them the highest wages? Would it be possible for them to take advantage of the public's whims from the depths of the provinces, to make and give it a product based on transitory fashions? Finally, I imagine that when they enjoy complete freedom they can spread into many different places; but when they are only free to work in the shelter of a privilege, do they not have to settle in the place where they are at hand to beg for this privilege, to have it renewed, and to prevent its being given to others? So then manufactures could only set up in the capital and, after the capital, in the large towns.

Once everything becomes more expensive in a great capital, goods that were made to be common there become scarce; and it is there that artisans direct all their energy to obtain for wealthy people the enjoyment of luxury articles, that is to say those pleasures sought through vanity, which boredom requires in one's idle existence.

The complicated levying of a mass of taxes, manoeuvres of exclusive companies, public paper issues, banks, speculation, and the grain monopoly were the paths open to fortune along which people hurried en masse. From there new men emerged, one after another, who, made wealthy on the spoils of the people, made a striking contrast with the beggars who multiplied from one day to the next.

The Great had set the example of luxury: but at least their luxury was limited by their means. There was no limit to that of the upstarts, because they could spend all the more lavishly, as they became wealthy all the more easily. Because at one and the same time they were made to be imitated and imitation was out of reach, they seemed to prepare the ruin of every rank of citizen.

Indeed, as one could only make oneself noticed through expenditure, disorder found its way in turn into all fortunes; and every rank became confused by degrees by the very efforts that it made to single itself out. From the trends people followed it seemed they had immense desires; and from the frivolities they were happy with, it seemed they had no wants. Whim set the price of the smallest things. If people did not enjoy them, they wished to appear to enjoy them, because they supposed others did; lacking enthusiasm they took its language and made fools of themselves enthusing about everything. However one was struck by it, one had to obey the whims of fashion. It was the sole arbiter of taste and feeling and set down for everyone what he was to want, say, do and think: because thinking was the latest fashion.

In this disorder people spoke out against finance since financiers had more ways of becoming rich. But did not citizens of every degree have cause to reproach themselves in the same way? If they obtained less wealth was it because they were less greedy or because they could not? It is the general morality one should condemn; but in a century of corruption every order inveighs against the others.

I wish a monarchy could never be too rich. Indeed, the vice that destroys it is not in excessive wealth: it is in the inequality of its division, an inequality that becomes monstrous in a century of finance.

But what! you will say, must one make a new division of land, and limit each citizen to the same number of arpents? No, indubitably; that project would be chimerical. Perfect equality can only be maintained in a republic such as Sparta; and I agree that in a monarchy men are not Spartans. What must be done, you will ask? Every citizen must be able to live from his work; and I say that wherever there are beggars the government is vicious.

I am very well aware that it is supposed that everyone can live from his work: because the rich man, who does nothing, says to the unhappy person without bread, "Go and work." Thus luxury which multiplies beggars hardens hearts, and there are no more resources for the needy. But let us see if every citizen can find work.

It is observed with reason that the luxury of the large towns gives a livelihood to many artisans, and consequently people say that luxury is a good thing. But how many men who would have been useful in the countryside flock to the capital to beg there, seduced by the profits that some make in a capital? Even some men of parts are reduced to wretchedness, because it is impossible for them to work in competition with those who set up before them, and who are in fashion. Is it not known that rich people, without knowing why, follow each other to the same shops, and that a skilful or lucky craftsman practises his own trade almost exclusively? Are you unaware that in matters of luxury the name of the workman is not unimportant?

Luxury creeps up imperceptibly on all conditions; and if a person is not rich he wants to appear so. Then he economises on necessities to be able to buy luxuries. So one takes away the work of the most useful artisans, and in consequence one takes away their bread. Besides, if in a time when wealth is spread too unequally, a small number of wealthy men cause costly manufactures to flourish, how few citizens are then rich enough to join in sustaining the commoner manufactures? If luxury gives some artisans a livelihood, it correspondingly reduces a greater number of them to beggary. There you have the results it produces in towns, especially in the capital. Let us move to the countryside.

The provinces have to pay at the capital the revenues of the landowners who live there and the Prince's revenues; a huge debt which grows every day with taxation. It is true that, through the vast consumption made there, the capital gives back to the provinces the money it has received from them; and it makes agriculture flourish there, in proportion as it draws products from them in ever greater amounts. But it cannot draw equally from each, and so agriculture cannot flourish equally in all.

Abundance is found in the countryside surrounding the capital, and there the most recalcitrant soil is made fertile. Abundance is also found in the most remote provinces when they have easy communications with the capital. But when they lack outlets, you can judge the poverty by the wan complexion of the inhabitants, by the villages falling into ruin, and by the fallow fields. They produce little, because the wealthiest consumers, to whom the lands belong, live in the capital where they consume the products of other provinces. They produce little, because these consumers prefer to the genuine wealth of a cultivated soil intrigue which opens the path to fortune for some, paper documents with which they have more income and greater ease in wasting it, in short luxury which ruins all. Not only do they fail to make the necessary advances to obtain more abundant crops for themselves, they also place the farmers in a situation where they cannot make them. They cause them expense: they take some of their animals away from them; in a word they seem to take from them every means of cultivation. However, the farmers, more numerous than the farms, are reduced by competition to inadequate rewards. As they are reduced to hand-to-mouth subsistence, they deny themselves what is necessary in order to pay a master who, in the bosom of softness, has as his maxim that peasants must not be in easy circumstances, and who does not perceive that the wealth of the ploughman would enrich himself. So it is only too true that the luxury of a great capital is a source of wretchedness and devastation.

# 17 Blows Directed Against Commerce: The Rivalry of Nations

IN ORDER TO judge what must happen to several rival nations who are each attempting to trade exclusively, I am moving the people we have observed into Asia Minor. I give it Mysia, Lydia, Bythinia and other provinces, and I make a kingdom with Troy as its capital.*

But since I only want to observe the results of the envy of nations, I assume, to remove every other cause, that this people no longer has in its customs or its government any of the vices with which I have reproached it. It will be at this moment an agricultural nation. It is fostering the skills that bear on agriculture: it is beginning to develop others: it is putting more refinement into the conveniences of life. But its habits are still simple, as is its government. It is unacquainted with tolls, customs, taxes, guilds, corporations or any kind of privilege, nor does it know what we call *grain police*. Each citizen is free to choose for his subsistence the type of work that suits him, and the government only demands a contribution which is adjusted to the needs of the state, and which the nation pays willingly. Such are the new Trojans. But you must allow me still more assumptions.

I assume, then, that in the centuries when they lived, centuries before all tradition, Asia, Egypt, Greece and Italy, as well as the islands scattered in the seas which separate these continents, were so many civilised countries whose peoples were beginning to have some trade with each other; while all the rest of Europe was still in barbarism.

Finally, my last assumption will be that the arts had not yet made as much progress anywhere as among the Trojans. Everywhere else they seemed in their infancy. Yet luxury was still unknown even at Troy.

The population must be large in all the countries I have just assumed. Many reasons contribute to it: the simplicity of manners, subsistence assured

*["The wisdom of the reader will have little difficulty in discovering in the course of this chapter that Condillac's imaginary kingdom of Troy is France." (Eugène Daire and G. de Molinari, *Mélanges d'économie politique* [Paris, 1847], 1:427.)]

in work of one's choice, and agriculture which makes all the more progress as it is prized more.

However, all the lands we have covered with civilised nations are not equally fertile; and, in consequence, all do not produce the means of subsistence for a similar population in a comparable area. Greece, for example, is nowhere near as fertile as Egypt; and many maritime coasts would be sparsely inhabited if they were confined to the produce of their soil alone.

But in places where agriculture cannot feed a large population, industry makes up for it, and trade enables a large populace to live there on the surplus of the agricultural nations. This people, to whom the soil seems to deny the essentials, becomes the carrier of the others. It deals with everyone's surplus; it brings back the means of subsistence to its own soil, and because it has acquired a habit of the thrift with which it was forced to begin, it ends up enriching itself. There you see what must happen to the nations that live on unproductive soil along the sea coast. Trading nations from their location, they are the first to carry out commission trade or trafficking.

Then all the ports were open to traders. All the peoples gave import and export complete freedom. The surplus was constantly poured from one to the other. Through the competition of every possible merchant, each good was at its true price; and the plenty which spread among all the nations seemed, through a kind of ebb and flow, to tend to set itself everywhere at the same level.

This trade was particularly profitable to the Trojans. The progress they had made in the arts drew to them all the merchants of every nation. They worked up both the raw materials of their soil and those which they drew from abroad; and their manufactures, which flourished more every day, gave subsistence to a host of artisans.

Happy in this position, the peoples did not know how to sustain it. Why, they said, send the Trojans those prime materials we can work up ourselves? Is it reasonable to carry our money and our products abroad to give subsistence to artisans there, who, by consuming in our midst, would increase our population and our wealth? So all the peoples considered ways in which each could establish the same manufactures among themselves.

But the trading nations particularly aroused envy. These nations, poor in their soil, were becoming rich and populous and seemed to owe their wealth and population to the blindness of others. Why should we leave them to carry out all the trade virtually alone, the envious peoples were saying? Shall we still suffer them for long to make profits out of us which we could make ourselves? It is we who make them subsist, it is we who make them wealthy. Let us close our ports to them, they will fall into wretchedness and soon they will no longer exist.

These reflections are not as well-based as they appear. The Author of nature, in Whose eyes all the peoples, despite the prejudices that divide them, are as one republic, or rather as just one family, has established needs amongst them. These needs are a consequence of the difference in climate which causes one people to lack things of which another has a surplus, and which gives each of them different types of industry. A curse on the people that would like to do without all the others. It would be as absurd as a citizen who, regretting the profits made from him in society, wished to provide by himself for all his needs. If a people did without the trading nations, if it destroyed them, it would be less rich itself through its actions, since it would reduce the number of consumers to whom it sold its surplus products.

Besides, the traders do not really belong to any country. They form a nation which is spread everywhere and which has its separate interests. A people is therefore mistaken if it thinks it is working for itself when it sacrifices all to its merchants. By excluding those of other nations, it sells its goods at a lower price, and it buys foreign goods at a higher one; its manufactures collapse, its agriculture deteriorates, and it makes fresh losses every day. It is only the competition of all the merchants that can make trade flourish to the benefit of each people. Do and let do [*faire & laisser faire*], there then is what should be the aim of all the nations. Trade that is always open and always free, alone can contribute to the happiness of all together and of each individually.

But that is not how people reasoned. A state, they said, is only rich and powerful in proportion to the money that circulates; and money only circulates in greater quantity in so far as one carries on a more extensive trade. Every nation that understands its real interests must therefore think of ways to become the sole trading nation.

This reasoning appears clear-cut and people act upon it. So there you have the peoples working to make each other poorer: because in wanting to take trade away from each other, each of them trades less. Let us see the effects of this policy.

The Trojans who had ports on the Aegean Sea, on the Propontis and on the Black Sea were still masters of all the islands adjacent to their continent. In this position, where they could carry on an extensive trade alongside the other peoples, they wished to engage in it exclusively. So they set up customs posts everywhere: they subjected foreign merchants who exported or imported to taxation; finally they closed the ports completely to them.

The people applauded the government's wisdom. It thought it was going to carry on all the trade by itself; and it handled no more than before, because it could not leave its manufactures and its fields to board ship.

Trade shrank considerably when it was no longer carried out through the intervention of the trading nations. This complete change brought with it the failure of many manufactures; and agriculture was damaged because there were fewer products, once the inability to export had made any surplus useless.

However, the government did not suspect the error it had made. On the contrary it believed that trade was bringing more wealth than ever into the state: it judged thus from the fortunes of some Trojan merchants.

But these traders were making themselves rich at the expense of the state: as they had no rivals when they bought and sold, they alone set the price of things. Every day they cut back the income of the artisan and the ploughman and sold dearly whatever they brought from abroad.

In their mutual rivalry, the peoples could not restrict themselves to closing their ports and denying each other trade in the hope of conducting it exclusively. They yet had to arm, and they armed. In wars that were disastrous for all, they congratulated themselves in turn on the blows they thought they were inflicting, and which only bore on trade to ruin it equally everywhere. Large armies by land, and large fleets at sea, made it necessary to snatch one section of the citizens forcibly from the plough and from manufactures, and to burden the other with taxes. These acts of violence were renewed with each war, always with new abuses because peace, which only came through exhaustion, never lasted long enough to allow the warring powers to make good their losses.

Trade, which had fallen during the war, did not pick up easily in peacetime. People did not dare to engage in enterprises demanding large advances, and whose prospects could evaporate in the first hostilities. None the less the government invited the people and even the nobility to carry out trade. It offered its protection to the dealers, and it seemed only concerned to make the trade flourish that it had wrecked and that it was to ruin further.

When one has power one believes that everything is possible. One does not mistrust one's intellect at all, and because one has given orders, one does not imagine one could find obstacles. There lies the reason why an error which has been made in public administration is made again and is made for a long time. It becomes a maxim of state and prejudices rule. The Trojans persisted in closing their ports to trading nations, they persisted in making war on them, and yet they were searching for what could be the cause of the decay of their trade.

They thought they had found it, when having meditated that enterprises needed even larger advances as they were exposed to greater risks, they imagined that trade could only continue to be carried on by companies which brought together the capital of several rich merchants. So they only had to allow as many to be formed as was judged fitting. But a company presented itself. It made the state see great advantages in the types of trade it projected. It exaggerated the advances it would have to make. It represented that after having made the outlay it would not be fair that it should be deprived of profit due to its hard work; and it demanded an exclusive privilege. It was given it.

This privilege was a blow directed at freedom since it gave one single company a right which belonged to all the citizens. The traders protested, but in vain. The new company gave the money, and the privilege was confirmed.

As soon as the government realised that these privileges could be sold, it sold more. As this abuse passed into custom it became the rule; and soon people regarded exclusive privileges as a protection granted to trade.

However, to sell exclusive privileges to craftsmen and traders was to exile those to whom none were sold. Many left the kingdom and bore away manufactures with them. It is true that the government forbade them to leave the state under severe penalties. But when they had passed over to a foreign land, it was no longer possible to punish them, and yet one could not prevent them from crossing there. This prohibition made them desert in greater numbers.

When manufactures in a kingdom enjoy complete freedom they multiply in relation to need. It is not the same when they belong to an exclusive company. As the interest of this company is much less to sell a great deal than to sell dearly, it thinks to make the largest profit with the least trading. Besides, it finds an advantage in reducing the number of manufactures, namely that the workers, remaining in larger numbers than it can employ, are reduced, if they do not want to beg, to working for almost nothing.

It was not only that labour cost these exclusive companies little. They also wanted to make a new profit on raw materials. They represented to the government how much the export of raw materials abroad was contrary to the interests of trade, and their sale overseas was forbidden. They therefore bought them at rock-bottom prices and as a result agriculture was more neglected every day.

While customs duties, taxes and exclusive privileges troubled trade and agriculture, luxury grew with wretchedness: the state, which no longer subsisted except through expedients, was continually contracting new debts: and financial speculation raised itself in the midst of the debris of public wealth.

There you have the condition in which the Trojan monarchy found itself. Such a condition was near enough that of all the monarchies which had armed to take from each other certain branches of trade. One would not have guessed from the means that they used that they wanted to become richer.

When the government is for ever borrowing, the interest on money is necessarily very high: it is especially so at a time when luxury, which sets no limits to needs, compels the richest to borrow.

If it is the citizens who lend to the state, capital leaves trade to let a host of rentiers subsist without work, men who are useless, whose number grows continually.

If it is foreigners, the capital not only leaves trade, it also leaves the state which ruins itself by degrees.

Then the traders who are finding it difficult to borrow, or who only find money at high interest rates, are powerless to form great enterprises. How should they form them? Their businesses are almost always tied up with that of the government to which the exclusive companies have lent their credit;

and in consequence mistrust of government banishes all confidence from trade. It is therefore very difficult for trade to flourish in such monarchies.

One did not see such drawbacks among the trading republics. On the contrary, great confidence reigned there because traders enjoyed complete freedom there and the government, without luxury and debt, assured their fortunes. They had a great advantage in trade over the traders of the monarchies because they could borrow at low interest rates, and having some saving, they thought less of making huge profits every time than to make small ones often. All the capital thus stayed in trade and made it flourish.

But of all the peoples, the wisest or the happiest were the agrarian republics. With little concern to carry out the trade themselves, they had not thought to close their ports to foreign merchants who came to carry away their surplus produce, and they lived in plenty.

This was the state of affairs, when new branches of trade changed everything.

The Phoenicians [the Dutch: Daire, *Mélanges*], a republican trading people, found to the east of Europe a country peopled by a host of cities, which seemed to them all the more barbaric, as possessed of plenty of gold and silver, they attached no value to them. This discovery, which gave them the means to carry out a much greater trade, soon gave them preponderance over all the trading nations.

In the Trojan monarchy, where exclusive companies had got hold of all the known trade, they had even greater need to make discoveries. It was the sole expedient for merchants who had bought no privileges at all. So as they were reduced to looking for some new branch of trade in unknown lands, they penetrated into the Caspian Sea; and from there by the Oxus, they went upstream to India. It was a vast, fertile country where the arts were cultivated, and where labour was all the cheaper, as a large population lived there in plenty with few needs.

This discovery introduced a new form of luxury into the monarchy. People admired the beauty of the fabrics made in India, and novelty giving them a value which grew in some way by reason of the remoteness of the country, the merchants who were the first to open up this trade earned from 150 to 200 per cent.

So this trade appeared very lucrative: indeed it was for the merchants. It would have been for the state itself, if people had gained 150 per cent on the goods they carried to India; because, on this assumption, it would have made the manufactures of the kingdom flourish. But the Indians had no need of articles which were made in the West; and gold and silver were almost the only goods which one could give them in exchange for theirs. So it was on the return journey that the merchants made a profit of 150 per cent; and consequently they made it at the state's expense.

People were not used to making such distinctions. The merchants were making their fortunes by carrying on a trade that was burdensome for the state, and people said, the state is becoming wealthy.

Once this trade seemed to be conducted with so many advantages by some individual merchants, it was not hard to prove to the government that it would be conducted with still more benefit by an exclusive company. It was even proved to the government that the individuals who were carrying on the trade could not conduct it; and although it was convinced of their impotence, so that it followed that it was pointless to forbid them the trade, the government prohibited them, and gave an exclusive privilege for fifteen years to a company.

So there you have many merchants excluded from a trade which they had discovered at their own risk and with their own capital, and yet the company did not carry it on. Companies are slow in their operations: they lose a lot of time in debating and they incur many expenses before starting. The latter did not start at all: it simply prevented the trade being carried on by others.

A second company was formed, a third, several in succession, and the government which was making a habit of forming them still believed that it was to its advantage to form more. It was so convinced of this that it finally formed one to which it gave the greatest help, down to advancing it the capital it needed.

The last named, despite some intermittent success, had soon used up the greater part of its capital. It could see the moment when it was going to lose its credit; and because it was important for it to conceal its losses, it had the idea of making a distribution to its shareholders as if the trade had produced a profit. But this fraudulent shift, which patched up its credit for a while, made an even greater hole in its coffers. Soon it was reduced to borrowing at high interest rates, and it only kept going through the help it received from the government.

But why is the selfsame trade at the same time lucrative and ruinous? It is lucrative when individuals carry it on, because it is then run economically. It is enough for merchants to be in touch with the merchants of the countries where they trade. At the most they will have factors wherever they need to have depots; and they avoid all useless expenditure because they see to everything by themselves.

It is not the same for companies. In the capital they need administrators, directors, clerks, employees: they need other administrators, other directors, other clerks, other employees wherever they form establishments. They also need, in addition to the counters and the warehouses, buildings as a monument to the vanity of the directors they employ. Forced to such outlays, how much will they not lose in embezzlement, in negligence, in incompetence? They pay for all the errors of those they employ to serve them; and all the more arise, as the administrators who succeed each other at the whim of faction, and who each see differently, never allow a sensible, sustained plan to be made. They form badly contrived enterprises: they carry them out as though randomly; and in an administration that seems to tie itself up in knots, they employ self-interested men to complicate it further. The direction of these companies is thus necessarily vicious.

But the India Company had further vices beyond that of its constitution. It wanted to be warlike and conquering. It interfered in the quarrels of the Indian princes: it had soldiers, forts: it acquired possessions; and its employees thought themselves sovereigns. It is thus easy to understand how its direction absorbed more than the products of trade.

However, this company persisted in wanting to keep its privileges; and it based its case on the assertion that this trade was impossible for individual traders. But it spoke for the interests of its employees who alone were amassing wealth. Indeed, its experience proved that it could no longer carry on this trade itself. So what risk was there in freeing the trade? The worst is that everyone would have abandoned it. But they would have carried it on, since they had done it before. [*1798 addition:* If it is possible to conduct the trade profitably individuals will carry it on, otherwise it will not be carried on.]

The Indian trade excited the greed of the trading nations. The Red Sea opened it to the Phoenicians. They were not slow to engage in it, and they carried to India the gold which they drew from the west of Europe. But it seemed that exclusive companies were to set up everywhere. One was formed to which the Phoenicians abandoned this trade.

This company had in their republic, as in a monarchy, the vices inherent in its constitution. However, it maintained itself better than that of the Trojans, because it found itself in more favourable circumstances.

The Phoenicians had conquered several islands, the only ones where spices grew; and they had believed they would keep to themselves the exclusive sale of these products, by giving these islands to a company that was concerned to close them to every foreign merchant. It was these products which supported their company. It would have been ruined, like all the others, if, without unique possessions, it had been confined to the Indian trade. Enlightened Phoenicians were not unaware of this. They did not count at all on the lasting nature of a company that was at one and the same time warlike and trading, and they judged with reason that it would have been more advantageous for their republic to leave complete freedom to trade, and to share even that of spices with foreign nations.

However, the example of an exclusive company among the Phoenicians was a great argument in Troy for protecting the India Company. How, people said, can this company be contrary to freedom and trade since similar ones are being established among free, mercantile peoples? But if those who made this objection foresaw the reply, they were in bad faith; and if they did not foresee it, they were very ill-informed. Nevertheless, similar reasoning blinded the government to the extent that it did not tire of making fresh efforts constantly to support this company.

The Egyptians [the English: Daire, *Mélanges*], situated so advantageously for trading from East to West, found it hard to see without envy the riches that the trade was bringing to the Phoenicians. So they tried to share them, and they opened up the same routes for themselves. Bit by bit the other peoples of Asia, copying each other, devoted themselves to the trade, and all arrived in India by different routes. The latecomers counted on the same profits as the first had made. They did not foresee that the competition of so many trading nations would make everything more expensive in Indian markets; and that the goods that were bought there at a higher price would resell at a lower one, because they were becoming commoner. On the contrary, with the great movement that was growing in the trade, people were convinced every day of the maxim that a state is only powerful in so far as it is rich, and that it is only rich in so far as it trades.

It is not that I blame the trading. I think one should allow a people to do whatever it thinks right. The government has nothing to prescribe in this respect. It certainly must not encourage trading exclusively, nor even agriculture. All its protection is limited to watching what is happening, to allowing it to be done, to lifting obstacles and maintaining order. So the country districts should not be trampled on, they will be repopulated with a surplus which will flow again into the towns to fill them with craftsmen, and into the ports to fill them with sailors. Then all will be brought to worth by an effort which will be applied to everything, and the nation will be truly powerful.

But, in order not to trample on the country districts, must one remove all the taxes? Doubtless not. Because it is the lands which must pay the taxes, since they alone are able to pay. As we have noted, whatever tax we place on them, the artisans and the merchants never pay, because if they work they are reimbursed and if they do not work they beg. In a word, whatever way one sets about to make them contribute, it is always the landowners who pay for the wage-earners, since it is the owners who pay the wages: we have already said so. One must therefore place taxes on the lands: one must give industry complete freedom, and one must not allow any of the abuses to arise which we have seen in governments.

All these abuses were to a greater or lesser extent introduced among the nations of Asia; and when they removed all freedom from trade, and with the repercussion ruined agriculture, they wanted to become trading nations and each wanted to be so exclusively. From that came frequent wars in India, in Asia, and continued upheavals in trade. It fell in turn everywhere, and it only picked up feebly among the nations which had had more success. All contracted debts, all multiplied taxes; and to support trade they all seemed to compete in ruining agriculture, without which, however, there was no trade at all. Disorder was the same everywhere, or near enough.

At last people realised that land is the greatest source of wealth; and it was proposed among the Trojans to encourage agriculture by allowing export and import of corn at the same time. Our soil, they said, is naturally fertile, and, if well cultivated, it will be an inexhaustible resource for us. Competition between the nations will set corn at its true price. Assured of the sale of their grains, cultivators will clear all the lands; and each year we shall have a greater stock for trade.

In Egypt, export alone was allowed: frequently the government even encouraged it by bounties. Wealthy through their soil, the Egyptians were so also through their trade, and they then dominated on the seas. Following this example, many people among the Trojans wanted export at least to be allowed: others opposed it, and the public, who did not know what to think, was fearful, whether it was allowed, or whether it was forbidden.

Among the lines of argument sustained on this matter, the best did not convince, and the worst had the advantage of being numerous. The government which, like the public, did not know what to think, obeyed the cry which appeared the strongest, allowing and forbidding export in turn; and because for lack of principles it conducted itself timidly, it usually only granted a freedom that it circumscribed, and which for that reason it left open to the greatest abuses. In a word, one would have said, by its behaviour, that it wanted to cause dearth to favour the monopolists.

In the meantime it was learnt that the Egyptians had just forbidden export; and this news seemed to make those who laid the blame on it in Troy win the argument.

We have proved that it is in the interest of all the nations to grant freedom to import and export: we note here that this freedom must procure the greatest advantages, or at least procure them more promptly, when it comes together with all the causes which can contribute to the progress of agriculture.

Although there were abuses in Egypt, old customs still caused agriculture to be respected. They had as a maxim that taxes should never be set except on the net product of the land, and this product was assessed in the way that was most favourable to the cultivator. A farmer knew what he ought to pay. Confident that he would never be asked for more, he lived in comfort. He was left all the advances he needed to cultivate the fields and to improve them; and the tax could never, on whatever excuse, be levied on these advances. He even had an opportunity to make himself wealthy, which contributed to the progress of agriculture. The fact is that leases lasted for twenty, twenty-five or thirty years. So, during the first four or five years of a lease, rich farmers could direct all their profits into plantations, into clearance of land, into increasing their livestock. They could even use some of their property for this purpose, and they often did so, because they were guaranteed being able to withdraw with profit the advances they had made, in fifteen or twenty years' time. In a word, through the length of their leases, they were able to cultivate a farm with the same self-interest as if it had been their own; and the proprietors themselves found a great advantage in it, because at each renewal of the lease they considerably increased their revenues.

There you have the causes which came together with the freedom to export in Egypt, and you can imagine that great advantages must have resulted from them.

In Troy, for quite some time, a large number of abuses contributed to the deterioration of agriculture. Leases were for nine years: the law did not allow longer ones to be fixed; and even if it had allowed it, agriculture would have drawn few advantages. What could one expect from the farmers? In general they only earned enough to subsist wretchedly. Little assured of their advances, they were often reduced to selling their animals, or even down to their ploughs, in order to pay their taxes. Poor as they were, they pretended to appear even poorer; because the taxes, which were arbitrary and fell on the individual, grew the moment a ploughman allowed any comfortable living to show. In this state of affairs, the fields fell fallow: people only cultivated in so far as they were forced by necessity; and the majority of farms were far from productive. One may judge from this exposition that, in the Trojan monarchy, time was needed to obtain for themselves all the advantages one must expect from the freedom of trade in corn.

You will no doubt ask why the Egyptians had forbidden export after encouraging it: the fact is that they had not allowed import. There was dearness following a bad harvest and foreigners brought no corn, or did not bring enough. In these circumstances, the government thought it should take the useless precaution of forbidding export, which was not happening and which could not happen.

The Trojans ought to have given the corn trade complete freedom, and they ought also to have made all the causes which can contribute to the progress of agriculture come together. But when a state falls into decay, people think neither about agriculture, nor of the causes which bring damage to it, nor of the ways to set it right. The sole maxim held is that one must make money; and when one has made it, one thinks one has more power, because one can raise larger armies. But in supposing that large armies create power, one must know how the monarch has the money, to judge if his power is well founded.

Is it the cultivators who give the money; and after having given it, do they live in ease? I can conceive that the sovereign is rich; and if he puts his wealth to use he will be powerful. But does he only have money because he has borrowed it? Then he has none. He only has debts. In order to pay them, he will ruin his people; and before he has paid them, he will already have contracted new ones.

Nevertheless, that is the position in which the chief powers of Asia found themselves. Everywhere one spoke of making money enter the state: one spoke of preventing it from leaving: in a word, one only spoke of the need to have it; and governments, which only conducted themselves by the principles of finance, could not think of ways to make agriculture flourish.

With this financial policy, monarchs believed themselves powerful, or prided themselves on becoming so. But the distant centuries in which I make them live must forgive them this error. They did not foresee how easily the richest empires, especially those of Asia, would be overthrown; and they could believe that some day there would be financial conquerors. They deceived themselves.

# 18 Blows Directed Against Commerce: How Traders' Speculations Have as Their Outcome the Ruin of Trade

WHEN TRADE enjoys complete freedom, it is possible to have a large number of competitors; and then the undertakings are exposed to greater or lesser risk, in proportion as they are more or less large scale. Let us see what the trader's speculations can be in such circumstances. What matters for them is to ensure the greatest possible profit.

A farmer who takes land on a lease estimates its return on the basis of the crops in normal years, and according to the current price of foodstuffs in the markets.

There you have his first speculation. It is founded on a supposition that is more or less probable: but the outcome is uncertain. He will make a profit if he gathers as much produce as he has expected, and if he realises the price on which he has counted. In the opposite case, he will make losses. He will have few products to sell should hail take away some of his harvest; and yet he will be obliged to part with them at a low price if his neighbours have produced plentiful crops.

Such is the danger to which he is exposed when he acts according to the commonest speculation.

If he thinks of a new form of cultivation and is the first to try it out, his speculations will be all the more uncertain. Because they will only have as a basis analogies which he cannot yet judge, and where experience alone can assure success.

Finally, should he see products which are at a higher price, because they are at one and the same time scarcer and more sought after, and he grows them in preference, his enterprise will be all the riskier. Either his soil will not be right for them, or they will cease to be so eagerly sought after, or they will become plentiful because other growers will have made the same speculation.

For the soundness of his undertakings he needs to have made sure of the nature of his soil, to have always grasped exactly the changing tastes of the crowd, and to have taken into consideration the endeavours of the other cultivators.

As they are unable to calculate all these things, the farmers always expose themselves to risk. They win, they lose; but they all contribute to the progress of agriculture, some by their mistakes, the others by their success; and finally in each region, a way of farming is established, which could often be improved in many respects, but whose excellence seems in general confirmed by experience. Then the cultivator conforms to custom and speculates less each day.

The craftsman also makes speculations. These bear on the current price of raw materials, on the wage that custom allots him, on the public's taste for certain works, and on the number of those who work alongside him in the same way.

The commonest artefacts which everyone uses are those where there are the fewest risks to incur. The price of the raw material varies little as it is always in good supply. The wage due to the worker is better known since these kinds of articles are always traded: they are there in large quantity, and it is a daily need that makes them sought after, not a passing fad. Finally, the number of craftsmen adjusts itself naturally to the needs of society, and consequently their competition, which is always much the same, puts little variation in their wages.

The profits in this type of work are thus better guaranteed: they renew themselves constantly. But they are insignificant. The worker whom they enable to live from day to day can only make small economies; and again he often makes them on his necessities, and could not change his condition without great difficulty.

These types of craftsmen have few speculations to make: for them to subsist it is enough for them to act as people did before them. But those who study the tastes of the rich, those who want to create new tastes, the craftsmen of luxury goods, in a word, if they can hope to earn greater profits, they also have more matters to take into account.

The raw materials on which they work normally being scarcer, and so costlier, become more and more expensive, as their articles become more fashionable. So they must limit themselves to smaller profits: too high a price could put off those who commission them.

Fashion, fickle by its nature, guarantees them nothing; and yet it is on this basis that they build all their speculations. Huge profits, if they make them, even come to work against them, because they soon see a host of rivals whom the lure of gain beckons to work in the same fashion. Then it often happens that one is hard-pushed to live from a trade which has made those who first carried it on wealthy.

Moved at random, and victims of fashion's whims, these craftsmen are often exposed to finding themselves resourceless. Those who have many competitors, because they came to it too late, have not been able to accumulate savings; and those who have worked in more favourable circumstances had not thought of making any. They did not foresee that there would come a time when their work earned them less.

As they do not have enough capital to wait for the moment to sell profitably, they have scarcely finished an article than they are sometimes reduced to selling it cheaply. Often they even find themselves unable to work because they cannot buy the raw materials.

Then a merchant who wants to extend his trade offers them his help. He agrees to guarantee them a wage provided they are happy to work for him exclusively. The craftsmen accept conditions that need dictates to them; and they come by degrees, one after another, to place themselves on the merchants' payroll.

Much the same is the case with the farmers: to fulfil their undertakings they need to have sold their products within fixed quarters. Besides, they are not normally rich enough to build storehouses where they might keep them, while they wait for the moment to sell them advantageously. So they believe themselves only too happy to be able to hand over to the merchants those products for which they cannot find a sale in the markets; and yet these merchants only buy them when they are at a low price, and they can count on selling them on at a profit.

Thus everything seems to favour the merchants who form great undertakings. Masters of all the tradable goods, they seem to have all the wealth of the state in their hands to make themselves rich from the toil of the ploughmen and the skill of the craftsmen. There you have a vast field of speculation for them.

You can see that these speculations bear on the need of the craftsman to be paid his wage, and the cultivator's need to sell his products, and the need the public will have for the works of the craftsman and the products of the grower.

It is in the merchant's interest to buy at the lowest price and to sell at the highest. So it matters to him that there should be a large number of artisans of every description, so that by their competition they bring themselves down to lower wages. For the same reason it also matters to him that many cultivators should be in a hurry to sell. Finally, it is important to him to have few competitors in the undertakings in which he is engaged.

You may conceive that with an exclusive privilege, he will easily obtain all these advantages; and that in contrast he will often be frustrated in them if trade enjoys complete freedom. Then speculations will be all the harder for him, as the success of his undertakings will depend on a host of circumstances that one cannot feed into a calculation, or that it is impossible to foresee.

However advantageously he has dealt with the craftsmen and the growers, he can be mistaken in his expectations. Because if it is with foodstuffs of prime need that he has filled his storehouses, an abundant crop which causes their price to fall will rob him of all his anticipated profit. It may even be that their sale will not reimburse him the costs of purchase and carriage.

Besides, there is absolutely no way to be sure of the consumption of them that must be made in the places where he counts on selling. A thousand accidents may reduce consumption as they may increase it; and when he knows what to rely on in this respect, how is he to know the proportion between the goods he is buying and the consumption to be made of them? Is he to know the quantity with which his rivals are furnished? So it could happen, against his expectation, that he had bought too much, and that he found himself reduced to having to sell at a loss. There are absolutely no speculations which could guide him with certainty in this respect. So he will be forced to conduct himself in these enterprises as though groping, following experience.

Such are the dangers to which he is exposed when he trades in goods of primary need; and yet those are the ones whose sale is most certain.

Second-order goods, of which we create so many needs, are not all equally necessary. Their use may be recent, and sometimes they are passing tastes which give way to others. So there is often a moment to grasp. If they are too ordinary, people will get tired of them; and if they are too scarce, the high price will limit the number of consumers. So by what calculations would it be possible to ensure for oneself the promised profits in this type of trade?

These difficulties which are found especially in the great commercial undertakings should trouble the government little. For it is not through a small number of entrepreneurs, who make themselves exclusively wealthy, that trade must be carried on. Rather, it is important that it is carried on by a great number who are content to live comfortably, and who enable a large number of craftsmen and cultivators to live in the same comfort.

Now when trade enjoys complete freedom, it is naturally conducted by a large number of entrepreneurs who share between them all the branches of trade and all the profits. Then it is difficult and almost impossible for a merchant to obtain wealth that is markedly disproportionate to that of his rivals. He would have to engage in undertakings where his speculations would be accompanied by too many uncertainties: he would not dare to venture it.

There you have the chief advantage of freedom of trade. It multiplies traders: it makes competition as considerable as possible: it shares out wealth with less inequality, and it brings every good down to its true price.

But if it matters to the state that there should be a large number of entrepreneurs, it matters to the entrepreneurs to be few in number. All difficulties are smoothed in the path of an exclusive company, because its undertakings, whatever they may be, call for few speculations. Since it alone has the right to buy from the producer and to sell on, it sets the wage of the craftsman and that of the cultivator at will; and because with the smallest trade it is assured of the greatest profit, it will burn some of the goods it has in the warehouses, if it fears that by making them plentiful it will lower their price.

Such then is the secret motive which causes exclusive privileges to be solicited; it is that people want large, guaranteed profits: still larger ones are always desired, and people always want them with fewer risks. So it is that the speculations of merchants always have as their final point the ruin of trade itself.

This motive is found again in finance whose speculations, as straightforward as they are easy, seem to leave nothing to chance, and ruin trade in its essence, because they ruin agriculture. If it undertakes to raise taxes, it acts so that for each million it pours into the king's coffers it levies two. If the state asks it for money, it lends it at 10 per cent and borrows at 5. If it acts as the king's banker, its profit is all the more assured as it makes itself mistress of all the government's operations. All depends on it, because one can do nothing without money, and it is it alone that can find money wherever it is needed.

Just reflect on the companies of merchants and financiers and you will recognise that they must imperceptibly draw to themselves all the money in circulation. If they pour it out constantly, it never ceases to return to them. On each occasion they take a new part of it. People owe them money, people owe even more: their credits mount up, and finally it happens that the state has contracted debts with them that it cannot pay. There you have, at bottom, what the speculations of high finance come to, and there you have too what they must produce.

Political speculations would present great difficulties if one had to study every component part of government, and direct them to the general good. But in a century when it is believed that all can be done with money, they become easy, because they are only concerned with the transitory devices which prepare the state's ruin: that is what we have shown. The ruin of everything. There then, you have the final outcome of the speculations of trade, high finance and politics in centuries where abuses have multiplied.

# 19 Conclusion of the First Two Parts

WE HAVE SEEN how wealth spreads everywhere when trade enjoys full and permanent freedom. It pours continuously from one province into another. Agriculture is flourishing: people cultivate the arts even in the hamlets: each citizen finds a comfortable existence in work of his choice: all is brought to value; and one does not catch a glimpse of those fortunes out of all proportion which bring luxury and wretchedness.

Everything changes in step with different causes which bring blows to freedom of trade. We have run through these causes, which are wars, tolls, customs, guilds, exclusive privileges, taxes on consumption, variations in coinage, exploitation of mines, every kind of government borrowing, the grain police, the luxury of a great capital, the rivalry of nations, finally the spirit of finance which enters every part of the administration. [*1798 addition:* Doubtless there are still more causes.]

Then disorder is at its height. Wretchedness grows with luxury: the towns fill with beggars: the countryside loses population; and the state which has contracted huge debts appears to have no further expedients except those which bring about its ruin.

We have been able to see in the first part of this work that Economic Science, which is difficult because it is naturally complicated, becomes easy when it has been simplified, that is to say when one has reduced it to some elementary propositions which, being determined with precision, appear trivial truths. Then this science develops by itself. Propositions arise one from the other, as so many consequences or as propositions that are in turn identical; and the statement of the question shows its solution so visibly, that one finds it in some fashion, without the need to reason.

In the second part I have reduced the reasoning to a simple narration. There I show the advantages of an entire and permanent freedom: I make known the causes which may undermine it: I make their results known: I do not hide the faults of governments, and I confirm the principles which I have established in the first part.

However, I have only picked up the principal abuses. It was all the more pointless for me to dwell on others as there is a means to destroy them all, that is to give trade full, complete and permanent freedom. I believe I have proved that.

Above all I have wished to spread light on a science which seems unknown, at least in practice. If I have succeeded in that, it will only remain to know whether the nations are capable of conducting themselves according to the light. This doubt, if it came from a man who had more talents and greater fame, would perhaps open their eyes, but, as for me, I know well that I shall only make those who have eyes see.

Nations are like children. In general they only do what they see to do; and what they have done, they go on doing for a long time, sometimes for ever.

It is not reason that makes them change, it is whim or authority.

Whim corrects nothing: it substitutes abuse for abuse, and disorders come always in increasing number.

Authority could correct: but usually it alleviates rather than corrects. It is still remarkable for it to alleviate. It has its passions, its prejudices, its routine, and it seems that experience teaches it nothing. How many mistakes have been made! How many times have they been repeated! And they are still repeated!

However, Europe is becoming more enlightened. There is a government which sees abuses, which thinks of ways to correct them; and it would please the monarch to demonstrate the truth. So there you have the moment when every good citizen must seek out the truth. It would be enough to find it. We are no longer in a time when courage was needed to speak the truth, and we live in a reign where its discovery would not be lost.

*THE END*

*The initial 1776 edition concludes:*

END OF THE SECOND PART

The third part of this work has not been written. The author will work on it, if the first two parts create a demand.

# BIBLIOGRAPHY

Allais, Maurice. "The general theory of surpluses as a formalization of the underlying theoretical thought of Adam Smith, his predecessors and his contemporaries." In *Adam Smith's Legacy,* edited by Michael Fry. London: Routledge, 1992.

Baudeau, l'abbé Nicholas. "Observations économistes à M. l'abbé de Condillac par M. l'abbé Baudeau." *Nouvelles Éphémérides,* Avril–Mai 1776. Reprinted in Lebeau, *Condillac,* 423–25.

Bédarida, H. "Lettres inédites de Condillac." *Annales de l'université de Grenoble* (1924): 231–44.

———. *Parme et la France de 1748 à 1789.* Paris: Champion, 1928.

Belin, Jean-Paul. *Le commerce des livres prohibés à Paris de 1750 à 1789.* Paris, 1913.

———. *Le mouvement philosophique de 1748 à 1789.* Paris, 1913.

Benassi, U. "Il precettore famoso d'un nostro Duca." *Bollettino Storico Piacentino* 18, no. 1 (1923): 3–19.

Blanqui, A. "Bibliographie Raisonnée de l'Economie Politique continuée jusqu'à nos jours." 1844. Included in Say, *Cours complet,* 688–725.

Bongie, Laurence L. "Diderot's femme savante." In *Studies on Voltaire and the Eighteenth Century,* 166:15–224. Oxford: The Voltaire Foundation at the Taylor Institution, 1977.

Cantillon, R. *Essai sur la nature du commerce en général.* Paris, 1755.

Condillac, l'abbé Étienne Bonnot de. *Le Commerce et le Gouvernment considérés relativement l'un à l'autre.* Paris, 1776. Nouvelle édition published in Paris in 1795. Extended edition published as vol. 4 of Condillac, *Oeuvres de Condillac.* Reprinted as vol. 4 of Condillac, *Oeuvres complètes de Condillac.* Reprinted in Daire and Molinari, *Mélanges d'économie politique,* 243–448. Reprinted in vol. 2 of Condillac, *Oeuvres philosophiques,* 239–367. Reprinted in 1980 from 1795 edition, Paris and Geneva: Slatkine Reprints.

———. *Cours d'études pour l'instruction du Prince de Parme.* 1775. Reprinted as vols. 5–21 of Condillac, *Oeuvres de Condillac.*

———. *l'Essai sur l'origine des connoissances humaines.* 1746. Reprinted as vol. 1 of Condillac, *Oeuvres de Condillac.*

———. *Lettres inédites à Gabriel Cramer.* Edited by Georges Le Roy. Paris, 1953.

———. *Oeuvres de Condillac.* 23 vols. Paris, 1798.

———. *Oeuvres completes de Condillac.* 16 vols. Paris, 1821–22.

———. *Oeuvres philosophiques de Condillac.* Edited by Georges Le Roy. 3 vols. *Corpus générale des philosophes françaises,* vol. 33. Paris: Presses Universitaires de France, 1947–51.

———. (1755) *Traité des animaux.* 1755. Reprinted in vol. 3 of Condillac, *Oeuvres de Condillac.*

———. *Traité des sensations.* 1754. Reprinted in vol. 3 of Condillac, *Oeuvres de Condillac.*

———. *Traité des systèmes.* 1749. Reprinted as vol. 2 of Condillac, *Oeuvres de Condillac.*

Daire, Eugène. *Collection des principaux économistes.* Tome 2: *Physiocrates.* Paris, 1846.

Daire, Eugène, and G. de Molinari. *Mélanges d'économie politique.* Vol. 1. Paris, 1847.

Decker, Matthew. *An Essay on the Causes of the Decline of the Foreign Trade.* Edinburgh, 1743.

Dermigny, Louis. "La France à la fin de l'ancien régime: une carte monétaire." *Annales* 10, no. 4 (Oct.–Dec. 1955): 480–93.

Diderot, Denis. *Apologie de l'abbé Galiani.* 1770. Reprinted in *Oeuvres politiques,* edited by Paul Verniere, Paris: Garnier, 1963.

———. *Oeuvres complètes.* Introduction by Roger Lewinter. 15 vols. Paris: Le Club Française, 1969–73.

Du Pont de Nemours, Pierre S. "Mémoires sur la vie, l'administration et les ouvrages de M. Turgot, Ministre d'État." Vol. 1 of *Oeuvres de M. Turgot.* 9 vols. Paris, 1808.

Eltis, Walter. "L'Abbé de Condillac and the Physiocrats." *History of Political Economy* 27, no. 22 (1995): 217–36.

———. "France's free market reforms in 1774–5 and Russia's in 1991–3: the immediate relevance of L Abbé de Condillac's analysis." *European Journal of the History of Economic Thought* 1, no. 1 (1993): 5–19.

———. "François Quesnay: a reinterpretation. 1: The *Tableau économique.*" *Oxford Economic Papers* 27 (1975): 167–200.

———. "The *Grand Tableau* of François Quesnay's economics." *European Journal of the History of Economic Thought* 3, no. 1 (1996): 21–43.

———. "Le rejet de Condillac par les physiocrates: une occasion manquée." *Economies et Sociétés, Série Oeconomia.* Histoire de la Pensée économique. P. E. no. 22–23, 1–2 (1995): 177–93.

*Encyclopédie des gens du monde.* Paris: Treutel et Wurtz, 1836.

Faccarello, G. "*Nil Repente!*': Galiani and Necker on economic reforms." *European Journal of the History of Economic Thought* 1, no. 3 (1994): 519–50.

———. "Turgot et l'économie politique sensualiste." In *Nouvelle histoire de la pensée économique.* Vol. 1, 254–88. Paris: Éditions la Découverte, 1992.

Faure, E. *La Disgrâce de Turgot, 12 mai 1776.* Paris: Gallimard, 1961.

Frugoni, Carlo I. *Opere poetiche.* Collected and published by P. Manara and C. C. Rezzonico. 10 vols. Parma, 1779.

Galiani, l'abbé Ferdinando. *Correspondance: Ferdinando Galiani with Louise d'Épinay.* Edited by Georges Dulac. 5 vols. Paris: Desjonquères, 1992–96.

———. *Delia Moneta.* Rome, 1751.

———. *Dialogues sur le commerce des bleds.* Paris, 1770. Reprinted in 1959, edited by Fausto Nicolini, Milan and Naples: Riccardo Ricciari.

Gide, Charles, and Charles Rist. *Histoire des doctrines économiques depuis les Physiocrates jusqu'à nos jours.* Paris, 1909. 2nd ed., 1913. 3rd ed., 1920.

Groenewegen, Peter D. "Condillac, Etienne Bonnot de, L'abbé de Mureau." *The New Palgrave: A Dictionary of Economics,* 1:564–65. London: Macmillan, 1987.

———. *The Economics of A. R. J. Turgot.* The Hague: Martinus Nijhoff, 1977.

———. "Turgot, Anne Robert Jacques, Baron de L'Aulne." *The New Palgrave: A Dictionary of Economics,* 4:707–12. London: Macmillan, 1987.

Guillois, A. *Le salon de Mme Helvétius, Cabanis et les idéologues.* 2nd ed. Paris, 1894.

Hayek, Friedrich von. "Richard Cantillon (c. 1680–1734)." In *The Trend of Economic Thinking.* Vol. 3 of *The Collected Works of F. A. Hayek,* 245–94. London: Routledge, 1991.

Hecht, J. "La vie de François Quesnay." In *François Quesnay et la physiocratie.* 2 vols. Paris: Institut National d'Études Démographiques, 1958.

Helvétius, Claude-Adrien. *Correspondance générale.* Vol. 3. Oxford: Voltaire Foundation and University of Toronto Press, 1991.

Herbert, Claude-Jacques. *Essai sur la police générale des grains, sur leurs prix et sur les effets de l'agriculture.* Paris, 1753.

Hume, David. *The Letters of David Hume.* Edited by J. Y. T. Grieg. 2 vols. Oxford: Clarendon Press, 1932.

Hutchison, Terence. *Before Adam Smith: The Emergence of Political Economy, 1662–1776.* Oxford: Basil Blackwell, 1988.

Jevons, Stanley. *Theory of Political Economy.* London, 1871.

*Journal de Trévoux.* Geneva: Slatkine Reprints, 1968–69.

Kaplan, Steven. *Bread, Politics and Political Economy in the Reign of Louis XV.* 2 vols. The Hague: Martinus Nijhoff, 1976.

Kenessey, Z. "Why Das Kapital Remained Unfinished." In *Perspectives on the History of Economic Thought,* edited by William J. Barber. Vol. 5, *Themes in Pre-Classical, Classical and Marxian Economics.* Aldershot, Hants.: Edward Elgar, 1991.

Klein, Daniel. "Deductive economic methodology in the French Enlightenment." *History of Political Economy* 17, no. 1 (1958): 51–71.

Knight, Isabel F. *The Geometric Spirit: The Abbé de Condillac and the French Enlightenment.* New Haven, Conn.: Yale University Press, 1968.

Labrousse, Ernest, Pierre Léon, Pierre Goubert, Jean Bouvier, Charles Carrière and Paul Harsin. *Histoire économique et sociale de la France, 1660–1789.* Paris: Presses Universitaires de France, 1970.

Larousse, Pierre. *Grande Dictionnaire universel du XIXᵉ siècle.* 17 tomes (34 volumes). Paris, 1866–79. Reprinted in 1982, Paris-Genève: Slatkine.

Law, A. "Louis d'or." In *Dictionary of Political Economy,* edited by R. H. I. Palgrave, 2:646. London, 1894–1900.

Lebeau, Auguste. *Condillac: Économiste.* Paris, 1903.

Lefèvre, Roger. *Condillac, ou la joie de vivre.* Paris: Seghers, 1966.

Le Roy, Georges. Introduction and editorial notes to *Oeuvres Philosophiques de Condillac.* Vol. 2 of *Corpus général des philosophes français.* Paris: Presses Universitaires de France, 1947–51.

Lespinasse, Julie de. *Lettres inédites.* Introduction by M. Charles Henry. 1887.

Le Trosne, G. *De l'intérêt social.* Paris, 1777. Reprinted in Daire, *Collection des principaux économistes,* 885–1027.

Lodge, R. "Livre." In *Dictionary of Political Economy,* edited by R. H. I. Palgrave, 2:617–19. London, 1894–1900.

Lough, John. "Lemonnier's painting, *Une soirée chez Mme Geoffrin en 1755.*" *French Studies* 45, no. 3 (1991): 268–78.

Malesherbes, Chrétien-Guillaume de Lamoignon de. *Mémoires sur la librairie, Mémoire sur la liberté de la presse.* 1809. Reprinted in 1994, with introduction by Roger Chattier, Paris: Imprimerie nationale éditions.

Malthus, Thomas R. *An Essay on the Principle of Population.* London, 1798.

Marmontel, Jean François. *Mémoires.* Vols. 1 and 2. In *Oeuvres complètes.* 18 vols. Paris: Amable Costes, 1819.

Marx, Karl. *Capital.* Vol. 1. Hamburg, 1867. Reprinted in 1970, London: Lawrence & Wishart for Moscow: Progress Publishers.

———. *Theories of Surplus Value.* 3 vols. 2nd printing. Moscow: Progress Publishers, for London: Lawrence & Wishart, 1969–71.

Mathias, Peter, and Patrick O'Brien. "Taxation in England and France, 1715–1810." *Journal of European Economic History* 5 (1976): 601–50.

Meek, Robert L. *Turgot on Progress, Sociology and Economics.* Cambridge: Cambridge University Press, 1973.

*Mémoires secrets.* 36 vols. (The initial volumes are by Louis Petit de Bachaumont.) London: Adamson, 1777–89.

Menger, Carl. *Grundsätze der Volkswirthschaftslehre.* Vienna, 1871. Translated and edited in 1950 by J. Dingwall and B. Hoselitz as *Principles of Economics* (Glencoe, Ill.: The Free Press).

Mill, John S. *Principles of Political Economy.* 2 vols. London, 1848.

Mirabeau, Victor Riqueti, marquis de, and François Quesnay. *L'Ami des hommes.* 7 vols. Avignon, 1756–60.

———. *Philosophic rurale.* Amsterdam, 1763. Reprinted in 1972 by Scientia Verlag Aalen.

Morand, Emile. *La Théorie psychologique de la valeur jusqu'en 1776.* Bordeaux, 1912.

Morellet, André. *Lettres d'André Morellet.* Edited by Dorothy Medlin, Jean-Claude

David and Paul Leclerc. 2 vols. Oxford: Voltaire Foundation and Taylor Institution, 1991.

Moureau, François. "Condillac et Mably: dix lettres inédites ou retrouvées." *Dix-huitième siècle* 23 (1991): 193–200.

Murphy, A. *Richard Cantillon: Entrepreneur and Economist.* Oxford: Oxford University Press, 1986.

Necker, Jacques. *De la législation et du commerce des grains.* 2 vols. Paris, 1775.

Pack, S. *Capitalism as a Moral System: Adam Smith's Critique of the Free Market Economy.* Aldershot, Hants.: Edward Elgar, 1991.

Piva, F. "Condillac a Venezia. Con alcune lettere inedite." In *Studi Francesi,* no. 64 (1978), Anno 22 (1): 76–84.

Plumart de Dangeul, Louis-Joseph. *Remarques sur les avantages et désavantages de la France et de la Grande Bretagne par rapport au commerce.* Leyden, 1754.

———. *Remarques sur les avantages et les désavantages de la France et de la Grande-Bretagne* (supposedly translated from the English of John Nickolls). Paris, 1754.

Proust, Jacques. *Diderot et l'Encyclopédie.* Paris: Armand Colin, 1962.

Puchesse, Count G. Baguenault de. *Condillac, sa vie, son oeuvre, son influence.* Paris: Plon-Nourrit, 1910.

Quesnay, François. *Essai phisique sur l'oeconomie animale.* 1736. 2nd ed., Paris, 1747, 3 vols.

———. "Évidence." 1756.

———. "Fermiers." 1756.

———. "Grains." 1757.

———. "Hommes." 1757.

These four articles are reprinted in Salleron, *François Quesnay,* 2:397–573.

———. *Physiocratie, ou constitution naturelle du gouvernement le plus advantageux au genre humaine.* 2 vols. Edited by Pierre S. Du Pont de Nemours. Paris, 1767–68. Reprinted in Daire, *Collection des principaux économistes,* 41–304.

———. *Le Tableau economique avec ses explications.* 1760. Published as vol. 7 of Mirabeau and Quesnay, *L'Ami des hommes.*

Raynal, l'abbé, baron Friedrich Melchior Grimm and Denis Diderot. *Correspondance littéraire.* Edited by Maurice Tourneux. 16 vols. Paris: Garnier Frères, 1877.

Ricardo, David. *Principles of Political Economy and Taxation.* London, 1817.

Rousseau, Jean-Jacques. *Confessions.* 1781. Translated with introduction by J. M. Cohen, London: Penguin Books, 1953.

———. *Correspondance complète de Rousseau.* 51 vols. Edited by R. A. Leigh. Geneva and Oxford: Voltaire Foundation, 1965–95.

———. *Correspondance générale.* 20 vols. Edited by Théophile Dufour. Paris, 1924–34.

———. *Émile.* 1762. Edited by François and Pierre Richard. Paris: Garnier Frères, 1964.

———. *Histoire du précédent écrit.* 1782. In *Rousseau, Juge de Jean Jacques, Dialogues,* texte présénté par Michel Foucault. Paris: Armand Colin, 1962.

―――――. *Rousseau, ses amis et ses ennemis, correspondance.* Edited by M. G. Streckeisen-Moultou. 2 vols. Paris, 1865.

Salleron, Louis. Editorial notes in *François Quesnay et la physiocratie.* 2 vols. Paris: Institut National d'Ètudes Démographiques, 1958.

Say, Jean B. *Cours complet d'économie politique pratique.* Paris, 1828–29. Reprinted in Brussels, 1844.

―――――. *Traité d'économie politique.* Paris, 1803.

Schelle, Gustave. *Turgot.* Paris, 1909.

Sgard, Jean B., ed. *Corpus Condillac (1714–80).* Geneva and Paris: Slatkine, 1981.

Smith, Adam. *An Inquiry into the Nature and Causes of the Wealth of Nations.* 2 vols. London, 1776. Reprinted in 1976, edited by R. H. Campbell, A. S. Skinner and W. B. Todd. 2 vols. Oxford: Clarendon Press.

―――――. *Lectures on Rhetoric and Belles Lettres.* Edited by J. C. Bryce. Oxford: Clarendon Press, 1983.

Spink, John S. "Un abbé philosophe: l'affaire de J.-M. de Prades." *Dix-huitième siècle* 3 (1971): 145–80.

Steiner, Philippe. "L'économie politique du royaume agricole François Quesnay." In *Nouvelle histoire de la pensée économique,* edited by Alain Béraud and Gilbert Faccarello, 225–53. Paris: Éditions la Découverte, 1992.

Steuart, Sir James. *An Inquiry into the Principles of Political Oeconomy.* 2 vols. London, 1767.

Streissler, Erich W. "The influence of German economics on the work of Menger and Marshall." In *Carl Menger and His Legacy in Economics,* edited by Bruce J. Caldwell. Annual Supplement to vol. 22 of the *History of Political Economy* (1990), 31–68.

Théry, A. F. "Notice sur la vie et les ouvrages de Condillac." 1821–22. In vol. 1 of Condillac, *Oeuvres complètes de Condillac.*

Turgot, A. R. J. Introduction to "Arrêt du Conseil établissant la liberté du commerce des grains et des farines à l'interieur du Royaume et la liberté de l'importation." In Turgot, *Oeuvres de Turgot,* 4:201–9.

―――――. *Oeuvres de Turgot et documents le concernant.* Edited by G. Schelle. 5 vols. Paris, 1913–23.

―――――. *Réflexions sur la formation et la distribution des richesses.* 1769–70. In Turgot, *Oeuvres de Turgot,* 2:533–601.

―――――. "Valeurs et monnaies." 1769. In Turgot, *Oeuvres de Turgot,* 2:79–98.

Vaggi, G. *The Economics of François Quesnay.* London: Macmillan, 1987.

Voltaire (François-Marie Arouet). *Correspondance.* 106 vols. Edited by Theodore Besterman. Geneva: Institut et Musée Voltaire, and University of Toronto Press, 1968.

Walras, Léon. *Eléments d'économic pure.* Lausanne, 1874. Translated and edited by William Jaffe in 1954 for the American Economic Association and the Royal Economic Society, London: Allen & Unwin.

Weulersse, Georges. *Le Mouvement physiocratique en France (de 1756 à 1770).* 2 vols. Paris, 1910.

―――. *La Physiocratie: à la fin du règne de Louis XV (1770–74).* Paris: Presses Universitaires de France, 1959.

―――. *La Physiocratie sous les ministères de Turgot et de Necker (1774–81).* Paris: Presses Universitaires de France, 1950.

Young, Arthur. *Travels During the Years, 1787, 1788 and 1789 with a View of Ascertaining the Cultivation, Wealth, Resources and National Prosperity of the Kingdom of France.* 2nd ed. 2 vols. London, 1794.

# INDEX

abundance, 97–98; effect on value, 100; from free trade, 181–84; means of obtaining, 104–5; and population growth, 206. *See also* surplus

agents, 115–16. *See also* government commissioners

*agio,* 160

agrarian nations, 312

agrarian provinces, 250–53

agricultural societies, 211. *See also* hunting and fishing societies; land leases

agriculture: definition, 119; productivity and surplus from, 63–65; relation with manufactures, 226; relation with trade, 104–5; and subsidies to government, 220–24; trade-offs involving land use, 205–9

Alembert, Jean le Rond d', 7–8, 25, 49

Allais, Maurice, 67, 68

American economy, 210

animal husbandry and human population, 207–9

apprenticeships, 263–64

arpent, 84

artificial needs, 98–99, 103–4, 123

artificial value, 98–99, 103–4. *See also* luxury goods

artificial wealth, 130, 131

artisans, 124–25; choice of cities vs. countryside, 302–5; of metals, 142; and poverty in towns, 218; production of value by, 128; role in economy, 201, 211; speculation by, 321–22; successful, 213; wages of, 126–27; wealth acquired by, 132. *See also* manufactures

artists, wealth acquired by, 133

art works vs. crafts, 129

Autroche, Claude de Loynes d', 33

balance of power, 259

banknotes, 281–82

banks and bankers: effect on exchange rates, 166–68; exchanges involving, 160–63; exclusive companies of, 325; origin of, 160; source of profits, 164–65, 167–69. *See also* interest; loans

Baudeau, abbé Nicholas, 62, 63, 66

*Before Adam Smith* (Hutchison), 40–41

beggars and begging, 304–5

below par exchange of currency, 163

bills of exchange, 159; price of, 166

bills payable, 280–81; government manipulation of prices, 282–83

black market, 260

Bodoni, Giambattista, 17, 29

boisseaux, 84

Bonnot, Étienne. *See* Condillac, Étienne Bonnot, abbé de

Bonnot, François, de Saint-Marcellin (brother of Condillac), 6, 33

[ 337 ]

The typeface used in this book is Fournier, a digitized
version of the Monotype Corporation's 1925 release of
the font based on Pierre Simon Fournier's St. Augustin
Ordinaire, cut in Paris in the 1740s. Display ornaments in
this edition of *Commerce and Government* are from the font
Europa Arabesque.

This book is printed on paper that is acid-free and meets
the requirements of the American National Standard
for Permanence of Paper for Printed Library Materials,
Z39.48-1992. ∞

Book design by Barbara E. Williams, BW&A Books, Inc.,
Durham, North Carolina
Typography by Graphic Composition, Inc., Bogart,
Georgia
Printed and bound by Worzalla Publishing Company,
Stevens Point, Wisconsin